Real Estate and Globali

Real Estate and Globalisation

Richard Barkham

Group Research Director
Grosvenor Group

WILEY-BLACKWELL

A John Wiley & Sons, Ltd., Publication

This edition first published 2012
© 2012 by John Wiley & Sons, Ltd

Wiley-Blackwell is an imprint of John Wiley & Sons, formed by the merger of Wiley's global Scientific, Technical and Medical business with Blackwell Publishing.

Registered office: John Wiley & Sons, Ltd, The Atrium, Southern Gate, Chichester, West Sussex, PO198SQ, UK

Editorial offices: 9600 Garsington Road, Oxford, OX4 2DQ, UK
    The Atrium, Southern Gate, Chichester, West Sussex, PO19 8SQ, UK
    2121 State Avenue, Ames, Iowa 50014–8300, USA

For details of our global editorial offices, for customer services and for information about how to apply for permission to reuse the copyright material in this book, please see our website at www.wiley.com/wiley-blackwell.

Library of Congress Cataloging-in-Publication Data
  Real estate and globalisation / by Richard Barkham.
      p. cm.
  Includes bibliographical references and index.
  ISBN 978-0-470-65597-9 (pbk. : alk. paper) 1. Real estate business.
 I. Barkham, Richard, 1961–
  HD1375.R3723 2012
  333.3–dc23
                     2011045310

A catalogue record for this book is available from the British Library.

Set in 10/13 pt TrumpMediaeval by Toppan Best-set Premedia Limited
Printed and bound in Singapore by Markono Print Media Pte Ltd

1   2012

This document and the information herein have been produced internally by the Research Department of *Grosvenor Group Limited* ("*Grosvenor*") solely as a compendium of the monthly outlook reports. The monthly outlook reports are *Grosvenor*'s research perspective on the global real estate markets. This document is intended as a research resource for general informative purposes only.

The information has been compiled from sources believed to be reliable however its accuracy and completeness are not guaranteed. Readers are advised and informed that none of the information contained in this book amounts to investment, legal or other advice. Certain statements contained herein regarding the markets are of a forward-looking nature and are based on *Grosvenor*'s research team's assumptions about future developments and future events, and therefore involve certain risks and uncertainties. Actual results may vary materially from those targeted, expected or projected due to several factors, and there can be no assurance that the actual results or developments anticipated will be realized or, even if substantially realized, that they will have the expected consequences. *Grosvenor* does not assume any obligation to release any updates or revisions to any forward-looking statement and the delivery of this document at any time shall not create any implication that there has been no adverse change in the information set out in this document or in the affairs of the Company Group since the date of this document.

The opinions expressed are those of the Research Department of *Grosvenor* at this date and are subject to change without notice. Reliance should not be placed on the information or opinions set out herein for any purpose and *Grosvenor* will not accept any liability in contract, tort or otherwise arising from such use or from the contents of this document.

Contents

Foreword

There is something unusual – perhaps unhealthy – about an industry in which a 25-year-old with almost no prior experience can make a fortune overnight. The fact is that you can get into property with little more than a telephone and a total disrespect for risk. The industry abounds with stories of a few thousands turned into millions. Property investing attracts, because it is very straightforward and visual. Once we have bought and sold our own home, we have experienced the essential mechanics of property investing. This is reflected around boardroom tables as well, where there is only rarely a specialist but, apparently, many experts.

In large property companies, there should be experts of course. But even here there has been a traditional assumption that it is 'unconscious genius' that will bring greatest success, not dedicated research. I am a great believer in instinct, but when it comes to managing a 300-year old business, something more is needed. So, when we reorganised the property business of the Grosvenor Estate in 2000, we did something which was probably unique at the time for a large property company. We established a dedicated research group around the world. As an internationally diversified investor and developer, we believed strongly in the notion that real local decision-making was essential and that a model of managing from London (as various peers had done) was flawed. The primary role of the centre would be to decide how much capital should be invested in each local business.

The research teams, coordinated but answerable to their local management, would provide a common 'language', as well as the medium through which valuable knowledge could be refined and moved around our business. Part of the output of the team would be a monthly commentary for all the Boards and staff on a single topic of relevance and interest. It is expensive to run such a team and so its establishment was in itself a real example of managing for the long term; something which many profess, but few are really prepared to pursue.

After some years it became obvious that collecting the short papers together would be valuable, as both diaries and refreshers on topics that keep coming back. I am delighted that my wish to do this has been realised in a much more sophisticated way than I ever imagined.

I particularly want to commend Richard Barkham, Grosvenor Group's Research Director, and Darren Rawcliffe, his predecessor, for their work in establishing the team and the intellectual rigour they added to our strategy. While never allowing them to dictate, they and their colleagues have informed every aspect of strategy since 2000. Richard's expert editing and introductory commentaries have provided a fascinating 'look back–look forward' feel to the collection, which I hope will be a worthwhile addition to the rather thin collection of books about the complexity of managing an international property company at the beginning of the 21st century.

Jeremy Newsum
Non-executive Director
Grosvenor

Preface

Grosvenor is an international property company whose roots, in the areas of London known as Mayfair and Belgravia, go back more than three hundred years. In 2000, Grosvenor took the step of creating a research team to support its growing fund management business and international diversification strategy. Each month for the last 11 years Grosvenor's research team, which now consists of 12 real estate economists, has produced an article on an aspect of real estate economics which seemed topical at the time. The series is called the 'Global Economic Outlook' and is distributed internally and to contacts and clients of the company. Sometimes the articles are based on recent macroeconomic developments and the implications for real estate markets and sometimes they attempt longer-term projections or cross-country comparisons. Although the topics covered have varied a great deal, the aim has always been to undertake original analysis using the tools and techniques of economics. Individual articles are produced by Grosvenor's research economists in the UK, North America, Asia and Europe and must be no more than 800 words long. This word limit is stipulated by the board of Grosvenor which requires its economics to be pithy. There has been no particular attempt over the years to develop a long term theme or maintain a particular editorial line. First and foremost the articles are constructed to enable Grosvenor to deploy its own and its clients' capital to best effect, in a very turbulent world.

In reviewing the series it became clear that these articles, though never specifically addressing this issue, told a very interesting story about the impact of globalisation on the volatility and performance of real estate markets. Over the last 10 years national economies have become ever more intertwined. Emerging markets have taken a greater share of production, providing OECD consumers with ever-cheaper manufactured goods delivered through sophisticated supply chains. Capital has flowed from high-savings economies to low-savings ones, not only though public capital markets but also, less obviously, via banks' cross-border investments in the bonds and commercial paper of other banks. All the while, developments in communications technology, including the internet, have increased the volume of data delivered to consumers and businesses so that events in, say, Japan, quickly impact on sentiment and economic activity in the UK. These developments have brought many benefits, but they have also created huge economic distortions. Some countries have over-consumed and built up debt; others have saved too much and built up excess foreign currency reserves. The lack of an appropriate global fiscal and monetary policy framework has meant that the economic power of globalisation has been misdirected. One consequence of this has been very high levels of volatility in asset markets, including the real estate sector. The central purpose of this book is to use the articles to sketch out the link between globalisation, by definition a profound international process, and the dynamics of real estate markets, which until very recently have been dominated by purely local factors.

Although one of the by-products of globalisation is that economic and market data is increasing exponentially, it is still necessary in the real estate sector to spend time and effort ensuring a degree of consistency across markets. Only in this way can valid international comparisons be made for the purpose of asset allocation. Nevertheless, all research requires judgments to be made and nowhere is this truer than in the field of international real estate research. The second purpose of this book is to present Grosvenor's approach to the analysis of international real estate markets and the variety of methods we have used to analyse data and arrive at conclusions. Our hope is that students and possibly others will gain some insights into the way in which research can blend with practice to help shape the strategic agenda of a major company. Many of the research themes in the book need to be followed up, as they seem to us to have social as well as commercial relevance. Grosvenor's research team will continue to explore the impact of global economic change on real estate markets; we hope that others will be inspired to do so as well.

Richard Barkham

Acknowledgements

The monthly Global Outlook was devised by Darren Rawcliffe and edited by him between 2000 and 2005. Richard Barkham has edited the series since 2005. Richard Barkham designed this book and is responsible for the introductory and concluding chapters as well as the individual chapter commentaries. Ruth Hollies managed the global yield project, the results of which are included as an appendix to Chapter 11. Current or former members of the Grosvenor research team who have contributed by producing articles or analysis are as follows:

Ian Anderson
Dr Richard Barkham
James Brown
Dr Josep Camacho-Cabiscol
Manish Enaker
Richard B. Gold
Maurizio Grilli
Dr Beatrice Guedj
Ruth Hollies
David Inskip
Chi Lo
Fiona MacAonghusa
Graham Parry
Cynthia Parpa
Shabab Qadar
Darren Rawcliffe
David Roberts
Harry Tan
David Wasserberg

1

Introduction

A remarkable decade for real estate

The decade from 2000 to 2010 was the most exciting, remarkable and ultimately disastrous period for real estate since the end of the Second World War. Those dramatic ten years witnessed the world's first coordinated real estate boom and slump. Real estate cycles are a common feature of free market economic development and, from time to time, they badly destabilise individual economies. In the years before 2007, real estate values were driven to peak levels across the greater part of the developed world. When prices collapsed in 2008, by up to 60% in some countries, the global financial system was almost destroyed and a new Great Depression ushered in. At the time of writing (mid-2011), the aftershocks of the great financial crisis (GFC) linger on, in the sovereign debt crisis of Southern Europe and in the moribund housing market of the USA. Unemployment in the developed world, the social cost of the crisis, remains very high.

For real estate, the 2000s started rather unpromisingly amidst the global recession created by the bursting of the 'dot-com' bubble. Between 1996 and the end of 1999, on the back of easy money, buoyant global growth and widespread optimism about the potential of the Internet, global stock markets rose by 24%. Between 2000 and 2003, all of these gains were reversed, as world markets fell by 30%. The swings in value were much

Real Estate and Globalisation, First Edition. Richard Barkham.
© 2012 John Wiley & Sons, Ltd. Published 2012 by John Wiley & Sons, Ltd.

greater in the stock markets of the USA and the UK. Investment fell and unemployment rose. Contraction in the corporate sector led to a fall in demand for business and commercial space and a steep drop in rents. The real estate recession of the early 2000s was particularly severe in the office sector, because demand for offices depends directly on the state of the financial markets.

It is worth reflecting on the 'wreckage' of the dot-com slump, because it is here that the real estate story of the 2000s begins. Since the early 1990s, OECD central banks have been haunted by the spectre of Japan. Between 1950 and 1989, Japan was one of the word's fastest-growing and most dynamic economies. Towards the end of its long expansion, its stock market and land market dramatically boomed and slumped. Since then, Japan has been unable to shrug off slow growth, deflation and a chronic inability to create jobs. The reasons for Japan's 20-year deflation are complex, but most agree that monetary policy was too tight in the post-bubble period. This is a mistake that OECD central banks do not wish to repeat. So, in the wake of the stock market crash of 2000, interest rates were cut aggressively to support asset values, boost confidence and revive business and consumer spending. Figure 1.1 shows OECD real interest rates over the period: it is the key to understanding the events of the 2000s and the GFC.

It is often said that using interest rates to stimulate an economy is like dragging a brick with an elastic band: nothing happens for a while and then the brick jumps up and hits you on the back of the head. This is how it played out in the real estate sector. The period 2001 to 2003 saw depression

Figure 1.1:   OECD real interest rates
Source: IHS Global Insight

Weighted average of major world markets

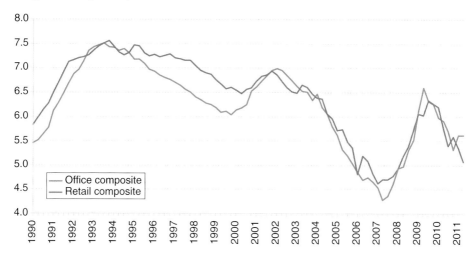

Figure 1.2:   Retail and office global composite yields
Source: CBRE

in most asset markets; confidence was weak as the global economy worked its way through the aftermath of the tech-crash. Suddenly, in 2003 a 'wall of money' hit the real estate sector. Investors, nervous of the stock market, were not prepared to tolerate the low returns on cash and bonds that resulted from super-loose monetary policy. The 'search for yield' was on and real estate was suddenly the most favoured asset class. The long, globally coordinated boom in real estate values had begun. Figure 1.2 shows a global composite yield for the retail sector and the office sector. The period from 2003 to 2008 saw a rapid and continuous appreciation of prices driven entirely by investment demand.

The first wave of investment was primarily driven by 'equity' investors; those for whom easy access to bank finance was not a key issue. These included pension funds and insurance companies, high net worth individuals, private equity funds and, increasingly, newly created sovereign wealth funds. Even small investors, through the medium of open-ended funds or other 'retail' vehicles, were clamorous for real estate. REITs (Real Estate Investment Trusts) were prominent investors; the ten years to 2007 had seen REITs or REIT-type vehicles approved in over eight jurisdictions (figure 1.3). The period also saw the very rapid growth in unlisted real estate funds (figure 1.4). These tax transparent vehicles provided a convenient means for professional investors to deploy capital in diversified pools of real estate assets run by professional real estate managers.

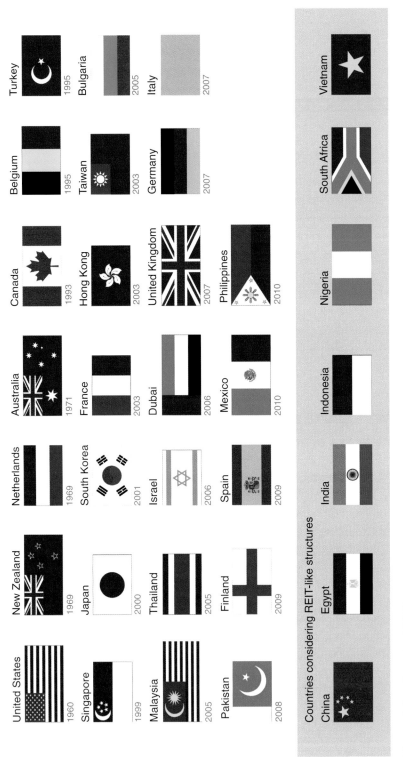

Figure 1.3:   Growth of REITs

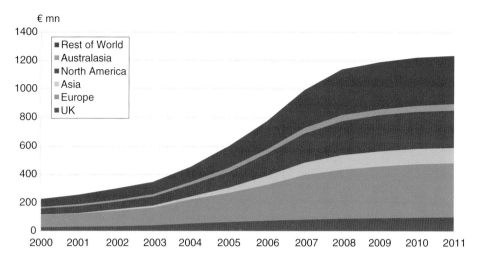

Figure 1.4: Growth in non-listed real estate funds
Source: Property Fund Research

'Behind the scenes', it was low interest rates that were fuelling the boom. Low interest rates (or expansionary monetary policy) have a 'double impact' on the attractiveness of real estate as an investment. First, they lower the cost of holding the asset. Second, by boosting the cash flow of occupiers, they improve the security of real estate operating income. At the time, the link between booming real estate values and super-loose monetary policy was not widely apprceiated. Indeed, many market participants preferred to think about the 'golden age of real estate'. Real estate, with its long duration and stable cash flows and increasingly good data provision, was the institutional asset of choice.

By 2005, the initial impetus to real estate values from 'equity' investors had been replaced by debt-driven buyers; namely, buyers with very high levels of leverage. Such 'players' are a feature of any rising real estate market, often originating in markets with low or negative real interest rates (where interest rates are lower than domestic inflation). In the mid-2000s, debt-driven investors from Ireland, Iceland, Spain, the USA and Israel flooded into the marketplace. Figure 1.5 shows money flows into real estate over the period, by type and destination.

Banks generally find real estate an attractive asset, but particularly when interest rates are low and economic growth is strong. Unlike businesses, real estate assets are relatively easy to appraise and assess for creditworthiness. Moreover, the market is large, and at times of rising values it can create additional lending opportunities very quickly. For instance, we

(a)

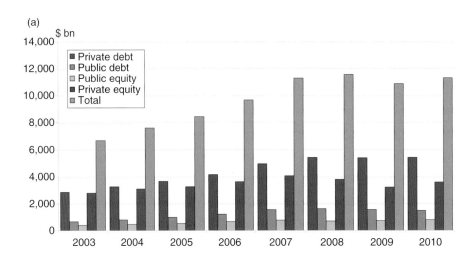

(b)

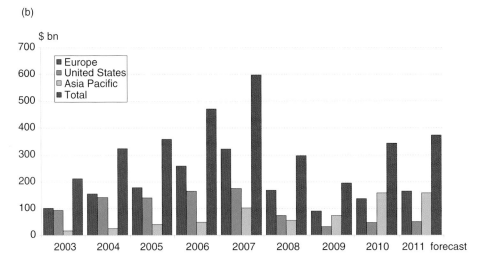

Figure 1.5: **(a)** Capital flows into real estate by type; **(b)** Capital flows into real estate by origin
Source: DTZ

estimate that the total value of real estate in the US is $7.7trn, so a 10% increase in values creates $770bn of additional 'lending opportunities'. No other sector gives banks the ability to increase their loan books as quickly as real estate. Compounding this, as we now appreciate, banks in the OECD can operate on the assumption that that they will not have to bear the full consequences of risky lending decisions. In any case, in the mid-2000s, it became quite clear that the major lending banks had replaced carefully considered lending with market share as their main objective function. Real estate was the sector of choice.

Two further factors facilitated the flow of debt into the real estate sector in the mid-2000s. One factor related to globalisation was the long-term growth in the usage by banks, in all regions, of the money markets for funding. Since the 1960s, customer deposits have fallen as a share of banks' liabilities and certificates of deposit, repurchase agreements and commercial paper have increased. As long as the money markets were open, the banks could expand lending way beyond the level that would be supported by their own domestic deposit base. During the 2000s, at least until 2007, it was very easy for banks in countries such as Spain, Portugal and the UK to tap the money markets in order to expand lending to real estate. Moreover, on the supply side, 'excess savings' in other parts of Europe and Asia saw the money markets awash with liquidity. This process, which might be called the globalisation of banking, is one of the key mechanisms by which real estate markets which are local in character can be swamped by international money flows. In the lead-up to 2007, banks in high savings areas invested in banks in low savings areas, allowing the latter aggressively to expand lending (Figure 1.6).

Alongside the globalisation of banking was the growth of loan securitisation. Securitisation is the process by which pools of loans, for instance

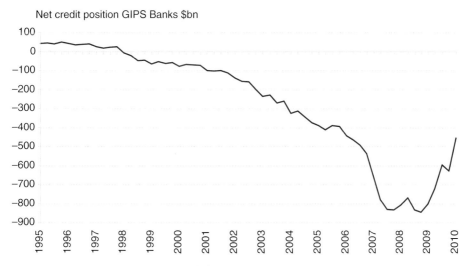

Figure 1.6:   Net credit position of Greece, Ireland, Portugal and Spain banks with banks in the rest of the world
Source: BIS

real estate mortgages, are 'bundled' together and the rights to receive the cash flows from these loans are sold to investors. The bank that sells this collection of loans receives cash (asset), which in due course it can recycle into additional lending and it deletes the loans (assets) from its balance sheet. In principle, there is nothing wrong with this; it has been a feature of the US mortgage industry for many years. Non-bank investors get access to stable investments with a good cash yield and banks get cash to help them engage in their primary task to provide loans to those that need them. However, there are two potential flaws in securitisation. First, in the circumstances of lax supervision and extreme monetary stimulation that characterised the early and the mid-2000s, it created an incentive for banks to originate loans for the sake of creating investment products, rather than supporting commercially sensible business transactions. Second, it facili- tates the 'unseen' build-up in leverage within a market – in this case the real estate market – because the loans are 'off-balance sheet'. Loan securi- tisation was a major part of the 'shadow banking sector', which ballooned in the five years prior to the GFC. Figure 1.7 shows the growth of securitised real estate.

The worst excesses in real estate loan securitisation took place in the US housing market in the six years to 2007. Here, mortgage lending to the general public became aggressive to the point of being fraudulent.[1] To create loans that could be securitised and sold to investors as quickly as possible,

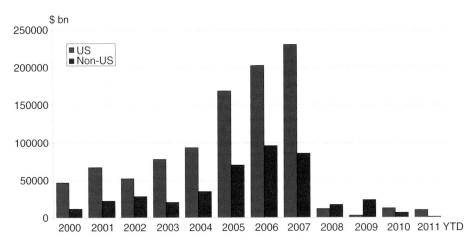

Figure 1.7:   Growth of securitised real estate debt (CMBS)
Source: CRE Financial Council

---

[1] *The Big Short: Inside the Doomsday Machine*, Michael Lewis, WW Norton & Co., 2010.

originators devised mortgage products that eliminated the need for lenders and borrowers to consider in any way, shape or form the ability of the latter to repay their debts. For instance, 'the stated income loan' or, as it is more notoriously known, 'the liar loan' allowed mortgage finance to be advanced to house buyers in extremely marginal occupations.[2] Not surprisingly, US house prices, which had in any case been rising strongly since the mid-1990s due to strong job growth, surged. At the same time, the capital markets, concerned as they were to secure 'yielding investments', received an enhanced flow of just the sort of product they were after: mortgage-backed securities. Figure 1.8 shows the rise and fall of US house prices.

The economic factors that drive the price of houses are: the cost of mortgages (interest rates); the rate of job creation (consumer incomes); expectations of future price rises (investment motivation); and the rate of construction of new premises (supply). In late 2006 rising interest rates, falling job growth and surging new construction hit the US housing market and sent prices, albeit slowly at first, into decline for the first time in the postwar period. The impact of the fall in US house prices on global capital markets took some time to emerge, but it was profound when it did. As it turned out, numerous financial institutions, including some of the world's

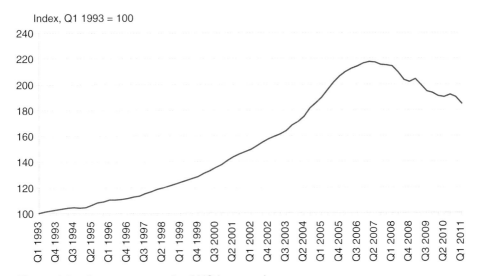

Figure 1.8: Long term growth of US house prices
Source: Global Property Guide

---

[2] When a 'stated income loan' is advanced, the lender takes the borrower's declared income 'on trust' and makes no attempt to verify it by recourse to pay slips (stubs), income tax returns, company records, utility bills or any other source.

best-known banks, had invested in mortgage-backed securities in general and US residential mortgage-backed securities in particular. The scale of this investment and the fact that the banks themselves had historically high levels of leverage meant that the global financial system was under serious threat. In addition, certain key insurance companies were in jeopardy, because they had insured mortgage-backed products. Capital had poured into the US housing sector and driven it to the point of implosion; globalisation ensured the rapid and widespread transmission of the shockwaves.

From a narrow real estate perspective, the interesting fact is that the boom in US house prices was far from the most extreme in the OECD. The long and relatively consistent run of GDP growth (and job creation) that took place in much of the OECD in the period after 1992 provided the housing markets of the developed world with a significant growth impetus. The decline in inflation and consequent fall in long-term interest rates over the period made mortgages more affordable in many countries. In some areas, such as the USA, boosting the rate of home ownership was a key government objective, which was manifested in the tax-deductibility of mortgage interest payments. For all of these reasons, housing markets in most of the OECD 'did well' in the 1990s (see figure 1.9). In fact, by the end of that decade house-price-to-income ratios were at an all-time high.

The relatively mild recession that ensued in the wake of the tech-crash of 2001 had two effects on global housing markets. Initially, because of the rise in unemployment and the fall in confidence, there was a period of stagnation. By 2003 however, interest rate cuts had begun to revive the

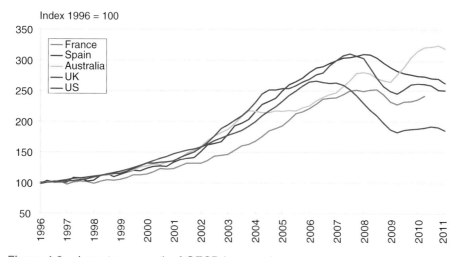

Figure 1.9: Long term growth of OECD house prices
Source: BIS, ABS,National sources, Global Property Guide

market and, shortly afterwards, growth resumed. Britain, Spain, Ireland and Australia experienced a particularly strong period of house-price appreciation, which led to a fall in underwriting standards and a generalised reduction in risk premiums. In 2008, as interest rates peaked, these and other housing markets in the OECD came to a juddering halt. At the time of writing, Spain and Ireland are still struggling to recapitalise commercial banks that are having, as a result, to write down huge quantities of real estate loans.

In September 2008, Lehman Brothers, an important US investment bank, filed for Chapter 11 bankruptcy protection. This event neither initiated the GFC nor signalled the bottom of the market. However, in the demise of Lehman Brothers due to high gearing and over-exposure to the US housing market, the world began to see the full extent of the banking and real estate crisis that it was facing. Two remarkably destructive negative feedback loops, both driven by sentiment, were initiated. The first was in the manufacturing sector. Companies, fearing a collapse in demand, immediately cut stocks and fixed capital investment, which produced a steep fall in global output. Companies and consumers, fearing a generalised collapse in the banking sector, withdrew their savings, further undermining the banking system. Economic confidence collapsed, as did stock and real estate values (Figure 1.10). By the end of 2008 it seemed as if the developed world was on the verge of a 1930s-style Great Depression.

As momentous and fearful as the events of 2007 and 2008 were, the more remarkable event was the scale and rapidity of the bounce-back. By the end of March 2009, it was becoming clear that a disaster had been averted and

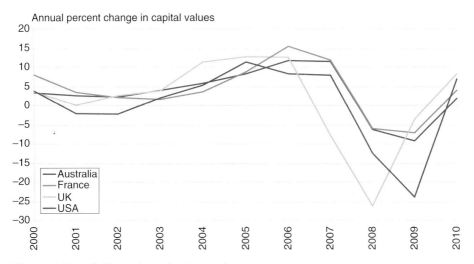

Figure 1.10:   Collapse in real estate values
Source: IPD

that some sort of recovery was under way. The situation was stabilised by the bank rescue packages put in place in 2008. The US government initially flirted with the idea that companies – even banks – should bear the economic consequences of their own actions, but in the end a full-scale bail-out was offered to the sector, as it was in the case of the UK and the Euro zone. In order to revive growth OECD governments collectively mounted the biggest fiscal stimulus in history. In order to revive asset markets and prevent deflation taking hold, central banks cut interest rates to zero and initiated the policy, developed by Japan in its long battle with deflation, of quantitative easing. The policy worked: in the first quarter of 2009 asset markets, including real estate, staged a surprising rebound. Shortly afterwards, economic growth resumed and by mid-2010 inflation was trending back to its target level in the OECD.

Based on a flawed global economic model

Real estate markets are always driven by economic growth. If the period 2000 to 2010 was remarkable, it was because the underlying global economic situation was, too. The great coordinated boom in real estate values, which peaked in 2007, reflected a global economy which was growing more strongly than ever but was increasingly prone to instability in asset prices. The GFC, which was due to excessive real estate lending, was the direct linear descendant of the dot-com boom and slump and the Asian currency crisis in 1998, which preceded it. These highly unstable economic conditions are still in play today and will substantively impact the real-estate research agenda for the next 10 years.

One of the dominant themes of the 2000s was the robust and increasingly self-sustaining growth of Brazil, Russia, India and China (collectively known as the BRICs). When demand in the OECD collapsed in the wake of the GFC, the BRICs quickly adjusted their economic policy settings and continued to grow. Without the BRICs' contribution to global demand, the recession of 2008 would have been much worse than it turned out to be. Figure 1.11 shows the growing contribution of the BRICs to global demand.

In seeking to understand the instability of OECD asset markets over the last 10 years and the next 10, we should focus on one BRIC in particular: China. China's free market reforms date back to the early 1990s, but in 2001 it was admitted to the World Trade Organisation, giving it greater access to world markets. Cheap and abundant labour has attracted investment by multinational manufacturing companies from the OECD, particularly America and Japan.[3] China's competitive advantage in world markets

---

[3] Approximately 30% of Chinese exports are transfers within American multinationals.

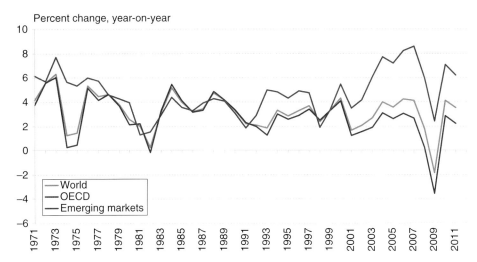

Percent change, year-on-year

Figure 1.11: Real GDP growth
Source: IHS Global Insight

is assisted by a degree of currency manipulation on the part of the Chinese government. Although China's trading partners – for instance the USA – make a fuss about this, it suits the interests of their consumers to have access to cheap manufactured products and the interests of their politicians to have downward pressure on inflation.

In order to hold the value of its currency down, China provides an unlimited quantity of RMB to world markets and, as a result, accumulates foreign currency reserves (figure 1.12). The dollars that China accumulates in vast quantities are used to buy US Treasury stocks. In small and balanced measures, these international capital flows are not problematic. However, the scale of Chinese investment in US bonds over the last 10 years has been sufficient to substantially reduce the cost of capital to US consumers and US businesses. The rise of China is directly linked to the build-up of debt in the US economy and the emergence of a large, persistent trade deficit. China, by contrast, runs a large current account surplus.

China is not the only Asian nation that supplies funds to the USA and the rest of the OECD. The Japanese economy is also characterised by export dependence and weak domestic demand. Japan, like China, has a high savings rate due to the lack of a universal social welfare and pension system. Globalisation allows Japanese savings to flow into OECD asset markets, helping to maintain the value of currencies that should be weaker and depress the overall cost of capital within the OECD, particularly in the United States.

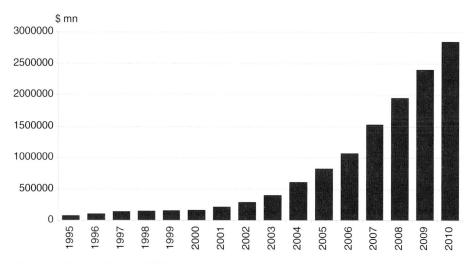

Figure 1.12:   Build up of Chinese foreign currency
Source: IHS Global Insight

In some ways, the flow of Asian savings into the USA is a very rational response to the risk-adjusted returns on offer. Within the OECD, the USA has the highest growth rate of the mature western economies, because of the rapidity with which it adopts new technology and its willingness to accept high rates of immigration. Moreover, US economic and military dominance means that the dollar has unchallenged status as the world's reserve currency. US bonds are regarded as the safest interest-bearing securities in the world, even in times of substantial economic turbulence in the US financial system. Low interest rates have been a mixed blessing: they have aided innovation and growth, but have also allowed a huge build-up in consumer and government debt.

The rise of China has had a destabilising effect on the economies of the West which is even more subtle. The years between 1992 and 2007 were ones of unparalleled economic success. This success was assumed to be due to the macro-economic policy mix that emerged from the Thatcher/Reagan reforms of the 1980s. The key elements of this were: (1) the successful control of inflation with short-term interest rates; (2) state provision broadly limited to public goods; (3) flexible labour markets because of reduced union power; and (4) a pragmatic approach to public finances within the constraints of a maximum debt-to-GDP ratio. The period became know as the 'great moderation', because of the decline in the rate of inflation throughout the OECD, combined with steady GDP growth[4] and employment creation.

---

[4] More technically, the period saw a fall in the standard deviation of quarterly GDP growth rates.

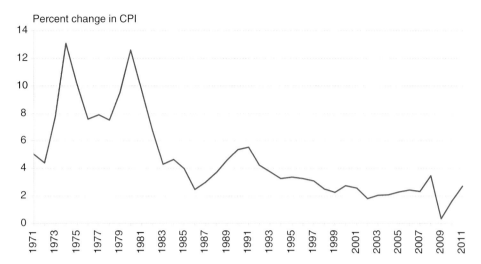

Figure 1.13: OECD inflation
Source: IHS Global Insight

Figure 1.13 shows OECD inflation over the last two decades. The importance of this fall in inflation cannot be overstated. Not only did it lead to a long period of falling interest rates, leading to a long boom in government bonds, but it gave policy makers a sense that they were fully in control of economic events. Real estate, being for the most part a bond type investment also experienced a long period of stable high returns. The problem was that the decline of inflation was not only due to macro-policy success but also to the flow of cheap manufactured goods from China.

The European response to the economic success of North America and Asia was to consolidate and, to a certain extent, protect the European economic region by the creation of a single currency. The creation of a single currency, it was argued, would allow the single market to allocate resources more efficiently and, in particular, to allow the development of large enterprises, which could compete with American multinationals in using cheap Asian labour.

As it has turned out, the creation of the Euro zone has had a devastating impact on many of the countries that adopted the single currency. The interest rate that was suitable for the northern European countries, such as Germany, with low rates of inflation and relatively sound public finances, was simply too low for those on the periphery: Ireland, Spain, Portugal and Greece. Falling interest rates precipitated a long boom in real estate prices, which stimulated growth in the volatile construction sector and, of course, the build-up of debt. Gains in competitiveness, which were the original aim of the single currency, have not materialised. In fact, it has been the banking sector that has made most use of the opportunities created by the single currency to consolidate and internationalise. Unfortunately, European banks used their increased access to world money markets to lend into an unsustainable real estate boom.

The crisis in the southern European economies arising from excessive real estate and consumer debt is compounded by a profound fiscal crisis. The governments of the Peripheral-4, with the possible exception of Spain, have fiscal deficits that are so large that they threaten the ability of these countries to borrow in the international capital markets. This situation is only partly the result of the structural flaws within the Euro zone, namely: (1) no mechanism or will to impose fiscal discipline on members of the single currency; (2) implicit guarantee of bail-out, leading to moral hazard, because of a history of fiscal transfers between core and peripheral countries; and (3) over-reliance on real estate markets to drive tax revenues. Something more fundamental is at work: governments, like banks and consumers, have over the last 10 years been seduced by the ready availability of cheap capital. Instead of developing policies to counter the economic challenge of Asia, governments have preferred to maintain the living standards of their electorates by borrowing from it.

In summary, there are three strands to the argument that the 'architecture' of the global economy is fundamentally flawed. First, currency manipulation by the Chinese is seeing the OECD rapidly lose its share of world manufacturing markets. Second, the combination of rapid economic growth in Asia, particularly China, combined with high savings rates in the region, is flooding the global economy with cheap capital, depressing long-term interest rates in the OECD[5]. Third, the era of cheap capital, as it has been described, has encouraged the build-up of personal, corporate and government debt in the OECD, making this region highly vulnerable to asset price movements in response to the interest rate cycle. So, when the OECD economy weakens, as in 1998, 2001 and 2007, in response to a collapse in asset prices, the first choice of policy markers is to cut interest rates to reflate asset markets. Low levels of inflation, in part due to the rapid expansion of production in Asia, make, in the short and medium term at least, constant monetary stimulation a viable, if short-sighted strategy. These three strands can be summarised as: high growth, excess savings and low interest rates. When combined with weak regulation of the highly dynamic and rapidly globalising banking sector, then it is quite obvious

---

[5] In due course, the growth of consumption in China will provide a powerful stimulus to the global economy that will offset the current negative trade shock. However, the full benefits of Chinese consumer spending growth will not be felt until its currency rises and broad social welfare provision reduces the impetus to save.

what caused the Great Financial Crisis. The problem is that, apart from some heavy-handed reform of the global banking sector, since 2007 none of these conditions have changed. OECD policy-makers are relying on low interest rates to restart economic growth and, as night follows day, are creating the conditions for the next boom and slump in the global economy.

The real estate research agenda

The purpose of this book is to review a remarkable decade in the history of real estate. If there is a conclusion or a 'message', it is that real estate research needs to be more aware of the big issues in the global economy, such as the 'rise of China' and the impact in the West of the Asian 'savings glut'. Perhaps the message is even more radical; real estate research is only likely to produce accurate forecasts when it is fully cognisant of the influence of geopolitics on asset market performance. As globalisation proceeds, real estate outcomes at the city or even neighbourhood level are ever more influenced by politics and economics on the other side of the world. Real estate research that does not imaginatively and creatively deal with these themes runs the risk of being irrelevant.

Academic real estate research, although it provides many carefully analysed case studies and useful theoretical insights, has seemed to be pursuing an ever narrower micro-economic and finance-driven agenda in recent years. So, whilst it is able to provide us with a better appreciation of, for instance, the complex times series processes that describe the evolution of real estate prices; the relationship between real estate traded in the public and private markets; the impact of mature trees on nearby house prices; it was not able to forecast the over-valuation of real estate markets that created the Great Financial Crisis. Nor has there been a great deal of useful retrospective analysis.

So one of the key lessons for real estate research from the events of the last 10 years is that it needs to be far more intelligently informed about the key underlying drivers of the global economy. This is not merely a matter of taking macro-economic forecasts and plugging them into rental models. There may well be a fairly robust statistical relationship between retail sales and retail rental value growth. If, however, retail sales are being driven by 'super-loose monetary policy' in an era of cheap capital, then the broader 'forces acting' need to be understood. Real estate outcomes are substantially impacted by savings rates, money supply growth, the output gap, labour markets' flexibility, taxation and fiscal policy. These macro-economic concepts need to be fully understood by real estate researchers and applied to real estate market data.

Such a research agenda is not easy: the pace of globalisation is rendering many traditional macro-economic relationships unclear, or, at least, capable of misinterpretation. For instance, in the period leading up to the GFC it was common to hear talk of the 'great moderation'. Some politicians even referred to having overcome the economic cycle. After the fact, it is easier to see that inflation was partly held in check by widespread migration (keeping wages down); and the penetration of OECD markets by goods manufactured in low-cost China. Meanwhile, surplus savings in Asia were recycled, via the bond and money markets, into a vast build-up of debt: corporate, government and consumer. Many of these trends were evident prior to the crisis, as many of the articles in this book show; but they were never quite organised into a coherent critical analysis. In any case, these trends will continue to have the most powerful effect on real estate markets. Globalisation is rapidly altering the basics of the world we live in and it needs to be fully part of the real estate research agenda.

A more controversial point, perhaps, is that real estate research needs to be informed by, and interested in, geopolitics. Although it never features in textbooks, macro-economic outcomes are profoundly affected by geopolitical developments. For instance, any hint of waning US military power or its precursor, waning economic power, will affect the value of the dollar, the equilibrium level of US interest rates and, therefore, US real estate prices. The fall of communism, including its abandonment by China, is another example. As it was seen at the time, the chief benefit was lower defence spending and greater resources for social purposes. The more important effect by far was the incorporation into the global trading system of nearly 1.5bn additional workers, allowing a long period of low inflation growth and asset price inflation. A final example is the formation of the Euro zone. Despite the rhetoric about economic efficiency, there is no doubt that ancient concerns about the balance of power in Europe were at the heart of that project. One interest rate for all Euro zone countries has had profound macro-economic and real estate consequences. Geopolitics tends to render economic models irrelevant, so it is a legitimate part of the broader real estate research agenda.

Background to this book

Over the last 10 years, Grosvenor Research has produced an article a month on some aspect of real estate economics. Although the topics covered and the research methods deployed have been very varied, the aim of the series has always been to assess the 'forces acting' on global real estate markets, whether local, national or geopolitical. The articles, almost always written in a rush, are on topics that appeared at the time to be of interest to Grosvenor, its partners and investors. Quite often, we hit on some of the decade's most important issues, but did not fully predict the full implications of these. Collectively the articles describe and analyse the ongoing impact of globalisation on real estate markets. Each chapter contains an introduction which sets the individual articles in a broader context. The articles appear in the order they are referred to in the text.

2

Macro-economics and real estate

A central theme of Grosvenor Research over the last 11 years is that real estate markets – specifically, rental growth and yield fluctuations – are only properly understood in a macro-economic context. Real estate research and advice is only as good as the appreciation of the macro-economic conditions of the time. Of course, we have also recognised the impact of rental and construction cycles, capital market 'bubbles', herd behaviour and, at the meta and micro levels, the impact of urban growth and change; but, ultimately, these are all driven by growth in GDP. This said, given the woeful state of macroeconomic forecasting technology and macro-economic theory, for that matter, it is not sufficient to rely on forecasts of the main macro-economic variables produced by governments, central banks, commercial forecasting houses and 'the consensus'. Consensus thinking is lazy thinking. A deep appreciation of the uses and limitations of macro-economic theory is required, alongside constant awareness of new economic data.

'Text-book' economics typically links real estate outcomes to GDP growth, via 'derived demand'. Real estate is not required for its intrinsic qualities, but because it contributes to the production of goods and services. As output increases so, after a lag, does the demand for real estate and its price. However, the influence of the macro-economy on real estate

Real Estate and Globalisation, First Edition. Richard Barkham.
© 2012 John Wiley & Sons, Ltd. Published 2012 by John Wiley & Sons, Ltd.

is much more comprehensive than this. Macro-economic conditions affect the level of interest rates and, most importantly, the market discount rate. This boosts values because a positive sequence of macroeconomic events tends to reduce the premium investors require for holding risky assets such as real estate. On the supply side, a rise in economic confidence tends to increase the supply of finance to the real estate development industry, increasing the rate of new construction and, in the future, the level of vacancy in the marketplace. When growth is too strong and inflation builds up, investors acquire real estate because of its putative ability to hedge inflation. For all of these reasons, we have devoted considerable resource to examining, over time and between countries, the precise impact of GDP growth on real estate returns. The general discussions of GDP growth and real estate performance are in the articles of: November 2001; January 2004; November 2004; and January 2010. Interestingly, in the article of November 2004, our commentary picks up the fact that the US economy was being over-stimulated by monetary policy which, as we later found out, was a significant factor in the sub-prime crisis that developed later.

Our general approach to interpreting macro-economic events for the purpose of forecasting real estate markets may be termed 'output gap monetarism'. This view sees aggregate demand as fluctuating about a rising trend of supply. In situations where aggregate demand is above aggregate supply, inflationary conditions exist and central banks use monetary policy (mainly interest rates) to slow economic growth. When aggregate demand is below supply and a negative output gap exists, inflation starts to fall and interest rates are cut. Fiscal policy, subject to micro-economic and political objectives, may also be pursued by governments to augment or restrain demand. Central banks generally have symmetrical inflation targets, meaning that overshoot and undershoot are, at least officially, considered equally undesirable. Unofficially, Japan's long struggle against deflation and recession has probably seen a greater fear of deflation than inflation in OECD central banks over the last 15 years. This fear has been magnified by a long series of positive supply shocks in the global economy, which have delivered an extended period of low-inflation growth but also, from time to time, the real threat of deflation. In the articles of December 2001 and October 2002, we discuss the possibility of deflation taking hold in the global economy. The former article concludes that a deeper recession would be required for such an event to occur. The GFC, six years later, was just such a recession. That later made one of the first attempts to consider the implications of deflation for real estate returns; a theme others have considered in depth in the last three years. In January 2010 and March 2010, we examined the way in which central banks have targeted asset markets, including real estate, to force the pace of recovery in deflationary conditions; our tentative conclusion is that an asset market revival provides a relatively ephemeral boost to economic activity.

Economic cycles are seven to eight years long, on average. In our framework, this means two years of rapid growth with relatively high unemployment, as the economy moves out of recession; two to three years of trend growth and falling unemployment; two years of rapid growth and accelerating job creation; and, finally, two years of falling output and rising unemployment. The article of July 2001 deals with the recovery from the relatively mild recession of 2001 and makes some interesting points about how economic weakness in one country is quickly transmitted to another in the modern era, because of globalisation. The progress of the recovery from the 2009 recession is considered in the article of January 2011. All of these articles demonstrate that, in their early stages, recoveries are volatile and uncertain. From a real estate perspective, one of the key indicators that a recovery is gaining traction is an upturn in business investment, because it signals the fact the businesses are confident to expand and take additional space. The articles of December 2002, July 2003 and January 2010 deal with the resumption of investment following recession. The path of economic growth is rarely quite as smooth as earlier comments suggest and most economic cycles have a mid- or late-cycle 'hiccup'. This is a slump in asset markets and economic activity that feels like a new recession, but actually isn't one. The article of November 2004 deals with a mid-cycle hiccup, although the writer does not quite realise it at the time.

The savings rate is the proportion of national income that is not spent in the current year by consumers, businesses and the government. It is an important variable in the analysis and forecasting of real estate markets, because of its close correlation with consumers' spending, in particular, on retail goods. As consumers become more confident after the end of a recession, they save less and spend more. At the peak of the cycle, consumers can become over-confident and spend too much by dis-saving and taking on debt. This happened *in extremis* in the economic boom of 2004 to 2007. Consumer confidence is related to a number of factors, but the most important ones are unemployment (or job growth) and asset values. As the economy moves through the cycle, unemployment falls and asset values rise, which drives rising consumer confidence and falling savings rates. Other things being equal, retail markets are safer, with greater growth prospects, in countries where the savings rate is high than where it is low. The articles in September 2002 and December 2009 deal with the causes and consequences of movements in the savings rate.

The framework outlined above posits the cyclical movement of demand around the rising trend of supply, generating GDP growth. There is another source of GDP growth: positive and negative economic shocks. Economic shocks can substantially raise or lower the level of aggregate demand or aggregate supply. Positive supply shocks might arise from technological developments such as the internet, which has substantially improved productivity or geopolitical events, such as China acceding to the World Trade Organisation. The latter brought a vast, hitherto untapped pool of labour into the world economy. In turn, the relocation of manufacturing activity to that area has created scale economies in production. The formation of the Euro zone, in that it has to a certain extent enabled a degree of industrial restructuring in Europe and greater scale economies, is also a supply-side shock. In any case, from a real estate perspective, it is important to distinguish an economic shock from a cyclical movement. The latter implies a temporary change in the rate of growth of the economy, the former suggest something more permanent which might affect user demand for real estate assets. In October 2000 and October 2005, we looked at the consequences of rising oil prices – creating both a supply-side and demand-side shock. We have tended to conclude that oil price movements are far less influential in the global economy than they were in the 1970s. However, we note in passing that there remains quite a strong correlation between raised oil prices and economic weakness, which suggests that oil prices are more influential than currently supposed.

The GFC is not commonly considered a negative supply-side shock, but this is what it is. The need to recapitalise the global banking system and, to an extent, improve the regulation of it, is substantially impeding the ability of the financial sector to lend to businesses. Our August 2010 article deals with the post-crisis developments in banking markets and, presciently enough, points to Europe as being a source of further instability.

Of equal importance to the rise of China over the last decade, was, in economic terms, the creation of the Euro zone. Our commentary at the time in the articles of January 2002, April 2002 and April 2003 mainly focuses on the impact of this event on the economy and the competitive position of Germany, which at the time was also struggling to integrate the ex-communist East German state. We correctly foresee that Germany would regain its competitive position by holding down its unit labour costs and practising fiscal restraint. We did not anticipate quite how dominant this would leave Germany within the Euro zone post-GFC.

Impact of the recession on US property markets – evidence so far (November 2001)

Since the beginning of the year, the slide into recession of the US economy has generated a very fast response from commercial property markets.

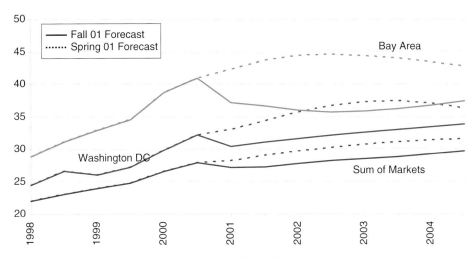

Figure 2.1:   Rental forecasts have been adjusted downwards . . .

Office vacancy rates have lifted much more quickly than usual and rental rates have consequently suffered. This effect has not been uniform across the country, though, and the west coast has been particularly badly hit. Now that data for the third quarter is available, it is possible to try and put the current downturn in some sort of historical perspective.

Compared with the last real estate recession in the USA, the current downturn is having a big impact on vacancy, but a relatively small impact on rental levels (Figure 2.1). From Q3 1989 to Q2 1991, average vacancy across Torto Wheaton's sum of markets rose from a low of 17.9% to a high of 19.1%, using CB Richard Ellis data. This very subdued change was partly because the recession moved slowly across the nation from coast to coast, so that the rise in east-coast vacancy happened while the west coast market was still thriving. By contrast, this time average vacancy has risen from 8.1% in Q3 2000 to 11.8% so far in Q3 2001 and is expected to rise further, reflecting a much more synchronised downturn in the major cities.

Another reason for the difference may be that rents weakened much more sharply at the end of the 1980s, which will have supported demand. Average nominal rents dropped 14% from peak to trough, but so far have only dropped 3%. The implication is that rents are likely to drop a great deal further across the nation as a whole, but not in all areas. In San Jose, for example, which has been particularly badly hit so far, average rents have dropped 24% from Q4 2000. In areas like this some further drop is likely, but much of the final impact has probably already been felt. The major market showing the least response to the downturn is, of course, New York. Vacancy is expected to remain tight and rents should carry on increasing,

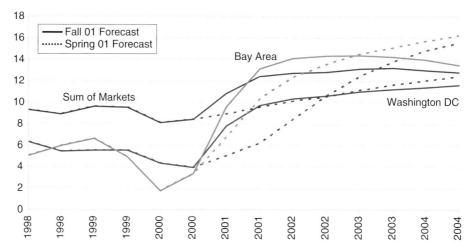

Figure 2.2:   Vacancy rates moved upwards

as the effort to find new space continues for occupiers hit by the September attacks (Figure 2.2).

The forecasting community, though, appears rather unconcerned by the prospects for the overall USA market going forward. Rent predictions from Torto Wheaton have been brought down, but only by around 6% for the first half of next year, increasing to a 7% downward adjustment by late 2003. One reason for this is that new completions are expected to reduce, so that the overall amount of new product delivered over the next three years falls by 14%; but this level of downward adjustment is likely to be outweighed by the amount of sublet space that started to come to the market earlier this year. In fact, there seems to be a clear downside risk to these forecasts, but the risk is mainly present in southern and east coast markets.

State of global property going into 2004 (January 2004)

Players in the international property markets can afford to feel a little more relaxed going into 2004, with the global economy in better shape. The US outlook is still clouded to some extent by the upcoming easing of growth that seems inevitable once the 2003 policy boost peters out, but corporate profits are high, household savings rates have at least partially recovered and the weaker dollar will help manufacturers increase net exports. The chances of the Federal Reserve spoiling things by raising rates back to more normal levels are extremely low. Core inflation is now close to 1%, with headline inflation following it down fast, so any significant increase in overnight rates or bond yields looks distant. In Japan, a sustained expansionary monetary stance combined with stronger world trade conditions is carrying the economy into another year of around trend growth and the Euro zone looks to be over the worst – even if a solid recovery is still uncertain.

Property markets are not going to feel an immediate benefit from this improving environment, though. As usual, labour markets are showing a lag in their reaction to the improving economy, meaning that greater demand for space from occupiers will be slow to materialise. In the office sector, stronger investment banking activity in the second half of 2003 has helped to stabilise demand, but a generalised recovery of employment in finance, business services and other office-intensive sectors cannot be expected until at least the second half of 2004 and possibly later. At that point, stronger demand will first of all look to take up the high levels of vacancy in most major office markets – both reported vacancy and space officially let to tenants, but unused and ready to be released to the market. In many markets around the world, the office sector is close to a turning point, but the end of rental decline will be followed by an extended period of stability, before sustained rental increases return after two, three or even four years, in some cases. Successful re-entry to the office investment and development markets will therefore depend very much on choosing markets where vacancy levels are within reach of levels low enough to allow rental growth.

High-end residential markets in international urban centres are in a similar position to the office market and rental recovery will depend, largely, on the level of vacancy. In the wider residential rented market, the outlook is much more stable, but development in the owner-occupied sector is exposed to the risk of collapsing prices in the previous high growth markets in North America, the UK, Spain and Australia, once interest rates begin a sustained rise. Although interest rate hikes still look several months distant in North America and the Euro zone, that is within most projects' time spans. UK and Australian rates could rise more quickly. Hence, developers should be particularly careful in markets where current pricing is above the levels implied by fundamentals.

Retail property is more influenced by very local factors than the office market and, even in economies facing stagnant consumer spending, many retail projects have been able to generate rental increases. But, on average, rental growth has flattened out in the face of the slower economy and increased pressure on retailer margins. The improving economy should prevent any worsening of this situation, but it may take some time before we see the significant increases in employment, increases in real earnings and falls in unemployment needed to stimulate rising average retail rents.

Having said that, retail rents should generally recover before office rents, although they can be expected to rise more gradually.

Is the global recovery running out of steam? (November 2004)

The current global recovery has become less certain since the middle of the year, which has caused a number of observers to question its resilience. However, this recovery was always going to be an unusual one, just because the preceding downturn (can we still call it a recession?) was so mild. Japan suffered most, but the USA and the Euro zone saw growth pause, rather than reverse. In many countries, including the UK, growth weakened, but the economy kept on expanding, whilst China and India expanded at a robust pace. Following such a mild downturn, there was not the normal scope for a vigorous recovery.

However, the strength of the US economy in 2003 did persuade many observers that we were about to see a classic upswing, even if the rapid US growth last year was mainly driven by an over-zealous policy response. Both the Fed and the federal government reacted as if the USA were in deep recession, rather than the mildest recession on record. The resultant pump-priming of super-low short-term interest rates and large increases in the federal budget deficit generated robust growth in 2003. It was always to be expected that the USA economy would draw back to more normal growth rates, and in fact we are seeing the USA economy expanding around trend at the moment.

One of the main concerns, though, is that what we are currently experiencing may be more than just an easing back to cruising speed. The main difference between this recovery and more classic recoveries is that the downturn did not resolve all of the economy's imbalances and this has reduced the potential for growth. The most important of these is on the consumer side. The USA's personal savings rate did not recover during the downturn, largely because the Fed's low interest rate policy kept households spending, when confidence plummeted and jobs were being shed quickly. In Japan, zero interest rates and demographic change have helped contribute to a transformation of household savings patterns, so that Japan is now a low-saving economy in the Anglo-Saxon camp (figure 2.3). There is little scope, in fact, for consumers to spur growth by reducing their savings ratios in the USA, Canada, Australia, the UK or Japan. Where there is scope, in the Euro zone, German and Italian consumers are unlikely to react until the labour market has stabilised and French savings rates have been on a trend increase since 1988.

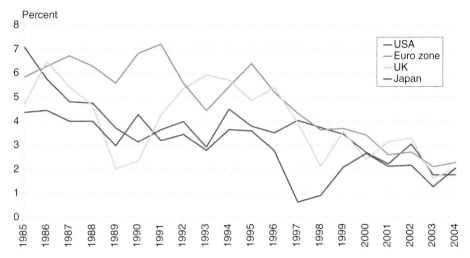

Figure 2.3:   Long term real interest rates are at historic lows
Source: Global Insight

Growth, then, must come from other sources. As usual, budget deficits are in a difficult position coming out of the downturn and there is almost no scope to use government spending to increase growth. Rather, deficits are under pressure almost everywhere to reduce and this would be a net drag on growth.

Apart from consumers and the public sector, the other main domestic sector of demand is investment spending, which is often the main stimulus to growth at this point in the cycle. As activity stabilises following a recession, firms find that their capacity limits are hit relatively quickly, because of a failure to maintain capital stock and employment levels during the downswing. If interest rates are low and profits have been restored by efficiency measures, this causes a sharp acceleration in investment spending that increases overall demand – particularly in the manufacturing sector. This is, to some extent, what we have been witnessing. All the G7 economies except Germany produced an investment recovery towards the end of 2003 that has generally continued. The outlook for investment spending remains good, given that inflation-adjusted interest rates, both short-term and long-term, are at historically low levels. In addition, corporate profits are high in the USA and the Euro zone, at reasonable levels in the UK and, although low in Japan, have staged something of a recovery there since 2000 (figure 2.4).

Corporate spending should, therefore, keep the global economy from falling back into recession, so long as interest rates stay low enough to

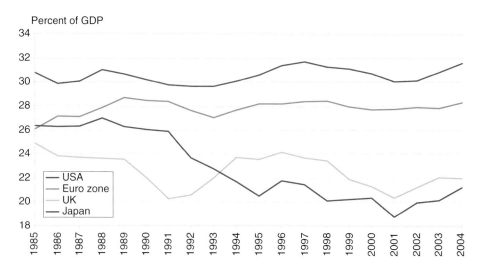

Figure 2.4: Profits have recovered across the OECD
Source: Global Insight

prevent a downturn in investment and/or a consumer retrenchment. Could exports provide additional growth? Not for the global economy as a whole. One country's (positive) exports are another's (negative) imports, so aggregate global growth is driven by domestic demand.

Although the short term seems secure, the next stage of growth will be disappointing. Once investment has expanded capacity, firms should then increase employment levels, spurring better consumer spending performance, but the outlook for employment growth in the major economies is not optimistic. In Japan, further corporate restructuring to improve efficiency should prevent the number of jobs rising over the short to medium term. In the USA, firms are still adjusting to higher productivity levels, which will reduce their short-term demand for labour. In the Euro zone, inflexible labour markets prevented a shake-out of employment in 2001, so now firms are already over-staffed, leaving little room for new hires.

Risks do abound, of course, but should not be over-played. The oil price, for one, can't be ignored and, although it is still some way from being the major threat to the economy, the next few months will be important to see whether recent price increases have been enough to set off a renewed trend towards higher inflation that could force central banks to raise rates faster. A more important risk comes from China. Not only does China play a crucial role in buying the manufacturing output of the rest of the world to use as inputs to its own manufacturing processes, it also supports the global financial system through purchases of US Treasury bonds that relieve upward pressure on the renminbi. October's policy moves by the People's Bank of China suggest that an upward revaluation of the renminbi has moved closer (which could cause Asian demand for US securities to fall away) and that the chances of a pronounced slowdown in China are more likely. The former effect would cause enormous instability, whilst the latter would cause a noticeable contraction in global activity.

The outlook for private business investment in 2010 (January 2010)

In response to falling demand, reduced access to credit and falling profitability, businesses have slashed investment spending over the past 18 months. Investment has contracted by 15–20% across the USA, Japan, the UK, Canada and Spain in 2009, wiping two percentage points off growth. By contrast, investment is estimated to have grown by 12% in China, supported by tax incentives and injection of credit into the private sector. Reduced investment in the advanced economies also reflects the natural response of businesses to conserve cash during periods of extreme uncertainty. Now that financial markets are beginning to normalise and the outlook is less bleak, it is a good time to assess whether this recovery is likely to be given a near-term boost from revived investment spending.

Business investment is the accumulation of physical assets, such as factories and machinery, by the private sector and accounts for around 14% of global GDP. In the short term, investment supports economic activity and employment levels. In the longer term, maintaining reasonable investment rates is important in renewing the capital stock and supporting growth, as well as being of particular interest to suppliers of capital goods and associated services including commercial property.

Two opposing forces will determine the direction of business investment this year. On the plus side, the rebound in financial markets has lowered the cost of finance for business. Combined with a much improved economic outlook, more profitable opportunities will emerge over the year, providing support for investment (figure 2.5). The rebound in equity prices has also pushed up the value of installed capital relative to its replacement cost, encouraging some businesses to expand production by investment rather than through mergers and acquisitions.

However, large amounts of spare capacity will weigh on investment in the short term. World output levels are around 5% per cent below capacity (known as 'the output gap'), so many businesses are likely to expand production by re-deploying idle capital and labour. Despite the recovering world

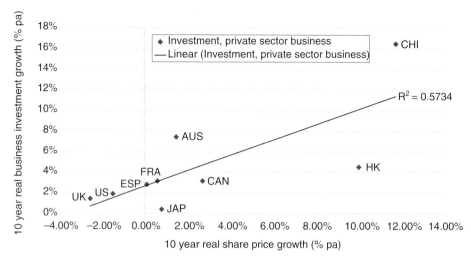

Figure 2.5:   Equity markets and business investment
Source: OEF

economy, profitability will remain under pressure, with output prices being constrained by subdued demand and intense competition. Weak profits and limited access to credit will constrain investment, particularly for small to medium-sized businesses. The positive impact of the stabilisation of financial markets may be negated by governments' borrowing requirements, with risk-free rates already drifting higher for economies with large deficits and no credible consolidation plans.

To help determine the shape of the recovery, business investment is modelled using interest rates, share price movements, the fiscal deficit and expectations of the output gap. Data from the USA, Canada, the UK, France, Spain, Japan, China, Hong Kong and Australia was used. The model explains around 60% of investment growth (see Table 2.1). Consistent with theory, the fiscal deficit is found to 'crowd out' investment, with higher deficits leading to lower levels of credit available for private sector use. Investment is found to be boosted by buoyant share prices, low real interest rates and a low level of spare capacity. Momentum is also important, with strong investment last year leading to strong investment this year.

After controlling for cyclical effects, the model indicates that OECD countries have been under-investing whilst China has been over-investing. China's decade-long investment binge has created excess capacity and deflationary pressures in many sectors (Figure 2.6). This is one of the main reasons for under-investment in the OECD and will continue to prevent investment from making a comeback in 2010. Even under the assumption that share prices appreciate 15% in 2010 and the output gap in 2011 narrows

Table 2.1

Variable	Coefficient	Std. Error	Significance	
Constant	0.05	0.01	0.0	R-squared (0.6)
Investment growth (−1)	0.27	0.05	0.0	
Investment growth (−2)	−0.26	0.05	0.0	F-Statistic Significance (0.0)
Real share price growth	0.06	0.01	0.0	
Real share price growth (−1)	0.07	0.02	0.0	
Real change in long-term interest rates	−0.50	0.20	0.0	
Fiscal deficit as % of GDP	0.41	0.08	0.0	
Output gap (+1)	0.39	0.18	0.0	
Fixed Effects	AUS (0.02), CAN (0.0), CHI (0.08), FRA (−0.02), HK (−0.01), JAP (−0.05), ESP (0.01), UK (0.0), US (0.0)			

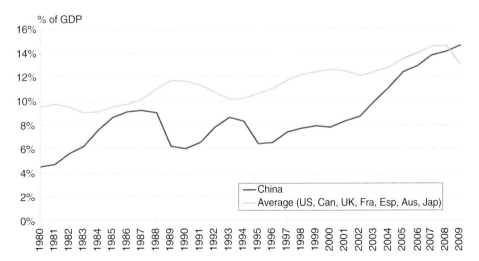

Figure 2.6:   Business investment as % of GDP
Source: OEF

by one-third, the model suggests that world investment will be flat in 2010. The conditions for a full investment revival will not be in place until 2011. So we expect the recovery to weaken in the second half of 2010 and only become firmly entrenched in 2011.

Are we heading towards global deflation? (December 2001)

Deflation is when prices fall systematically and persistently across the economy, as has been happening in Japan, Hong Kong and the Chinese consumer sector for some time. At the country level, it is highly unusual and creates huge problems for economic growth. If prices are on a falling trend, consumers and companies are often better off to wait before making a purchase, because they know prices will drop further and this acts as a drag on growth (Figure 2.7). The ability of policy makers to do anything about this is weakened, because negative inflation means that real interest rates are always positive, which prevents central banks adopting the level of easing currently being seen in the USA, for example. In addition, nominal GDP can start falling because prices are falling, which raises the ratio of debt to GDP and makes it harder for governments to maintain a policy of fiscal expansion. For real estate investors deflation presents particular problems, because ERVs and retail sector turnover are closely linked to inflationary trends. Upward-only rent reviews clearly provide a large measure of

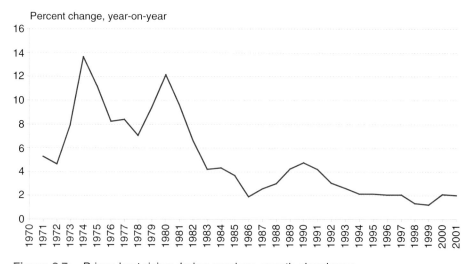

Figure 2.7:   Prices kept rising during previous growth slowdowns

protection in the UK; but elsewhere, deflation should translate into falling rental growth and therefore falling returns on capital, unless yields drop.

With monthly declines in the inflation numbers for the major Western economies, some analysts have begun to talk about global deflation. This has not happened in modern economic history, not even in the weakest periods of global growth (Figure 2.7); but cannot be ruled out because the current economic slowdown is being caused by a huge capacity glut that could force prices of goods to keep falling. It is unlikely, though, that the level of current spare capacity is great enough to generate global deflation because, while the prices of goods are falling, service sector prices in the West are still rising healthily – continuing the pattern of the last few years. This is particularly evident in the USA and the UK, where household demand has remained relatively strong and tight labour markets have forced employers to pass on extra wage costs to their customers. Global deflation probably requires a severe recession in the household sector of a number of Western economies in order to reduce demand for services and increase unemployment and, therefore, the supply of workers to the service sector.

Deflationary conditions may be already present in parts of the West (October 2002)

Despite current signs of an increase in western inflation, the global down-turn continues to raise the prospect of worldwide deflation following fast on the heels of the reality of deflation across most of the East Asian economy. In the West, inflation is running at just 1–2% in all the leading economies and has been close to 1% in Germany, the USA, France, the UK and Canada at points over the last year (Figure 2.8). But inflation estimates outside the USA probably overstate the true extent of inflation, because they do not adjust for product improvements. When product quality improves, a new product has theoretically been created and any price increases should be estimated net of product improvements. Most national price indices do not make the necessary adjustments, though, and this biases the inflation estimate upwards by around 1%, which suggests that in many economies prices have been largely static over recent months. In addition, within the overall inflation estimates, the prices of goods and of services have been behaving very differently. While prices in the service sector have been increasing rapidly as employee costs increase, goods sector prices have been falling, as excess capacity has translated into slimmer margins. Thus, in many purchase decisions, Western consumers are already faced with deflation.

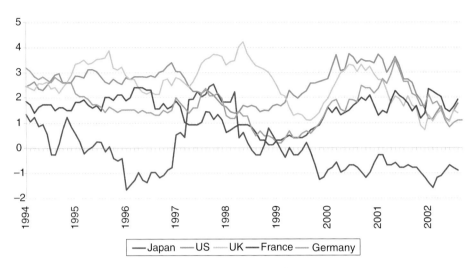

Figure 2.8:   Inflation in the world's leading economies

The significance of this is that consumers will behave differently when prices are falling compared to when prices are rising normally. Normally, consumers know that if they delay making purchases and hold cash, the real value of that cash is eroded as prices rise and the money does not earn any interest. This increases the costs to the consumer of delay, beyond the inconvenience of not being able to own the product in question, and helps make sure households keep spending. If prices were to start falling, though, the opposite would happen. As consumers hold on to their cash it grows, in real terms, because lower prices in the future mean that its purchasing power rises. Hence, the cost of delay is reduced and may completely disappear, making it rational for households to stop spending. A further effect is that deflation makes it very difficult to adjust relative prices. When one product needs to become cheaper relative to another, the easiest way for that to happen is for its price to rise less quickly than other prices. But when prices are stagnant or falling, a change in relative prices often requires an outright fall in nominal prices. As sellers are often reluctant to actually cut their nominal prices, deflation tends to mean that relative prices adjust more slowly, making the overall economy less efficient.

The implication for real estate returns is that deflation should be damaging, because it reduces demand, particularly in the sectors most exposed to the consumer. But there is a more direct effect, via rent-setting. Because rents are either formally related to movements in the consumer price index or nominal retail sales values, or informally adjust to changing inflation levels to keep real rents in line with the market demand/supply balance, falling inflation should mean falling nominal returns. Compensation could come via a yield improvement, if lower inflation is perceived to be permanent and bond yields decline. But the current bout of deflation is not likely to be viewed as permanent and is unlikely to cause a downward shift in yields.

Are buoyant asset markets enough to stimulate recovery? (March 2010)

In late 2007, global asset prices began to collapse, as the implications of the impending economic downturn became clear. The fall in asset prices triggered a global credit crunch, a slump in production and the real threat of deflation. Real estate was at the heart of the crisis, because of the amount of bank lending which it secured. Luckily, governments and central banks moved quickly to stabilise the situation. There were three choices: (1) create general inflation, to reduce the real value of debt; (2) allow the recession to run its course, with consumers rebuilding their balance sheets by increased savings; and (3) 'engineer' asset price inflation, to de-gear consumers and businesses. Whilst policy-makers clearly have an eye on (1) and (2), the main thrust of action has been on (3). So far, it seems to have worked.

Figure 2.9 shows the peak to trough decline, the recovery and the overall standing of each market compared to its previous high. Of course, the

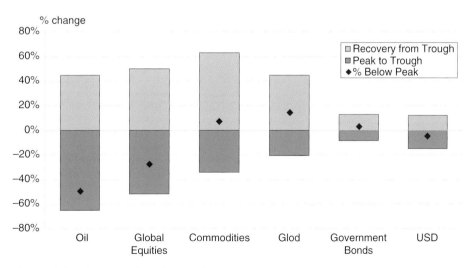

Figure 2.9: Asset markets have reflated
Source: HIS Global Insight

factors behind the resurgence of each type of 'asset' vary. Stocks have risen, because the risk premium fell after the financial system was rescued. Bonds have been boosted by quantitative easing and the flight to safe assets. Oil and commodities have risen on resilient emerging market growth and speculation. Broadly speaking, however, the recent asset market surge has been due to huge monetary stimulus.

Since about Q3 of 2009, real estate markets have also begun to reflate. Figure 2.10 shows the office sector, which has shown the strongest revival; Figure 2.11 shows retail markets; and Figure 2.12 the housing market. Although quantitative easing does not impact real estate directly, ultra-low interest rates and increased liquidity have forced investors to look for alternatives to bank deposits at the safer end of the real estate market. The office sector has shown the strongest rebound, because it has been affected not just by 'the search for yield', but also by the revival in fundamentals associated with rising stock prices and freer capital markets. The retail and residential sectors are more dependent on economy-wide employment growth and so are more sluggish.

Real estate markets are a key part of the 'transmission mechanism' from monetary policy to the real economy. In commercial real estate markets, according to Real Capital Analytics, $247 bn. of debt is 'in distress': $150 billion in the USA, $69 billion in Europe and $29 billion in Asia. As real estate values increase, the incidence of distress falls and banks restart

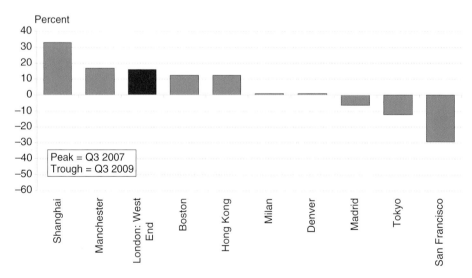

Figure 2.10:   Office values are in recovery
Source: Various agents, Grosvenor Research, 2010

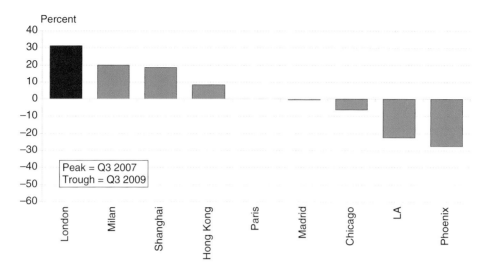

Figure 2.11:   Retail values are in recovery
Source: Various agents, Grosvenor Research, 2010

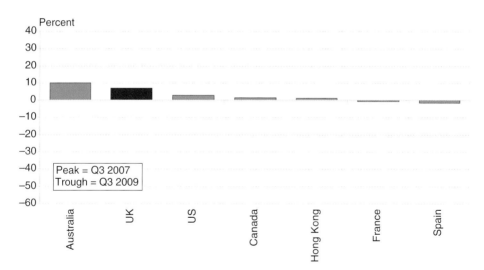

Figure 2.12:   Residential value growth is sluggish
Source: Various agents, Grosvenor Research, 2010

lending. There is also an impact on the demand for loans, as corporate sector loan capacity increases. In the household sector, rising asset prices (stocks and housing) helps to offset accumulated debt and to stimulate spending on goods and services. Another important boost comes from revived construction activity, as house-building begins.

So, although the impact is indirect, rising asset prices have played a significant role in the recovery of the last six months, particularly in offsetting the slump in economic confidence that took hold in 2008 and 2009. The fall in consumers' spending has been nowhere near as deep as expected. Moreover, as confidence has improved firms have moved quickly to rebuild stocks. However, with the first phase over, continued recovery requires growth in consumption and fixed capital investment. Again, the health of consumer and business balance sheets will be crucial. Unfortunately, the global fiscal stimulus is ending and extensive government borrowing is beginning to push long-term interest rates up. Fundamentals are probably not yet strong enough to support asset prices. The second half of 2010 will provide a testing time for asset markets and economies. So we conclude that asset price inflation provides a powerful, but ultimately only temporary boost to the global economy.

Has the global economy passed its worst? (July 2001)

Throughout the first half of 2001, most economists and forecasters were expecting the US economy to relaunch in the second half of the year and for the European economy to remain strong. That assessment now looks optimistic, so this article is devoted to examining the G7 economies, which account for most of global output. Much of the gloom has been caused by falling profits and large redundancies in the industrial sector, so it is important to realise that the industrial sector typically accounts for just 20–25% of a G7 economy, and that each of the G7 can easily shrug off a manufacturing recession, unless the sector's problems are shared by the service sector or a manufacturing contraction reduces confidence enough to stop consumers spending.

How bad is the outlook for industrial production? The manufacturing sectors of the G7 countries are closely linked. Outputs are traded in the same global marketplace and there is a high degree of product similarity between countries. In addition, the outputs of one country's industrial sector are often the inputs of another's. Given these linkages, it has come as little surprise to see a softening in the industrial sectors of each of the G7 economies (Figure 2.13). What has been surprising, to some extent, has

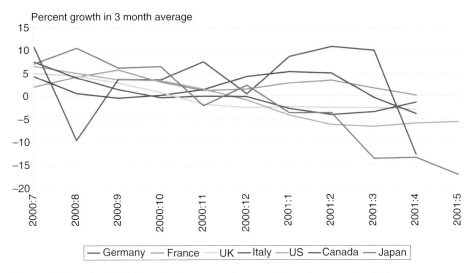

Percent growth in 3 month average

Figure 2.13: Industrial production on a downward trend across the G7

been the differential impact of the slowdown. Germany has suffered more than any other European economy, despite being a highly successful manufacturer. As during the 1998 Asia crisis, it is showing itself particularly sensitive to weakening global demand for manufactured goods. In the USA, the sector is still shrinking, despite stabilisation in Canada.

The driver of the downturn was the build-up of over-capacity in the sector, following the investment spending spree of 1999/2000. The contractions reflect an unwinding of that spree, which is clearly continuing. There is little evidence that the contraction is about to end, and indeed may be worsening outside North America. Another weak quarter for industrial production seems inevitable.

It is well-known that the US economy has survived recession because the consumer has kept spending. Consumption spending makes up around two-thirds of total spending in the industrialised economies, so recessions are unlikely to happen if it remains solid. The over-capacity that has hit the manufacturing sector has little direct impact on US consumption and so the main transmission mechanism to the wider economy is likely to be through falling confidence. Although confidence has deteriorated in some economies, notably in the USA, it appears to be still high enough to maintain spending. The most up-to-date data on household spending comes from retail sales volumes, which is closely related to total consumer spending. Figure 2.14 indicates that the situation in Japan is deteriorating, but that most of the Euro zone is now recovering from a dip during the first quarter, while the USA is flat, but holding firm. In Canada volumes have strengthened significantly recently, while the UK has been generating extremely

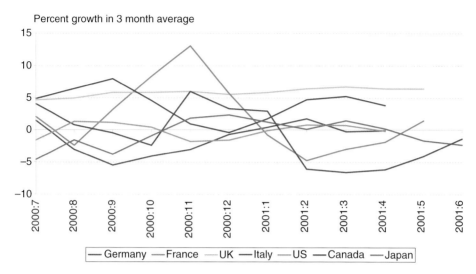

Percent growth in 3 month average

Germany —France —UK —Italy —US —Canada —Japan

Figure 2.14:   Retail sales volumes recovering or stable in most economies

strong activity throughout the year. The problems in Japan are as much a function of domestic factors as international ones and will probably persist throughout 2001.

The reason for this generally upbeat picture is that manufacturing recessions have not generated big increases in joblessness. Employment has actually been growing in Canada and the USA over the last two quarters, as the service sector has taken the opportunity to eliminate long-standing staff shortages. With the unemployment rate hardly affected by the downturn and wages continuing to rise, consumption looks fairly solid at first glance. The big uncertainties are the outlook for the stock market in North America and real wage increases across the G7. The unsustainability of low savings rates in the USA and the UK are only a concern if unemployment rises. Although much has been made of the negative savings rate in the USA, this is because of inconsistencies in its calculation which includes taxes on capital gains (reducing the rate) but not the capital gains themselves (which would increase the rate). Hence negative savings is to some extent an illusion and could well continue.

Falling stock markets do reduce wealth and should damage consumer spending. But the relationship between wealth and spending is not clearly defined and declines seen so far have not been enough to trigger a consumer retrenchment. Pessimists argue that the run-up in the market in 1999 requires a larger downward correction to restore balance. If they are right, we might yet see a negative wealth effect. But a bigger problem may be real wages. Settlements have generally remained under control, particularly in the Euro zone, but at the same time inflation has risen, cutting real wage increases. This will improve the medium-term profitability of the corporate sector, but is already eroding gains in household purchasing power. The probable result is continued softness in consumer spending in the Euro zone, and perhaps a softening in the USA if inflation there goes above 4%. But inflation is unlikely to exceed nominal wage increases and without that, real wage increases should remain positive, preventing a recession in the wider economy.

How will rising interest rates impact real estate markets? (January 2011)

The legacy of the great financial crisis (GFC) is no less evident today than it was a year ago. The Euro zone banking system, particularly in the peripheral countries, is undercapitalised and exposed to non-performing real estate loans. Certain Euro zone governments lack the resources to recapitalise their commercial banks. In the USA, the construction sector remains depressed, because of the stagnant housing market, depriving the economy of the normal cyclical employment boost. In Asia, the Chinese authorities have had to act to restrain inflation in goods and asset prices, resulting from earlier policy measures. Against these negatives, the global economy seems to be growing around its trend rate of growth of 4%. The Grosvenor indicator of current economic activity, which is composed of the timeliest monthly data, shows that, despite volatility, the global recovery is solid (figure 2.15). Moreover, a modicum of inflation is returning to the system.

The rebound in economic activity has been led by the production sector, as companies have restocked and consumer spending has responded to low interest rates and rising asset prices. Going forward, we expect falling unemployment and reviving business confidence to drive further gains in consumption and investment. Renewed fiscal and monetary stimulus in the USA should fuel above-trend growth in 2011. Prompt and effective action by the ECB and the IMF is likely to see the Euro zone through the inevitable banking and sovereign debt crises of 2011. Notwithstanding inflation, the Chinese authorities are politically committed to maintaining growth of between 8% and 10%, which will maintain momentum in emerging markets. All of this adds up to the start of the next rate cycle.

Taylor rule analysis also suggests that OECD interest rates are set to rise. The 'Taylor rule' is a mathematical formula that links policy rates, which control inflation, to the current level of inflation (relative to its target rate) and the output gap. Thus, if inflation is rising and/or unemployment falling, the Taylor rule indicates by how much interest rates need to rise and vice

Figure 2.15:   Trend growth in the global economy
Source: IHS Global Insight, Grosvenor Research, 2010

versa. Over the long term, the rule has quite a good track record of predict-ing actual movements in short-term interest rates. Importantly for this analysis, the Taylor rule indicates that interest rates are too low for current economic conditions. Figure 2.16 shows the average OECD short-term interest rate alongside the rate of interest recommended by the Taylor rule. The analysis indicates that, because of recent growth, OECD interest rates should now be increased. At the moment, central banks are more concerned about the downside risks to growth, so they are holding rates down and allowing monetary policy to become 'super-loose'. But the pressure to increase rates is building.

So how will rising interest rates affect global real estate markets? In the first phase of the tightening cycle, when short-term interest rates rise slowly and growth dominates, the chief impact will be via the bond market. Bond yields have already risen and we think they will rise further, as markets sense the end of quantitative easing and more substantive inflation pres-sures. This shift in bond yields could come as early as mid-2011, but will certainly be in place by 2012. Rising bond yields will put upward pressure on real estate yields. Emerging markets and resource-based economies, which are further ahead in the tightening cycle, will probably be affected first. Prime real estate markets, which have seen substantial inward yield shift over the period of quantitative easing, are also vulnerable. We do not foresee a major correction in real estate markets, because of three factors. First, growth will dominate, generating user demand for space. Second, one

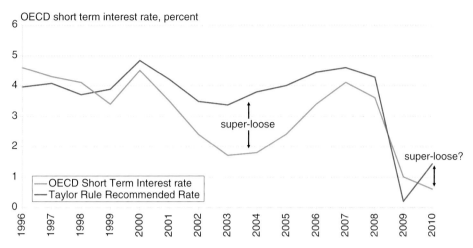

Figure 2.16: Monetary policy is 'super-loose'
Source: OECD, IHS Global Insight, 2010

of the few benign legacies of the GFC, at least from a real estate investment perspective, is that construction of commercial property is at a virtual standstill. Falling availability over the next few years will lead to rental growth. Third, relatively generous income returns gives real estate a degree of protection from rising interest rates. Towards the end of 2013, as short rates approach the peak of the next rate cycle, we would see an impact on real estate feeding through from weakening economic activity. Countries like the UK, where variable mortgage rates are important, will suffer housing-market and retail weakness. To a greater or lesser extent, however, all markets will be affected by a pronounced 'mid-cycle' fall in activity. What are the investment implications of this analysis? Timing is important. Investors will need to opt for short 'tactical' hold periods of up to three years, or longer ones of five to six years, which avoid the peak of the next rate cycle. Passive investment strategies focused on prime real estate are also increasingly risky; more nuanced strategies based on changing patterns of real estate use are better. More broadly, investors should be long on equities, short on bonds and neutral on real estate.

Is the USA really in recovery? (December 2002)

The surprisingly good news coming out of the US economy in the third quarter has once again confounded the sceptics (including this writer), who were expecting the final data from September to be bad enough to cause a significant downward revision to the initial GDP estimate. The initial estimate is always based only on projections for the third month in the quarter and all evidence seemed to be pointing to a stalling of activity in September, compared with July and August. But, in the end, the Bureau of Economic Affairs (BEA) found that the economy was actually stronger in September than in the earlier parts of the quarter. There is some weakness in the release – much of the upward revision from the initial estimate of 3.1% came from higher stockbuilding that will only detract from growth in the coming quarters – but overall consumption spending remained strong, investment spending bottomed out and net trade was neutral. Perhaps, then, the economy is coming right sooner than expected? To gauge this, it is worth looking at the key imbalances that preceded the recession. The most important was an investment binge that generated over-capacity in a number of sectors and reduced profitability. The fall in fixed investment spending since 2000 has been a dramatic response to this binge and was the main driver of the 2001 recession. In Q3, fixed investment was up an annualised 0.5%, which is small enough to be considered 'no change', but meant that spending had stayed constant throughout the second and third quarters, after falling 7.6% since Q3 2000. In year-on-year terms, investment spending was still down, by 2.6%, but, given the rate of the recent collapse, this could well be viewed as stabilisation. The second key imbalance was the very low savings rate, that had been driven down to almost zero by massive wealth gains creating the expectation that wealth increases would continue indefinitely. A likely response to the recession was a sharp upward correction in the savings rate as unemployment rose and expectations of future wealth gains were eroded (Figure 2.17). This would have translated into a consumer recession. But instead, the sharp reduction in interest rates kept the housing market buoyant and protected household wealth from the fall in equity valuations. But spending did ease as incomes carried on rising, allowing the savings rate to increase gradually. It now stands at just over 4%, which is probably where it should have been at the start of the recession, rather than close to zero. There is still upward adjustment to come, but the savings rate is moving closer to balance now.

So does this mean that the fundamentals for the US economy are now good enough to provide a solid launch pad for future growth? Not quite. The share of investment spending in GDP still looks extremely high by historical standards, indicating that the binge has yet to fully unwind (Figure 2.18). In addition, the growth that is evident in the economy is the result of extremely low nominal interest rates that have pushed real interest rates below zero while core inflation is over 2% and headline inflation is rebounding. If growth continues over the coming months, inflation will increase further and the Fed will have to consider raising rates. This would

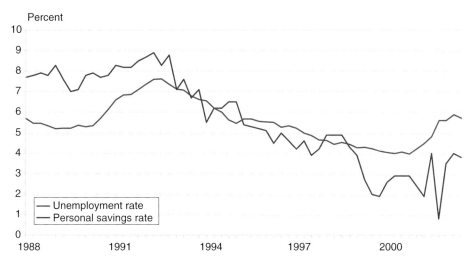

Figure 2.17:   US savings rate is set to increase

Figure 2.18:   Real fixed investment as percent of real GDP

hit all asset prices hard – both housing and non-housing – and increase the negative impact of the extremely high debt levels the economy has accumulated. Growth would fall back to the sort of weak recovery we have been expecting for some time. Even with the good news from Q3, hopes of a vigorous recovery look more optimistic than realistic.

Investment could lead the recovery – but not yet (July 2003)

The current global slowdown was triggered by a collapse in investment spending around the world, following a period of very strong demand, for ICT-related products in particular. The timing of the recovery is also likely to depend upon the demand for investment products, in line with basic macro-economic theory that highlights the resurgence of investment spending after a period of attrition, as the classic driver of an economic rebound. During recessions, investment spending falls faster than most other components of demand, driving a reduction in the size of the capital stock. Eventually, this means that even stagnant output levels cause rising levels of capacity utilisation, just because the capital stock is falling, so that when demand does increase slightly the capital stock is inadequate, driving firms to increase their investment spending. Just as falls in investment spending can be extremely rapid, so increases can also be dramatic. This volatility means that a pick-up in general demand can drive an investment rebound large enough to kick-start self-sustaining growth for the wider economy.

To assess whether the conditions are right for an investment rebound, capacity utilisation figures are most often used. But these, typically, focus on the manufacturing sector, which limits their usefulness as a guide to overall investment spending – although the data for the US economy suggests that utilisation in manufacturing is still too low for a rebound. Trends in the share of investment spending within GDP can give a more useful guide to possible rebounds, because there is some evidence that this ratio reverts back to a long-run average. Certainly, the late 1990s run-up in the share of real investment spending (excluding price effects) did give a clear signal of the recent investment recession in the USA and the UK (Figure 2.19). But this ratio has yet to fall far enough to give a clear indication that spending is about to recover, particularly in the USA.

Part of the reason, though, is that the prices of investment products have been deflating, while prices in the economy at large have not. This means that investment spending as a share of GDP, in real terms (excluding price effects), is behaving differently from the ratio, in nominal terms. Both ratios increased sharply during the mid-1990s, but the ratio in nominal terms was not as extreme and has come back to average levels already. The nominal ratio is the better version to use because if the prices of investment goods are persistently falling, firms should be buying more of them, which would cause a long-run rise in the real ratio, but leave the nominal ratio relatively stable. The nominal ratio suggests that investment spending

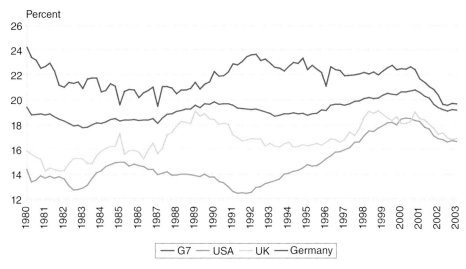

Figure 2.19:   Real investment as % of GDP looks far from a rebound outside Germany
Source: Global Insight

has moderated, but is not yet ready for a rebound (Figure 2.20). That would change, though, with another year of declining investment and subdued GDP growth.

UK savings rates have recovered, but the USA still looks out of balance (September 2002)

Of the various imbalances hanging over the US economy in the run-up to the last recession, one of the most serious was the low savings rate. This was also a feature of the UK economy, but one that was missing from the main Euro zone economies and Japan. Low savings rates arise when households spend more of their income than current and future economic conditions warrant – typically, when they assume that temporary boom conditions will persist. After this undershooting of savings rates occurs, an upward correction to more appropriate levels takes place. During this correction, households will spend less of their income than they would normally, causing low consumption growth that can often generate a recession. In the USA, estimates of the household savings rate (which is the proportion of disposable income that is saved and not consumed) fell to very low levels, as households spent wealth as well as their current income. The low point, of under 1%, compares to savings rate of around 15% in the Euro zone and even higher in Asia. In the UK, rates fell to just over 3%. Much of the decrease, though, was justified by reductions in the probability of becoming unemployed in both the USA and the UK (Figure 2.21). In the Euro zone, unemployment reductions were much less significant and less prolonged.

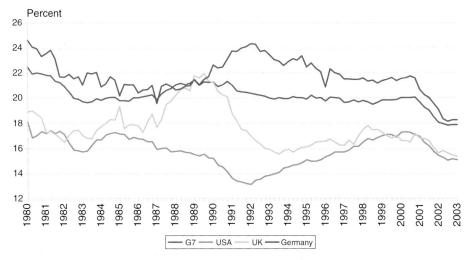

Figure 2:20:   A rebound in nominal investment looks closer
Source: Global Insight

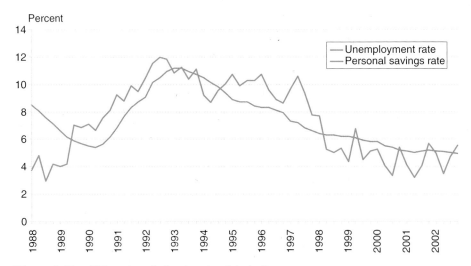

Figure 2.21:   UK savings behaviour back in balance
Source: Global Insight

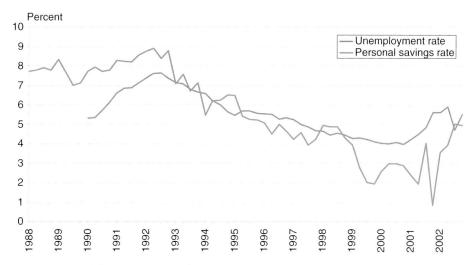

Figure 2.22:   US savings rate still looks too low
Source: Global Insight

But the final falls in savings of 1999 and 2000, particularly in the USA, were out of line with labour market conditions, raising the possibility of an upward correction in savings behaviour that could produce a US consumer recession (Figure 2.22).

Since the end of last year, savings rates have picked up in both the UK and the USA, but US rates still appear to be undershooting, while the UK looks to be back in balance. If confidence among US households continues to fall, this undershooting will become unsustainable and the savings rate should move further back towards an appropriate level, by perhaps three or four percentage points. This would cause either a sharp contraction of consumer spending or a prolonged period of very weak activity. In either case, the retail sector would suffer directly along with the housing market. But with consumption the largest element of the US economy, all sectors would eventually suffer further as the economy fell back into recession.

How to save the world: by not saving (December 2009)

One of the factors that drove global economic growth from the mid-1990s was falling savings rates. Around one-third of world growth over this period was driven by household spending in the USA, the UK, Spain and Canada.

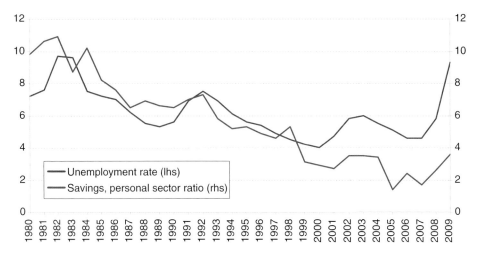

Figure 2.23: Unemployment and the savings rate in the US
Source: Bank of England

As the big economies saved less, they consumed more and production, particularly in emerging markets, responded to meet this demand. We can see the long decline in US savings rates in Figure 2.23. In the short term, there is a clear link between unemployment and savings: when jobs are plentiful, households spend and in times of recession, households retrench. But, in the longer term, the trend is downward. The current rise in savings rates in countries such as the USA, the UK and Spain, in response to rising unemployment, is taking a big chunk out of global final demand, so depressing economic growth. One of the ways out of the current crisis, it has been argued, is for those countries with historically high savings rates to enact policies to cut these and boost consumer spending. Put more simply, the once indestructible US consumer has been dealt a severe blow by the credit crunch and other countries, in Europe and the emerging markets, need to 'take up the baton'. Figure 2.24 shows savings rates across the OECD and the key emerging markets and, on the face of it, there seems to be plenty of room for increased consumption in the key emerging economies of China and India and the big OECD economies of France and Germany.

To assess the potential for high savings countries to boost consumption we conducted a 'cross-sectional regression analysis', to determine the key drivers of savings rates across the OECD and key emerging markets. The results are in Table 2.2. The coefficients are of the standardised 'beta' type, so they indicate the relative importance of each variable. Overall, the analysis accounts for 71% of international differences in savings rates. The model confirms that unemployment is an important driver of savings, but it is far

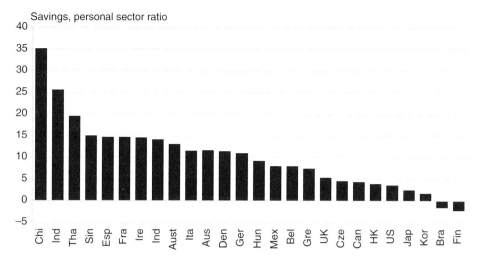

Figure 2.24: Global savings rates 2008

Table 2.2

Variable	Coefficient	Std. Error	t-Statistic	Prob.
C	0.16	0.11	1.56	0.14
Unemployment rate	0.22	0.11	1.97	0.06
% Service sector output	−0.49	0.12	−3.90	0.00
% Service sector output (emerging markets)	−0.48	0.26	−1.84	0.08
Age dependency ratio	0.26	0.12	2.24	0.04
Gini coefficient	0.48	0.13	3.73	0.00
R-squared	0.77	Mean dependent var		0.12
Adjusted R-squared	0.71	S.D. dependent var		0.94
F-statistic	12.24	Prob (F-statistic)		0.00

from the most important. More important than employment is the proportion of national output generated by the service sector. Service sector output probably represents a 'bundle' of key societal developments. The growth of the service sector is, in part, driven by the development of state welfare services and it is also associated with a reduction in the volatility of the business cycle. Service sector output is twice as important in the emerging markets as it is in the OECD, probably because these economies are just beginning the transition from manufacturing to services. The dependency ratio, measured as the number of people below the age of 15 and over the age of 65 divided by the number of people of working age, also has a material impact on savings. The higher the level of dependents, the more those of working age have to make provision against unforeseen events, such as higher medical and care bills and schooling and pensions. Finally, our model suggests that the level of inequality in society affects savings rates. This is measured by the – oddly named – 'Gini' coefficient. The greater the discrepancy between higher and lower income groups, the greater the savings ratio. This is because higher-income groups have a much higher propensity to save than low-income groups.

As our model explains only 70% of variation in savings rates across countries, we know that other factors are at work. We suspect that the level of home ownership, the availability of consumer credit, taxation, extended family networks and social attitudes to bankruptcy are all influential. These factors and those that have statistical significance in our model tend to change only slowly over time. So, it is highly unlikely that the 'high savings' economies will be able to expand consumption in the short and medium term to offset the loss of consumption (rise in savings) in the USA, the UK, Australia and parts of the Euro zone. In turn, this suggests that the world economy faces a longish period of weak growth. Not only this, but asset markets will remain volatile and over-inflated, as excess savings 'slosh' around the world, trying to find a home.

Events to watch – is OPEC about to set off a second oil crisis? (October 2000)

OPEC-inspired increases in oil prices have raised the prospect of a third oil crisis that could derail the world economy and plunge global property markets into recession. But while the political fallout has been heavy in many countries, the economic impact has been muted. A stronger economic reaction would be a highly negative factor for the main international property markets, as it would cause weaker economic growth and higher interest rates as central banks responded to the rising inflationary pressures. This combination would lead to reduced demand across all market sectors.

These dramatic effects are some way from becoming reality. Current oil prices are still low, once inflation has been taken into account (Figure 2.25), and in addition the industrialised economies are now much less reliant on oil than they were in the1970s. Thus the economic consequences have been relatively moderate. The price rises have added 0.5–1.0% to inflation across

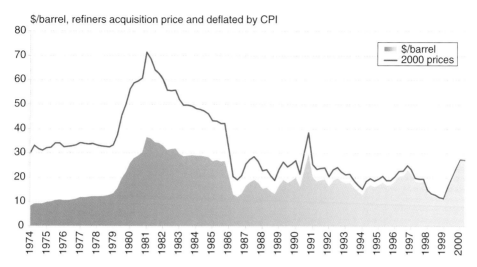

Figure 2.25: Oil prices are still low in real terms
Source: Global Insight

the industrialised world (even in the Euro zone, where the weakening euro/ dollar exchange rate that has meant that crude prices have quadrupled in Euro terms, while they tripled in dollar terms), and this impact should gradually subside over the coming months. There will be a negative growth impact, as the manufacturing sector suffers and central banks raise interest rates, but if the oil price stays around current levels, Standard & Poor's estimate that the growth impact will be around 0.5%, which is in line with estimates from the OECD. Such an outcome would have a relatively minor effect on the global property industry.

What would happen if prices rose further? Standard & Poor's have conducted a global scenario that looks at the possible impact of oil rising to an average of $40 per barrel over 2001 and, in this case, the growth impact is stronger, but nowhere near the scale of a recession. They expect this level of oil prices to take around 1% off global growth, bringing Europe back to trend growth levels (rather than the current forecast of strong growth next year), shifting the US economy back below 3% and preventing the Japanese economy escaping the 0.5–1.0% growth range.

The lesson is that it will take a much greater price rise than we have seen so far to send the global economy into recession. Is this likely to happen? Most commentators think not – but they also believed that prices would slip back to $20 over the summer of 2000. One of the main threats comes from Iraq, whose production levels are higher than the rest of OPEC's combined capacity. So if Iraq wanted to disrupt the world economy by cutting production, there is little that other OPEC members could do to compensate.

However, a key problem at the moment is that tankers and refineries cannot handle enough oil to satisfy global demand for refined products. Thus, if the global economy were to accelerate further, rising demand would push oil prices even higher. This is unlikely, though. Most major regions cannot grow much faster than current levels.

How is this oil shock different from the 1970s? (October 2005)

The current real price[1] of oil is above the level reached in the 1973 oil crisis, but below the all-time high of 1978–9. We estimate oil has to rise to about $100 per barrel in order to reach its previous high in real terms. With a slower rate of economic growth and oil companies' stated intentions to expand refining capacity, a rise of this magnitude seems unlikely.

Why has the higher oil price not generated inflation or extinguished growth this time around? There are several reasons. In 1973–4, during the first oil crisis, prices in the developed world surged, while this time around inflation and wages have hardly moved. Globalisation, flexible labour markets and improved monetary policy management have kept prices and wages in check. Today, companies are not held hostage by workers' demands for higher wages, because of the implicit threat that their jobs can be exported. Also, central banks have more credibility in fighting inflation and are less accommodating than they were in the 1970s and expectations of low inflation are well-entrenched.

As to the diminished impact of oil prices on economic growth, the OECD members ('rich countries'), which account for the lion's share of the global economy, have been shifting from energy-intensive manufacturing activities to services. These countries are also steadily improving their energy efficiency. The combined effect of these two trends is that, for a given unit of GDP output, energy inputs are declining by between 1.5% and 2.0% per annum,[2] so that an oil shock will not have as much of an impact on growth as it had in the 1970s. So demand for oil has been increasing at a rate of

---

[1] We use a global GDP deflator created by Global Insight. The real price of oil is highly sensitive to the measure of inflation used. For instance, some deflators may show the current price of oil to be at an all-time high.

[2] International Energy Agency, *The Experience with Energy Efficiency Policies and Programmes in IEA Countries*.

about 1.2% per annum among 'rich countries'. By contrast, non-OECD ('developing') countries' demand for oil has been increasing at a rate of 2.1% per annum.

This discussion highlights another difference between today and the past; the 1970s oil crisis was caused by a supply shock brought about by the unilateral action by a group of oil-producing nations. Today's experience has less to do with oil rationing and more to do with high levels of demand coming up against insufficient refining capacity. In addition, oil-producing economies were far less developed in the 1970s than now. The oil revenue they earned simply could not be spent, so it was banked. Today, increased revenues boost demand for goods and services in oil-producing economies and this creates increased demand for exports from non-oil producers, helping to offset the 'taxation' effect of higher oil prices.

If the foregoing discussions sound a bit optimistic, we should sound a cautionary note. The full effects of oil price rises may not yet have been felt in the global economy. In our statistical analysis, the seventh quarter after an oil price rise was found to be the most significant. In this cycle, the initial oil shock began at the end of 2003, in the wake of the invasion of Iraq, when the price of oil jumped about 20%. Subsequent demand shocks occurred earlier this year, so the full impact should be felt in greatest force in 2006 and 2007. We conducted another statistical exercise[3] that showed that the full effect of an oil shock takes three years to fully dissipate. Of course, if oil significantly declines in price in the future, this could counter earlier increases.

In addition to differing oil-intensity levels, currency and domestic resources affect oil impacts around the world. The oil market is dollar-denominated, so the fluctuation of a country's currency against the dollar impacts their energy costs. A country with a currency that's weakening against the dollar suffers additional pain from an increase in oil prices. Figure 2.26 shows that since 1970, the price that Germans pay for oil has increased most. Furthermore, the UK and the USA are oil producers and this has helped to defray the amount of oil they purchase on international markets. For about a decade, the UK was a net exporter of oil, though it has now begun to import to meet its needs. This and sterling's strength against the dollar has mitigated the impact of rising oil prices.

We analysed the impact that oil-price increases have had on economic growth in the four economies in Figure 2.26. In the USA, the UK and Germany, real oil prices had statistically significant impacts on economic growth, over approximately the same time frame. We then tried to establish if the relationship between oil and economic growth had changed since the crises in the 1970s. During the period from 1972 to 1985, the oil price rises

---

[3] Impulse response function on an unconstrained vector autoregressive regression.

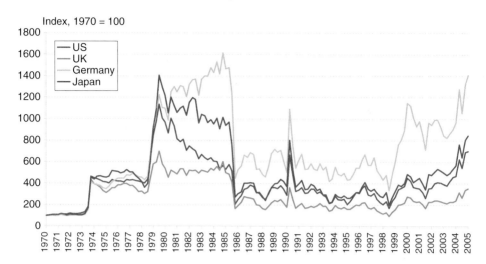

Figure 2.26:   Real oil price by country
Source: Global Insight, OEF, Grosvenor

appear to have impacted economic growth more rapidly and with more intensity. In the later period (1986 to 2005), oil's impact was clearly weaker. While these results point to a decline in oil's impact in today's economy, its impact on consumer and business sentiment should not be discounted. Although it appears that the global economy has navigated the current oil-price spike with limited damage, its full repercussions have yet to be played out.

Global financial markets – remaining challenges to a sustained recovery (August 2010)

Financial markets were at the epicentre of the crisis and their ongoing rehabilitation remains an essential part of a sustained global recovery. How far has this been achieved? There has certainly been a marked improvement in the health of the global financial system since the depth of the crisis. The global banking system has continued to improve, in line with stronger economic growth and the stabilisation of real estate and securities prices. The IMF (International Monetary Fund) estimates that banks have written-down the bulk of total losses from the crisis (around US$1.5 trillion of an estimated total of $2.3 trillion), with most of the remaining writedowns able to be covered from improved bank profits.

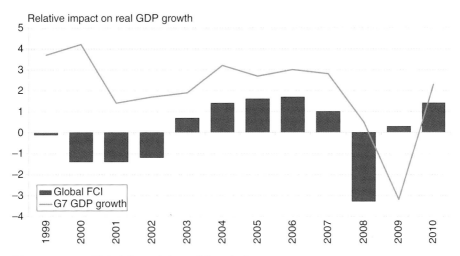

Figure 2.27: Global financial conditions index
Weighted average of (US, EU, Japan, China, UK, Canada and Australia). 2010 estimate is Q2 data.

As a result of this stabilisation, financial markets are now contributing strongly to short-term growth prospects by passing through the unprecedented central bank stimulus to households and business. This is captured by our global Financial Conditions Index (Figure 2.27),[4] which shows that financial stimulus will add around 2.5% to global growth over the next 12 months.

Nonetheless, there are still challenges to overcome before global financial markets return to full health. European banks face problems, given their large holdings of EU government bonds. While the ECB (European Central Bank) has been working hard in recent weeks to assuage market fears by purchasing EU government bonds and publishing its favourable bank stress test results, Europe faces a difficult road ahead and remains the most likely source of further disruptions in global financial markets.

European banking concerns are also complicating the refinancing challenge confronting banks. Globally, banks must refinance a sizeable US$5 trillion in maturing debt over the next two to three years (Figure 2.28). One concern is that they are still too heavily reliant on cheap central bank liquidity as a funding source. With central banks anxious to start winding back their liquidity support, banks will be forced either to shrink their assets or to turn to more expensive funding alternatives, such as corporate

---

[4] The FCI captures the combined effects of short- and long-term interest rates, bank lending, corporate bond spreads, asset prices and exchange-rate movements.

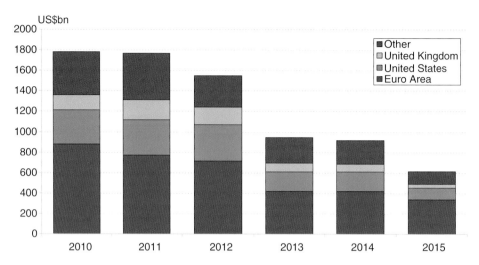

Figure 2.28: Bank debt maturity by region
Source: IMF

bonds, to plug their funding gap. This challenge will be made more difficult as banks will have to compete with a large issuance of government bonds for the next several years.

Another challenge is the need to restart securitised lending markets. Securitisation (e.g. RMBS and CMBS) was a particularly important source of debt for real estate, pre-crisis. Despite the improvement in financial conditions, new securitisation issuance remains at a fraction of its former level. These markets will need to expand significantly, further to support growth, or else bank lending will have to rise to take up the slack. Part of the difficulty in restarting securitisation remains the uncertainty over stricter new 'Basel III' prudential regulations, due for release in late 2010, which are being formulated to deal with pre-crisis regulatory failures. At the core of these changes will be higher equity requirements on bank lending and securitisation. This will raise the 'hurdle rate' of return that banks need for new lending. This will reduce the availability and raise the cost of debt, particularly for commercial real estate loans and particularly for development, which attract a relatively high risk weight.

Conclusion: All of these challenges suggest that it will still be some time before the financial system is back to full health. Indeed, we are probably now past the point of maximum financial stimulus for the global economy. While none of these immediate financial sector challenges are sufficient on their own to derail the recovery, a weak financial sector remains a source of instability that could amplify a negative shock. A self-sustaining recovery will only be possible when the financial system is able to grow in line with the real economy. Over the medium term, constraints on credit growth through higher capital requirements will also reinforce the sizeable deleveraging process that must still be confronted in many highly indebted OECD countries.

The Euro finally arrives – but will that make much of a difference? (January 2002)

The introduction of Euro notes and coins this month marks the final event in a timetable for Euro introduction that was set out in the early 1990s and has been moving on since 1997, when inflation and interest rates converged across the Euro zone. This had a major impact on property markets, because two of the underlying drivers of performance came into line across member states. The alignment was cemented from January 1999, when the ECB took over responsibility for setting a single interest rate across the zone and Treaty conditions preventing member states running large budget deficits kept government bond yields in line and prevented inflation accelerating because of high government borrowing. The most important factor, though, was the locking of currency rates between member states from January 1999, that made each national currency little more than a sub-unit of the Euro. These measures created a single monetary zone, even though the original member currencies were still circulating, so is the final introduction of Euro notes and coins anything more than symbolic?

From an investor's perspective, probably not. EMU does accelerate the process of market integration, helping to equalise prices across the Euro zone and improve efficiency as competitive conditions increase, but the key actions were those taken in 1999, rather than this month's event. Most prices of goods and services have already converged[5] and the main factors preventing further integration are labour market rigidities and regulatory barriers. Improving the free flow of labour is about reducing language barriers, societal constraints and differences in social security provision, rather than introducing Euro notes and coins, and national regulators are showing no trend to free up the EU business arena in response to the new notes and coins.

But what about the Euro's exchange rate? There will probably be a sentimental surge after the 1 January event, but this will be temporary. A more

---

[5] Major price discrepancies that persist are generally due to different tax and regulatory structures in the member states.

lasting boost will come from underlying economic conditions. The European economy is still doing relatively well and the weakest parts (namely Germany) are showing increasing signs of having turned the corner. The main negative effects last year were a reduction in household spending power and consumption as inflation increased, but wages did not, and an early response in the manufacturing sector to the tech recession. Both have run their course now, and the pick-up in unemployment they generated has not been enough to drive up savings rates. Barring another shock, and assuming the ECB continues to keep monetary conditions loose, activity should strengthen in the first half of 2002. Unless the USA quickly resumes growth of over 3%, which is unlikely, this should convince investment markets that the growth deficit between Europe and the USA will be smaller than they had thought, driving a (partial) recovery in the exchange rate.

Germany (April 2002)

The disappointing performance of the German economy since re-unification has raised fears that the European economy has lost its engine of growth – but Europe's largest economy has rarely been its main driver. In fact, Germany has not clearly outgrown the rest of Europe during the modern era. Labour productivity growth was in line with other large EU economies (and above North America), but employment growth was practically nil (Figure 2.29). What Germany did achieve, however, was growth with low and stable inflation, which gave the appearance of invincibility.

Re-unification with East Germany in 1991 changed the playing field by forcing West Germany to absorb millions of workers, who became massively overpaid once the old East German currency was accepted at a 1:1 exchange rate with the Deutsche Mark. Until then, Germany had significantly outperformed its neighbours in controlling unit labour costs, which justified an ever-strengthening DM. But re-unification produced a one-off downward shift in competitiveness that was compounded when unit labour costs spiralled out of control in 1992 and 1993. The best solution would have been to let the DM fall to restore German competitiveness, but the ERM (Exchange Rate Mechanism) and later EMU (European Monetary Union) required a stable DM, so the currency became structurally overvalued (Figure 2.30). This has left Germany struggling with an uncompetitive East German workforce, but without the flexibility needed to absorb that workforce. The rigidity in German labour institutions helped deliver wage moderation in periods of relative stability. But the same institutions

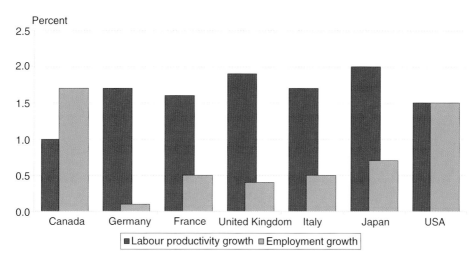

Figure 2.29:   G7 long term growth breakdown 1979 to 2001

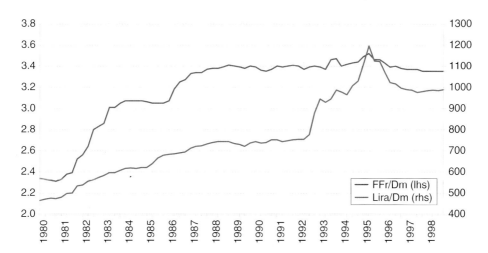

Figure 2.30:   Deutsche Mark entered EMU near all-time high

have held back the economy from a radical re-structuring that could have quickly restored competitiveness.

All is not doom, though. The current poor growth period is more likely to be part of the extended adjustment period following re-unification and EMU entry, rather than the start of a new era of low German growth. Since 1995 unit labour costs have increased by 6–10 percentage points less in Germany than in France and Italy and by around 20 percentage points less than in the UK. This process will eventually restore Germany's competitive position and will undoubtedly be accelerated by the changes in capital gains taxation that should free up the corporate sector to restructure more rapidly. But policy blunders, such as making it harder to hire part-time workers, have hindered the process and highlighted the importance of a pragmatic policy response to Germany's problems. The outcome of the upcoming election will decide whether a sustainable revival is imminent or not.

Germany's economic situation (April 2003)

2002 was another terrible year for the German economy, and the worst since the recession of 1993. The last time Germany was the top performer among the large EU economies (UK, France, Italy and Germany) was in 1992, during the boom following re-unification; and it has been the worst performer in seven out of the ten years since. Is Germany becoming another Japan? To answer that, we first have to find a cause of the poor performance and the first place to look is re-unification. The costs of re-unification were enormous, given the 1:1 exchange rate adopted between the old East German currency and the Deutschemark (DM). This made the East German economy hugely uncompetitive, by raising costs across the board with no accompanying increase in efficiency. Lower productivity in the East should have caused a depreciation of the DM to compensate. But, by then, the currency was the anchor of the ERM mechanism; market confidence in it was high; and so the DM remained firm. In time, the currency markets would have moved against the DM in the face of persistent under-performance, but the run-up to EMU came first and Euro conversion rates were calculated, based on an overvalued DM, that locked in the competitive disadvantage (Figure 2.31).

   This lack of competitiveness requires lower than average rises in wages and prices and/or better productivity growth. Germany has a good record of keeping prices and wages under control, but with low inflation in the rest of the Euro zone, there is a limit to what can be gained by keeping inflation relatively low. Increasing productivity is therefore at least as important, so that unit labour costs (which measure the cost of producing extra output and so take account of productivity and costs) rise more slowly than elsewhere. Germany is performing quite well on this measure, as it historically has. Over the 1980s Germany's unit labour costs rose much more slowly than in the UK, France or Italy, but this advantage was wiped out by the rising DM, which made German unit labour costs (in dollar terms) rise even more quickly than those in France. During the 1990s, Germany's usual advantage over France in local currency terms was overturned by the negative impact of re-unification, but this time currency movements did nothing to compensate. So Germany entered the EMU needing to rebuild an advan-

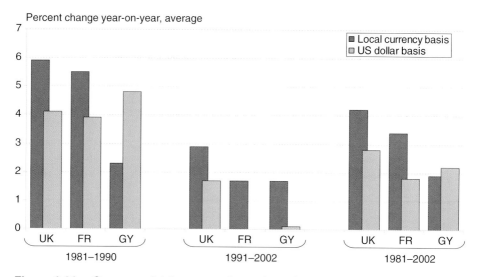

Figure 2.31: German unit labour costs have risen slowly, but currency overvaluation has dominated

tage and, while it has been gaining ground recently, there is still some way to go.

Will it get there? Germany's wage bargaining system may be notoriously inflexible, but it is extremely good at delivering low wage growth, with few strikes. Given this and the proven performance in controlling unit labour costs, Germany will probably regain a competitive advantage eventually, but we need to look to the medium term for that. The package of economic reforms being considered by the government will help by making it easier for small, growing firms to expand their workforce and output and by reducing the enormous incentives for the unemployed to remain out of work. But these reforms will have little impact in 2003 or 2004. In the short term, the outlook is dominated by a very weak labour market that generates very few jobs and by the budget deficit that is running too close to the EMU 3% of GDP limit to allow any tax cuts or spending increases to generate any significant momentum. Put this way, the parallels between Germany and Japan are clear and the property markets can expect little support from employment growth or rebounding retail spending. Job creation and consumer spending are set to remain around the worst levels in Europe, this year and probably next. Ironically, this is only exacerbated in the short term by Germany's success in keeping price inflation down. While that is crucial for long-run recovery, it is damaging the short-term outlook by keeping real interest rates higher in Germany than elsewhere.

3

Real estate and recessions

In the last chapter, we argued that real estate outcomes are substantially driven by real GDP growth. There is 'feedback': real estate markets can substantially enhance the upswing of economic cycles, particularly in the latter stages, and also exacerbate recessions. This is not true of all economic cycles, but was a particular feature of the most recent boom and slump, the GFC. For this reason, the subject of real estate and recessions is worthy of specific consideration.

How does real estate exacerbate the economic cycle? There are a number of mechanisms. In most cases, the most important impact on the real economy is through the construction sector. As real estate prices rise, the real estate development industry moves to bring new buildings to the market. Resources are pulled into the construction sector and there is an immediate boost to the real economy from increased employment. Local multipliers associated with the construction sector are high, so the impact of rising real estate prices on the economy is large. The danger comes when there are persistent rises in house prices. The housing sector is much the largest part of the real estate market and so, in a relatively short period of time, the construction sector output can become a relatively large proportion of total output. This is not harmful in itself, but when the real estate boom comes to an end, as it always does, activity comes to a halt in quite a large share of the economy, causing immediate recession. On average, in the OECD countries, construction is around 7% of national output. When

Real Estate and Globalisation, First Edition. Richard Barkham.
© 2012 John Wiley & Sons, Ltd. Published 2012 by John Wiley & Sons, Ltd.

construction output rises to above 10%, as it did in the US prior to the GFC and Spain and Ireland, it becomes a major contingent liability. Our article of November 2006, which looks at the housing boom in Spain, is quite accurate in its prediction of the looming negative consequences for the wider economy. The article of January 2009 provides comments on the US housing market when still in mid-collapse.

Another important mechanism by which upward momentum in the real estate market feeds into the real economy is bank lending. Banks always like real estate and at times they find it irresistible. Moreover, the real estate market is so large that even a small proportionate increase in value creates huge increases in lending opportunities. For instance, the total value of the US real estate market is estimated to be $7.7 trillion. So a 10% increase in value creates $770 billion of equity, against which loans can be advanced. This is in addition to any new stock that is created by development. Rising real estate markets provide banks with immediate opportunities to increase their loan books. As real estate booms develop, usually when monetary policy is stimulative, banks begin to compete with each other to put on loans and, typically, reduce their underwriting standards and increase their loan-to-value ratios. In the end it is bank lending itself which creates rising values, so the boom feeds itself.

This unholy alliance between the real estate and banking sector is not new; it is at least as old as industrial societies,[1] but in the recent GFC three elements meant that it nearly brought the global economy down. First, the real-estate lending boom was coordinated across countries. Previous real-estate lending booms have occurred in different countries at different times, so when they unwound it was painful for the countries concerned, but not for the global economy. Second, developments in financial technology and generally accepted accounting practice meant that the scale of the lending boom was hidden. The market can 'discipline' companies which take on too much risk but only if they have the information to be able to do so. Third, the lending boom afflicted the vast, but hitherto relatively stable US housing market. The US economy generally accounts for about 25% of global demand; so if it takes a hit, the global economy goes with it.

It is possible that the role of real estate in the economic cycle is growing over time. Rising rates of home-ownership in the OECD countries mean that real estate is, on average, a higher proportion of household balance sheets. So debt-fuelled price rises feed higher consumer spending growth than would otherwise have been the case, through wealth and access to credit affects. As societies become wealthier, the premium placed on the preservation of built and natural heritage rises, so land-use planning systems tend to restrict the rate of new development, which pushes prices higher.

---

[1] See Peter Scott (1996), *The Property Masters*, E&F Spon, 2–6 Boundary Row, London.

The most recent US housing bubble seems to have been somewhat focused on 'coastal towns and cities'; locations known to have become more restrictive in planning terms over the last 15 years or so. In the commercial real estate market there has been a long-term trend towards standardisation of buildings. This makes them less likely to be owned by their occupiers and more likely to be owned by professional investors, who revalue them annually and use them as security for loans.

That we have spent so much time considering real estate in a recessionary environment over the last ten years is testament to the volatility created by globalisation. Capital flows are growing rapidly as a proportion of world GDP and these interact with local economic cycles to produce powerful and destabilising asset market bubbles. Commentating on this type of market movement presents a real challenge for the property research community.

As well as evaluating the level of danger in world real estate markets, researchers will also be confronted by the need to emphasise risk in the outlook for real estate. This is never easy. There is frequently a commercial imperative in the advisory community to 'make the case for real estate'. The key is to link the real estate forecasts to an ongoing economic analysis which is cognisant of the big changes taking place in the global economy. Moreover, on a more optimistic note for analysts and investors, our evidence suggests that real estate, because of its stable long-term cash-flows, is a highly defensive asset, even in a severe recession. We consider the issue of real estate in recessions in the article of February 2009. In any case, the articles of October 2007 and August 2008 deal with the way in which the GFC spread from the USA to Europe. The articles of January 2009 and February 2010 deal with the long-lasting impact of the GFC on US economic growth and levels of unemployment. The very real danger that the global economy would fall into a long-lasting depression, rather than a 'mere' recession, is dealt with in October 2008. At the time, the fear of a new great depression with unemployment rising to 30% across the industrialised world was quite widespread. Our article argues, correctly, that a great depression was not inevitable, because the appropriate policy response was in place. The nature of this policy response, namely 'printing money', is considered in the article of April 2009.

An overheated housing market may cloud the Spanish economic landscape? (November 2006)

Since 1997, Spanish house prices have grown by around 100% in real terms. Compared with other countries, Spanish house price growth has been unprecedented in its steepness, its durability and its geographical breadth. The 'boom' has run in parallel with a series of substantial changes in key driver variables, such as: low interest rates; strong increase in household income; employment growth; and numerous fiscal incentives. However, the high level of housing starts, 700,000 over the past few years, suggests that increases in price have not, in aggregate, been driven by an under-supply. In Spain, the level of housing starts over the past five years has reached 14.7 per 1,000 inhabitants, compared with 6.1 in the United States and 4.5 in France.

Macroeconomic models that take a set of both macro- and demo-graphic variables, not surprisingly, suggest an overvaluation. But also, financial-type models that model houses as an asset that generates future income flows, in the form of rents or accommodation services, also suggest an overvaluation from 13% to 40%.

With one rate of interest for the whole Euro zone, arguably too low for Spain, borrowing has continued to increase and both indebtedness (115% of gross disposable income at the end of 2005) and the associated interest burden have risen strongly. The level of annual repayments has been on a rising trend, reaching a new peak of 28.5%. Consequently, the safety buffer available to households to absorb adverse shocks without their spending decisions being adversely affected, has been diminished.

The property wealth of the Spanish household has been on an increasing trend (as shown by Figure 3.1) and represents now five times GDP, compared with 1.5 in the United States and 2.3 in France. Net property wealth

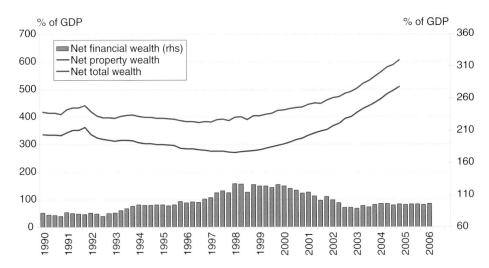

Figure 3.1: Household wealth in Spain
Source: Grosvenor Research & INE

is now 85% of total wealth in Spain, compared with 15% for financial wealth. As households' main asset is their home (the ownership ratio is 85%, the highest in Europe), the greater the difficulty in adjusting to the composition of their wealth in the face of adverse shocks.

The construction sector (13.5% of GDP) has sustained both economic activity and employment growth (both the construction sector and real estate have contributed 1.5% on the 4.4% annual employment growth over the past four years). The positive wealth effect, combined with both employment growth and lax financial conditions, have also driven household spending 4% per year above its long-term average (2.6% per year since 1980). Having set the background and the strong relationship between household consumption and total return in the retail property submarket (as suggested by Figure 3.2), the stellar performance of the retail property market is easy to see.

The scenario of a gradual rise in interest rates suggests a soft landing. However, a larger correction in house prices could spill over into a sharper retrenchment of consumer spending and business investment, which could in turn diminish demand for housing. Although parallels with other markets can be too simplistic, given differences across markets, loan structures, for example, the Netherlands is particularly interesting, because it is further along the housing market cycle. The Netherlands has seen a cooling housing market and has suffered a harder landing, with the downturn there reducing output growth by 0.5% a year for two years, but such a shock could be worse in Spain. Econometric analysis suggests that Spain has a higher

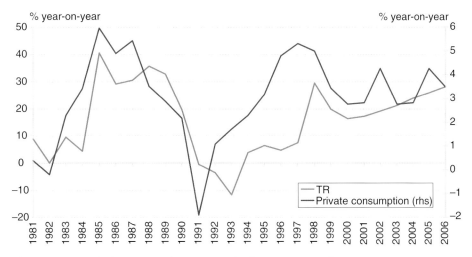

Figure 3.2:   Relationship total returns and private consumption
Source: INE and Grosvenor Research

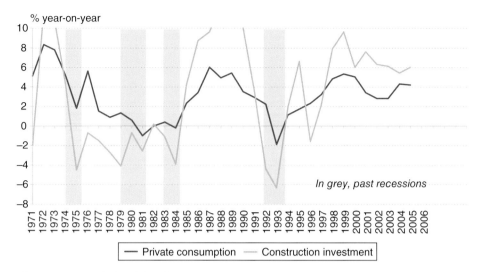

Figure 3.3:   Relationship private consumption and construction investment
Source: Global Insight

elasticity of consumption to construction investment (Figure 3.3) than the Netherlands. Thus a serious downward adjustment in the construction sector will definitely occur if the housing market slips.

All this considered, household spending is expected to fall back in 2007, thereby dampening retail rental income growth for the next two years. This, combined with a potential outward move in yields, will definitely undermine retail property returns. Such a bleak outlook has probably driven Spanish property companies to embark on a slew of take-overs, initial public offerings and foreign acquisitions. Such a move could be interpreted as an attempt to spread risk ahead of a slowdown.

When will the US housing market turn? (January 2009)

As we enter 2009, the US housing market remains in freefall. Major home price indices continue to erode and, on average, prices have fallen to their March 2004 levels, according to the Case-Shiller Index (Figure 3.4). In many markets in the South, Midwest and parts of California, prices have fallen in excess of 40% and the majority of home sales are for bank-owned or foreclosed properties (Figure 3.5). Housing starts are at their lowest level since World War II (Figure 3.6) and while mortgage rates are now at a 37-

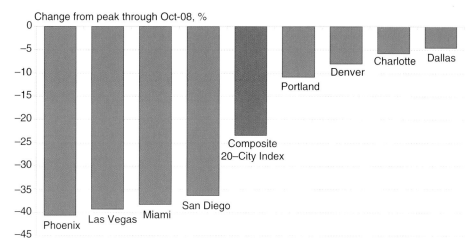

Figure 3.4: S&P/Case-Shiller home price indices
Source: Global Insight

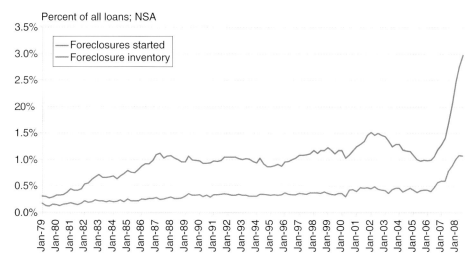

Figure 3.5: Foreclosures
Source: Global Insight

year low, there is little consumer appetite for risk. The Mortgage Bankers Association reported that almost 85% of all new mortgages issued in recent weeks were to refinance existing loans, not to purchase new homes. The only bit of good news is that the prime buying season does not begin until the spring.

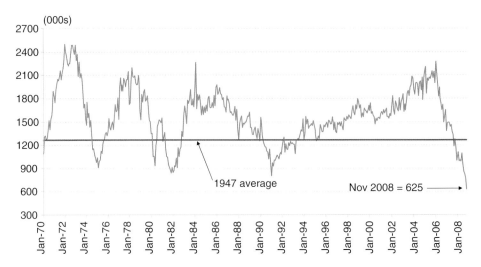

Figure 3.6: US housing starts
Source: Global Insight

Compounding the situation is housing's feedback loop on the economy. With its linkages to activity in virtually every industrial sector, from forestry to finance and from rebar to retail, the economy appears to be chasing housing and vice versa. Breaking this vicious cycle will prove to be difficult. Despite some press optimism, there is little hope for a turnaround anytime soon.

Housing price deflation, compounded by the worst recession since the Great Depression, comes with its own set of problems and hurdles. For example, low mortgage rates do little for current owners, who have no equity and cannot refinance. At the same time, deflation does little to encourage other households from entering the market if they believe that prices will continue to fall and/or they soon may be joining the ranks of the unemployed. Without a job, even low mortgage payments are unaffordable. Homebuilders have little incentive to build, since any new units will be worth less than when they started. Finally, beyond conventional mortgages, lenders have little incentive to lend and even then they are looking for bullet-proof borrowers with substantial equity, little debt, and secure jobs.

If there has been a bright spot, it has been the wave of government intervention which propped up the banking system, provided banks with limited and selective liquidity via the TARP program and lowered mortgage rates. Without the coordinated efforts of the Federal Reserve, Congress and the White House, we would be talking about a complex and prolonged Global Depression, with housing low on our list of concerns.

Given that we are in a deep, but manageable, recession, what is the outlook for the US housing industry? Despite the aforesaid tale of woe, there are some tantalising clues that a bottom will form sometime late this year. First, home values are declining, but at a slower rate. Second, employment growth is likely to turn positive late this year, a necessary requirement for a housing turnaround. Third, lower mortgage rates will eventually attract new buyers and help some, but not all, existing owners reduce their carrying costs. Finally, housing remains the single largest source of wealth accumulation for the average US household and, while appreciation will remain muted relative to its recent excesses, paying an amortizing mortgage off every month remains the most painless and efficient savings plan.

So when will the housing market begin to turn? With affordability improving and interest rates declining, one would think that the turn could be quite soon. If the employment picture were not so bleak, this might be the case. Unfortunately, employment levels are not expected to stabilise and begin to rebound until late 2009 or early 2010. Following that, we should begin to see some mild pick-up in housing starts and existing home sales and, by 2011, some substantial traction should be evident. However, home prices will not exhibit double digit increases once a recovery has begun. While some markets will inevitably outperform, the general consensus is that housing price inflation will be constrained, in part because of rising mortgage rates and their negative impact on affordability.

So there remains a glimmer of hope that housing will begin to show some signs of life very late this year or early 2010. There is undoubtedly more pain to come and uncertainty clouds the outlook, but low interest rates and depressed home prices will help spur the market once the employment picture turns positive.

The sub-prime storm – impact on Europe (October 2007)

This month we consider the impact of the sub-prime crisis. We will look at the direct impact on real estate and the 'knock-on' from depressed economic activity. Property-induced financial turmoil is not new. In 1974 the Bank of England had to prevent the collapse of the UK banking system, following binges of reckless real-estate lending. The early 1990s economic downturn was exacerbated by poor bank balance sheets, related to the downturn in property prices.

Since the 1990s, a motley combination of financial deregulation, rising asset prices, banking competition and, some might say, hubris, has led once more to aggressive bank lending to real estate. This time round a key factor is debt 'securitisation', which started in the United States and has spread rapidly across all financial markets. By packaging real-estate loans and selling in the public debt market, banks have been able to escape their own

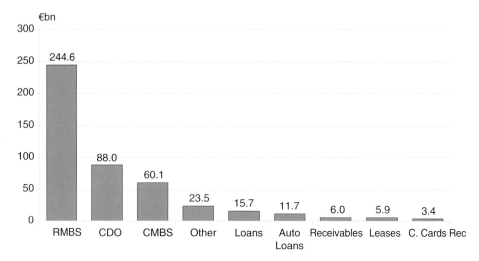

Figure 3.7:   European securitisation by origin
Sources: Thomson Financial, Dealogic, JP Morgan, Merrill Lynch, Structured Finance International, Bloomberg

balance sheets. In Europe, for instance, in-house research shows that the total securitisation issuance has increased by 37% per annum since 2000, to reach almost €459 billions in 2006.

In fact, securitised debt originates in a range of sectors; from commercial property to credit cards (see Figure 3.7). However, the lion's share in Europe is related to residential mortgages (RMBS), with a volume of €245 billion. Theoretically, pooling loans reduces the uncertainty of the cash flow, improves liquidity and increases investors' flexibility in exposure to real-estate markets. Risk is transferred from primary lenders to others with broader more diversified portfolios.

Once the debt has been packaged and sold on, banks are able to get on with the job of lending. The resulting fall in the cost of capital to banks permits more marginal lending and stimulates demand for it. So businesses and households take on debt when their ability to repay holds only in the most benign of economic circumstances.

Generally, the risk on commercial real estate products is assessed as low, because of fairly small default rates and recourse to physical assets. However, the complex nature of some products means the 'risk' has been so finely sliced and spread that it is hard to know where it currently sits. Moreover, the incorporation of Collateralised Deposit Obligations (CDOs) and the like into money-market instruments means banks are not as free of risk as they might have thought. The first response of banks in the current 'crisis' was

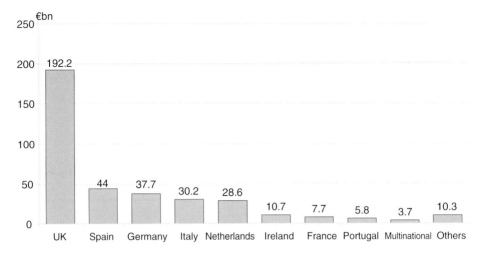

Figure 3.8: UK the largest issuer in Europe
*Sources: Thomson Financial, Dealogic, JP Morgan, Merrill Lynch, Structured Finance
International, Bloomberg*

to cut their lending to each other, forcing short-term inter-bank rates up;
central banks tried to ease this by injecting money into the system. The
resulting uncertainty created a flight to quality, making packaged debt unattractive; with spreads on Commercial Mortgage-Backed Securities (CMBS)
increasing significantly (to justify the risk as it is now seen).

As can be seen from Figure 3.8, the UK, with its more mature financial
sector, has a much larger share of the securitised debt market. Therefore,
the UK is likely to feel the knock-on effects more, although continental
Europe will not be immune.

The most immediate impact is difficulty in raising finance. Real estate
is a capital-intensive sector and the 'squeeze' on liquidity may have longer-
term impacts on construction activity, though this may prove beneficial in
some markets heading towards oversupply. Investment deals may be hit
and there is some evidence in the market that some transactions have been
postponed or shelved.

The household sector will face higher borrowing costs and credit availability, particularly from re-mortgaging, will reduce. With reduced funds, the
housing market and retail sector will be hit. However, in the UK, a cooling
was on the cards from past monetary policy, but also further hikes were
being factored in, which are unlikely now. Therefore, the impact in the
retail and residential sectors may be 'as expected'; the price of credit rising
through the market and not via central bank policy.

However, the cost of capital has increased across the board. The impact this has in terms of output lost or reduced investment is difficult to quantify at this point in time, but it may be material. Already, city job losses have been announced. OEF (Oxford Economic Forecasting) estimate that, with the market for structured products contracting in the UK and the USA, the GDP outcome might be 0.2% and 0.4% lower than they might otherwise be. Our estimate is that 0.1–0.2% of Euro zone growth is at risk. It is likely that the financial sector is going to shoulder the lion's share of the slow-down, so office returns will fall.

The initial reaction to the sub-prime situation has been a 'flight' to quality, easing government bond yields in the UK and the Euro zone. Across the market there will be a general re-pricing of risk (that is, paying attention to the nature of the underlying assets). In real estate this may mean a return to core assets. There have been previous 'liquidity' crises which have not been recessionary, but have hit asset prices. Uncertainty, compounded by complexity, has created a feeling of panic which may not be rational and some players may now be over-pricing risk, leaving opportunities for calmer (and cash-rich) players to pick up correctly priced assets.

A year on: the sub-prime crisis from a Spanish perspective (August 2008)

A year ago the 'sub-prime' crisis hit the markets. It started in the USA, where many thought it might have been contained. In the short-term it was mainly a liquidity issue, but as time has passed and asset values, real estate in particular, have fallen it has increasingly become a solvency problem, with a number of banks going under and more to follow. What some thought might be history, within the year is now a signal cause of a global economic slowdown, which is considerably more severe than expected. Furthermore, the banking crisis did move outside of US borders, crossing the Atlantic to the UK and Europe. Initially, many thought only a few directly-exposed German banks might suffer, but the crisis has been more widespread. Here, we consider how Spanish banks have fared and the implications for the real-estate sector.

In Spain, the banking crisis has been smaller than in the USA, with Spanish banks posting good results in 2007. However, growing uncertainties, such as the long-awaited residential price correction combined with the liquidity crisis, will make banks far more exposed in 2008. Not surprisingly, with increasing risks to profits, bank share prices have fallen (see Figure 3.9). This, despite the fact that bank performance in Spain is boosted

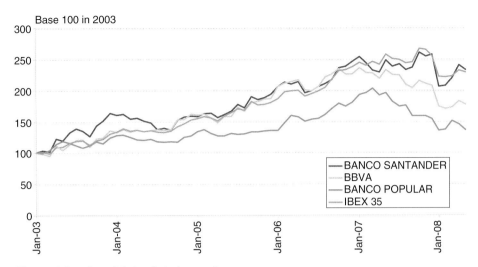

Figure 3.9:   Spanish banks' share price
Source: Grosvenor; Global Insight

by the high concentration of the sector, which distorts competition and produces more generous margins. In Spain, the Big Five: Banco Santander, BBVA, Banco Popular, Caja Madrid and La Caixa, account for 42% of total market share.

Another factor supportive of Spanish banks is the highly dynamic credit cycle over the past few years, which has further driven bank profits. The Spanish banking system is known for charging borrowers more and giving savers less, compared with both Italian and British banks. The average margin is around 2% across the Spanish banking sector, similar to Italy but higher than in Britain (1.61%), France (0.98%) and Germany (0.77%).

Also, the main Spanish banks are very well capitalised because they rely heavily on retained profits for their capital base expansion, plus the Spanish government forces them to make a high level of provision against losses. The coverage ratio of non-performing loans is above 200%, compared with an average of 60% for other European banks. The ratio of doubtful loans to gross loans stood only at 1.2% in 2007, compared with levels reaching 3%–6% in the core Euro zone countries.

All that said, the liquidity crisis in Spain was triggered by much the same factors as in the USA: rising interest rates and falling property prices. A reduction in credit availability following tighter financial conditions, plus the deteriorating economic background, will act negatively on banking activity, eroding total loan volumes and eroding margins.

One area where Spanish banks are slightly more exposed than their continental European peers is their use of securitisation to gain funds. Spain

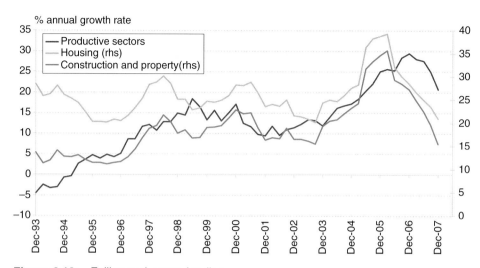

Figure 3.10: Falling real estate lending
Source: European Central Bank Grosvenor Research

has been behind the UK, but ahead against other EU countries, in terms of securitisation, with residential mortgage-backed securities (RMBS) reaching €42 billion, compared with the UK at €180 billion. Banks are now forced to refinance themselves on the 'expensive' interbank loan market, given the lack of asset securitisation, as well as the freeze of interbank transactions related to covered bonds.

So how's this impacting on real estate? Residential prices are falling, construction volumes and property transactions have decreased, with outward yield shifts in both the office and retail markets. This slowdown is a direct result of reduced credit availability (see Figure 3.10). The volumes of mortgages as well as loans to the property sector are decreasing so real estate in Spain will suffer more substantially than originally thought.

The downturn in the property market, plus the lower repayment capacity of borrowers, will lead to an increase in defaults as well as a lowering of recovery rates. Despite this bleak picture, the impact of a multiplication of defaults on the balance sheets and profitability of the institutions will be limited, for the following reasons: the requirements of the Bank of Spain regarding statistical coverage of credit risk, should guarantee a safety buffer against bad loans and losses related to depreciation of mortgage loans, which would not be solely carried by Spanish institutions (Spanish banks 'export' close to 30% of the counterparty risks linked to mortgage loans).

Our judgment is that the downturn in the economy and the severe down-turn in real-estate markets will impact on Spanish banks' profitability and appetite to lend. This in turn will lead to a deeper correction in real estate prices than previously thought. However, the highly regulated and some-what 'overprotected' banking system should be robust enough to survive intact.

Global headwinds – US real estate debt (February 2010)

Whilst the US economy started to recover in Q3 2009, it is not clear when this might be true of the property markets. First, employment is a lagging indicator. Employers are not willing to risk adding new employees until they are certain that the recovery is sustainable. Adding hours or temporary workers is the preferred path to increase output in the short run and this does not require additional space. Second, as the economy recovers, interest rates will start to rise, putting some upward pressure on yields. However, the biggest real-estate headwind is the looming wave of both traditional commercial real-estate (CRE) loans and commercial mortgage-backed secu-rities (CMBS) that need to be refinanced over the next several years (see Figures 3.11, 3.12 and 3.13).

Grosvenor North America Research estimates that approximately $770 billion of the $1.4 trillion CRE bank loans coming due in the next five years will be 'underwater'. Losses from these loans will range from $225 to $300

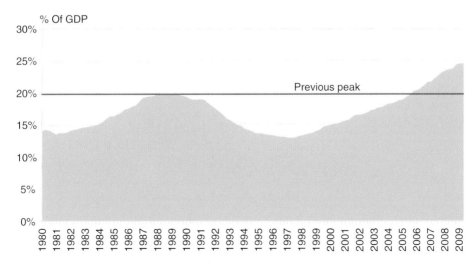

Figure 3.11:   Commercial and multifamily loans
Source: IHS Global Insight

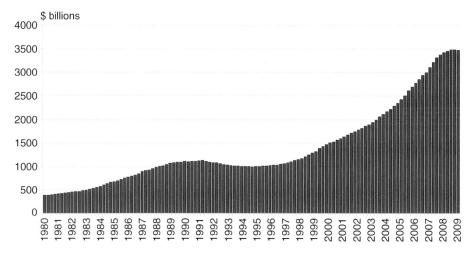

Figure 3.12: Commercial and multifamily loans outstanding
Source: Federal Reserve

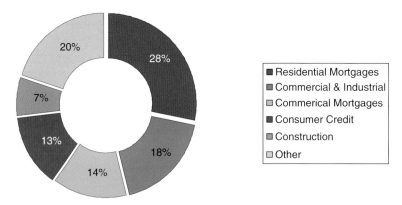

Residential Mortgages
Commercial & Industrial
Commerical Mortgages
Consumer Credit
Construction
Other

Figure 3.13: Banks' loan profile – June 30, 2009
Source: FDIC

billion and while it will be far less than the $1.1 trillion residential loan debacle, it will force the closure of scores of smaller local and regional banks, whose primary asset base is CRE loans. With commercial real-estate prices down 30% to 50% or more, depending on the market and/or land use, the biggest surprise is that none of the nation's 'super-banks' are on the Federal Deposit Insurance Corporation (FDIC) watch list. However, even these banks are now experiencing real-estate delinquency rates approaching ten percent, with more expected as the year progresses.

Federal regulators, in an attempt to avoid a crisis, are allowing banks to extend loans that are in 'technical' default, but whose cash flows are sufficient to cover the building's debt obligations after taxes. Unfortunately, this 'extend and pretend' approach to problem loans only works if the market recovery period is shorter than the 'extend' period. Since job levels are not expected to return to pre-recession levels until 2013, carrying these loans for an extended period will hamper lending and increase costs on future activity. This will hurt profitability and create a vicious circle that will delay the market's recovery. In another sign that the FDIC is moving to quickly deal with the issue, there are moves to resurrect a Resolution Trust Corporation (RTC)-style entity, which would allow the government to quickly and efficiently sell off commercial real estate paper to interested investors.

In addition to foreclosed and 'extended' CRE properties, the American property market must also deal with a rapidly worsening CMBS market. Virtually all CMBS pools securitised between 2007 and 2008 are underwater and delinquencies are quickly creeping into 2006 vintages as well. CMBS loans are much more complex than CRE loans, since they are syndicated and once they default, they are sent to a special servicer. Quite often, ownership rights become cloudy and alignment of interest issues quickly break down between the holders of various tranches. Like banks, special servicers can extend loans, but at some point they must act in the best interest of the investors and this will eventually mean selling properties in a less than receptive market environment.

CMBS maturities will not peak until 2017 and 2018, but CMBS pools represent over 20% of the $3.5 trillion commercial real estate debt market and $31 billion of it is expected to mature in 2010 alone. Fortunately, because of pay-offs, liquidations and defeasances, the actual 2010 refinancing needs are only approximately $18 billion. Not surprisingly, defaults are becoming commonplace, with the most notable being Stuyvesant Village in New York, an 11,000-unit apartment complex, which was bought for $5.4 billion in 2006 and is now thought to be worth only $1.8 billion, according to Fitch Ratings.

Whilst CRE and CMBS loan defaults will be a serious problem, they will not bring down the banking system. However, they will put additional downward pressure on commercial property prices. Whilst this will create opportunities for well financed investors, the broader impact, via bank balance sheets, is negative for the economy.

How close are we to a new 'Great Depression'? (October 2008)

This month we join the throng of commentators drawing parallels between the Great Depression in the 1930s and the current 'turbulence'. Here, we present a basic but systematic assessment of whether the forces acting in the Great Depression are present now and their magnitude. The good news is that many factors that contributed to the Depression are weaker or not present. The bad news is that some important ones are and, on balance, things are getting worse. The box below gives some of the key facts from the 1930s US depression. Finally, although the Great Depression is often thought of as an event in US history and, indeed, it reached its nadir in this country, it was a global event.

The Great Depression in the US was a true 'economic meltdown'. Unemployment rose from 3.2% to 25% by the mid-1930s: 1 in 4 had no job. Industrial output fell by almost 50% and family incomes contracted by nearly 40%. Many lost their homes and, although food prices fell by 50%, people were so poor foodstuffs could not be sold for profit. By 1932 investment was only 5% of its 1929 level. The USA was hit worst, but other countries also suffered. The mid-1930s showed some recovery, but unemployment in the USA was still at 14% at the onset of World War II.

Table 3.1 gives a list of the factors thought to have contributed to the Great Depression. The relative importance of these factors can be debated, but the following is a brief explanation of each factor. A cyclical downturn in investment, after a period in which firms had expanded strongly: the 1920s saw unprecedented productivity gains, driven by increases in capital at the expense of labour, as seen in automobile production. Such downturns are often abrupt and cause the capital goods industries to shed labour quite dramatically. Another example is the slump in production of ICT equipment in the late 1990s. A big similarity between the 1920s and now was the strong build-up of debt by consumers and businesses, particularly in the USA, related to a period of extremely low interest rates. In fact, the stock-market bubble of the 1920s was, in its latter stages, fuelled by bank lending to small investors. One short-term cause of the Great Depression was tightening monetary policy and current OECD interest rates started to rise around 2005, to restrain demand and keep inflation under control. In the 1920s there was no goods inflation, but the Fed started to raise rates in 1928 to curb the equity price boom. Monetary policy in other countries was geared to restoring the gold standard: namely, the ability to exchange currency for gold on demand. Generally, this implied a deflationary contraction of the money base. Today's equivalent is the fight against inflation, which has forced interest rates up across the OECD.

Rising interest rates will always hit asset values and this, combined with limited earnings growth potential, hit the 1929 stock market, with a decline of 85% in the USA over 30 months. US stock values did not regain their 1929 level until 1954. This is much worse than recent events: in 2000 markets fell about 45%, but bounced back by 2007. Since then they have declined by around 28%, but are still falling at the time of writing. In the

Table 3.1:   Current relevance of factors causing the 'Great Depression'

Present in 1930s Downturn	Present Now				Rank	Max	Actual
	1	2	3	4			
Cyclical downturn in investment			x		2	8	6
Massive build-up of debt in preceding decade				x	3	12	12
Tightening monetary policy in preceding 24 months				x	3	12	12
Tightening monetary policy during the crisis due to gold standard		x			3	12	6
Stock-market crash (85% down in 30 months)		x			3	12	6
Widespread bank failures		x			3	12	6
Absence of government support for banks	x				3	12	3
Decline in trade due to increased tariff barriers	x				2	8	2
Agricultural disruption		x			1	4	2
Deflation		x			2	8	4
Narrow economies based on capital goods industries	x				2	8	2
Highly unstable geopolitics (based on unresolved issues from WW1)	x				2	8	2
					Total	116	63

USA, as firms went bust and workers were laid off, banks which had lent excessively began to fail. Approximately 9,000 banks failed in the 1930s and depositors lost $140bn (approx. $850bn in today's money). The supply of credit to the economy ceased and, it is argued, the authorities failed to provide support to banks until it was too late. It's the same today; many banks are in trouble, following a period of 'reckless' lending, but this time a comprehensive 'bailout' package is coming to the rescue. A bizarre policy response in the 1930s to the economic turmoil was that the USA increased tariffs on imports, which brought retaliation, resulting in a 50% drop in world trade. There is no real equivalent today. Due to the slump in demand in the early 1930s a vicious cycle of deflation set in, which impacted negatively by increasing the real value of their debts. Japan experienced a similar bout of 'debt inflation' in the 1990s, but we are some way from that now.

Other factors creating the Depression include: a drought in the USA, hitting agricultural incomes; the rise of fascism and militarism in Europe and Japan; and the generally undiversified nature of national economies (i.e. a small number of main business sectors and a small public sector).

Table 3.1 shows the extent to which we think the 'Great Depression' factors are operating now (1 = not at all; 4 = strong basis). It also ranks the importance of these factors in the 1930s (1 = low; 3 = high basis). If all the factors were operating strongly today, the total from multiplying the presence score by the importance score would be 116. In fact, because not all of the factors are operating today, the score is only 63. So we have approximately 54% of the factors associated with the Great Depression in place now. This leaves us facing a nasty recession, but not a Great Depression. Also, things should begin to improve as inflation falls and interest rates are cut. The US big bailout is important; without it, our Great Depression score would be 72 (64%). However, it remains to be seen how effectively this injection of taxpayers' money can actually be deployed.

Printing money – will it work? (April 2009)

An emerging and potentially catastrophic feature of the global credit crunch is the inability of low interest rates to stimulate demand. This policy impotence is an inevitable consequence of continued weakness in banks' balance sheets. When banks have insufficient capital they cannot lend, no matter how much the central bank lowers rates. The financial downturn has already been exacerbated by problems in broader credit markets. Credit spreads remain significantly elevated, while issuance in securitisation and commercial paper markets remain depressed. Indeed, as part of this vicious cycle, the shortfall in bank capital has been compounded by exposure to these illiquid markets. This note evaluates the potential for quantitative easing or 'printing money' to be a solution.

Once central banks have cut interest rates to 0%, the next step is generally referred to as 'printing money'. Printing money is a broad term which captures a wide range of monetary policy options, where the central bank purchases assets funded through an increase in its own liabilities (the monetary base: see Figure 3.14). In its simplest form, quantitative easing involves the targeted increase in the level of commercial bank reserves at the central bank. This was the approach adopted (ineffectively) by Japan in the first half of the decade. Having learnt from the Japanese experience, central banks are now pursuing a more sophisticated approach employing a broader range of support measures. These include boosting short-term interbank liquidity;

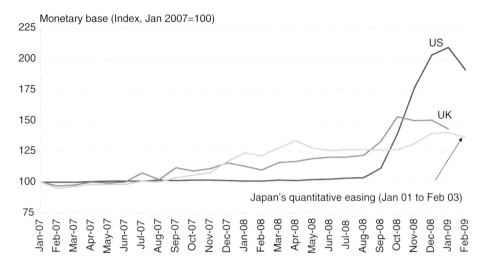

Figure 3.14: Monetary base growth
Source: US Federal Reserve, Bank of England, Bank of Japan

reducing long-bond yields by buying government bonds; and directly improving funding in dysfunctional credit markets. The US Federal Reserve has been particularly active in buying private financial assets (particularly ABS) in a bid to reduce credit spreads and revive funding.

The great fear with printing money is that it causes rampant inflation and a plunging currency. These fears are often overstated, but there are clear inflationary risks from any sustained expansion of the central bank's balance sheet. However, a temporary increase in monetary base is unlikely to be inflationary, particularly when the economy is slumping towards deflation. There is nothing magical about how printing money becomes inflationary; it arises from a strong increase in real activity leading to more demand than supply across a wide range of products. So, provided that any short-term increase in central bank liabilities is reversed as the economy recovers, there should be no enduring inflationary consequences from quantitative easing.

The bigger risk confronting the global economy is deflation, not inflation (Figure 3.15). Deflation is a major threat to any economy in recession and needs to be attacked pre-emptively, before it becomes entrenched. Falling prices increase the incentive for households to defer consumption, compounding the decline in aggregate demand. As prices start to fall the real interest rate rises. This represents an effective tightening of monetary policy when the economy is already in recession. Furthermore, because wages are relatively 'sticky', a fall in prices tends to push up real labour costs at a time when the unemployment rate is already rising. Deflation also compounds balance-sheet problems, since the real quantity of debt is rising as

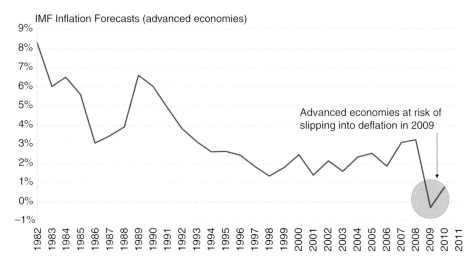

Figure 3.15:   Risk of deflation has increased
Source; IMF, March 2009

the ability to service that debt is falling, which can force further deleveraging and asset-price deflation.

Given the problems posed by deflation, recent moves by central banks to expand their balance sheets should be seen as a welcome step in the right direction. How long it actually takes for these unconventional policies to start boosting growth is difficult to say and depends very much on which specific measures are adopted and how aggressively they are pursued. Recent evidence from the USA suggests that the Fed's quantitative measures have already had a small positive impact on financial markets, with a moderate narrowing of spreads and increased issuance. However, the measures announced to date are still well short of a comprehensive recovery solution. Credit markets remain deeply distressed and announced central bank asset purchase plans are still fairly small, compared with the overall funding needs in these markets. Part of the problem remains poor communication; changing market perceptions is a crucial element of policy effectiveness, yet central banks are still to fully convince the market that quantitative action is sensible policy that will work, despite the recent revival in sentiment. Nonetheless, by establishing a framework for quantitative action, central banks are at least in a position to refine and extend quantitative policies as conditions demand.

Furthermore, although quantitative action can be a powerful aid to recovery, it is no panacea. In particular, central bank quantitative action does not replace the need for comprehensive resolution of lingering banking-sector problems. The quickest way to enhance central bank policy and speed up a broader economic recovery is to clean up banks' balance sheets, so they have sufficient capital to support new lending. A key criticism of government recovery policy remains the lack of a comprehensive disposal mechanism for liquidating toxic assets. While the US government has now announced plans for a Public–Private Investment Program to help fund the purchase of toxic assets from banks, it remains reluctant to take direct control of the problem by establishing explicit government-controlled asset management vehicles to dispose of toxic assets. Until the problems in the banking system are adequately resolved, central bank quantitative actions can only be a partial solution to a sustained recovery, even if quantitative easing can provide a substantive non-inflationary boost.

Are recessions bad for real estate? (February 2008)

Today's papers are full of gloom over the impending US recession. Will the other regions of the world follow the USA into recession and will they fare better, or worse? More to the point, what will be the impact on real estate returns?

What do we mean by a recession anyway? Many say a recession is two consecutive quarters of contracting growth. The authoritative US National Bureau of Economic Research (NBER) defines a recession as a significant decline in economic activity, lasting more than a few months, which begins just after the economy reaches a peak of activity and ends as the economy reaches its trough. From a real estate perspective, it is the feed-through from GDP weakness to unemployment that is most important.

Table 3.2 shows the two most recent recession periods, 1990–93 and 2000–03, in terms of length, persistence and depth of recession. In the 1990s, consecutive quarters of GDP contraction were evenly spread across the globe, but while the USA bounced back, other nations suffered further quarters of contraction – in the UK it was five consecutive quarters. Further, the UK suffered the biggest peak-to-trough loss of GDP. In GDP terms the early 2000s recession was mild and, largely, confined to the USA. In the early 1990s, interest rates were used to squeeze inflation from the system, but low inflation in 2000 allowed interest rate cuts to support struggling economies.

The recession impact on employment is generally longer (Table 3.3) and greater than the GDP impact. Office occupation and absorption are closely related to the health of the labour market; one mechanism by which real-estate markets are affected. Increasing levels of unemployment are also associated with lower earnings and less spending, combined with debt

Table 3.2: Economic growth – recessions compared

GDP	USA	UK	EU	China	Australia
1990–93					
Consecutive quarters	2	5	2	0	2
Total quarters	2	6	4	0	5
% peak to trough	−1.3	−2.5	−0.1	–	−1.8
2000–03					
Consecutive quarters	0	0	0	0	0
Total quarters	3	0	0	0	1
% peak to trough	−0.1	–	–	–	−0.8

Table 3.3: Employment – recessions compared

Employment	USA	UK	EU	China	Australia
1990–93					
Consecutive quarters	6	11	3	0	6
Total quarters	6	11	9	1	8
% peak to trough	−1.2	−6.1	−3.9	−1.0	−3.0
2000–03					
Consecutive quarters	4	0	2	10	0
Total quarters	7	2	6	12	2
% peak to trough	−1.2	−0.1	−1.1	−11.0	−0.8

default. All of these factors are closely aligned to the performance of retail assets.

Not only is the contraction important, but also the length of time to return to the same number of employed people. In the UK the peak of employment was in 1990, Q4, and it wasn't until 1998, Q3 that employment reached the same level. In the USA, job losses began a quarter earlier than in the UK, but returned to post-recession levels more rapidly, with the numbers employed returning in 1992, Q3. This highlights the flexibility of the US labour market. Interestingly, only the USA saw contracting GDP in the 2000–03 years, but there were mild job losses across all countries in this period. It doesn't take a recession to create unemployment; merely slow growth.

What are the linkages with real estate performance? Figure 3.16 shows annual average percent returns in four time periods: early 1990s recession; mid-1990s growth phase; 1999 and 2000s recession. The UK and Australia suffered the greatest losses in the early 1990s, with both experiencing three years of falling returns. The USA suffered losses in only two years and

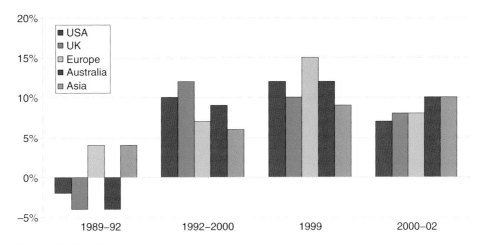

Figure 3.16: Real estate returns
Source: Grosvenor, IPD, NCREIF, PCA

Europe saw only a marginal loss in one year, but slowed significantly. The real-estate pain of the early 1990s is strongly related to the recession experience of the UK, the USA and Australia. The performance was also to be influenced by the supply conditions in each market. This was especially the case in the UK, which entered the recession with significant oversupply.

The recession of 2000–2003 had very little impact on percent per annum returns, compared with those experienced from 1992–2000, although there was a significant slowdown between 1999 and 2000. The severity of the recession was not as great in this period and not characterised by consecutive declines in GDP, which led to benign outcomes. Australian and Asian returns grew strongly from 2000–02, but were recovering from the 1997 financial crisis.

Where are we now? Probably worse than the 2000s, but not as bad as the early 1990s. Inflation is not entirely subdued, but is tame enough for some interest-rate cuts. Moreover, in the 1990s, and even the 2000s, there was only the USA to rely on; now, India and China are credible motors of the global economy. So real estate will not get away scot-free, but may escape with only one year of negative returns. The UK looks badly placed, because of high supply levels and an over-dependence on financial services, the focus of current problems.

4

Inflation and real estate

Alongside GDP growth and interest rates, the rate of inflation in the economy is the most crucial variable for determining real estate performance in the short, medium and long term. The effects of inflation act on real estate at a variety of levels. As the nominal value of tenants' cash flows rise, these feed into real estate cash flows via new and adjustable lease contracts (such as upward-only rent reviews) or new leases. This gives real estate the ability to preserve the real value of investors' capital in the longer term. At times of rising inflation expectations, investors tend to prefer real estate to other asset classes and so its risk premium falls and yields compress, providing a further performance boost.

Inflation also affects real estate indirectly, through the movement of other macroeconomic variables. In recent times, monetary authorities have relied heavily on interest rates to control the rate of inflation. So, as inflation rises, so also do interest rates; this tends to be bad for real estate, because it slows the rate of economic expansion and therefore the requirements of tenants for new space. This statement may seem to contradict those made in the first paragraph, but the real world is full of opposites. Asset classes are always subject to positive and negative forces acting at the same time. Our own work, in the article of September 2009, suggests that whilst real estate is a good long-term capital preserver, it does perform poorly in the short term when inflation is unexpectedly high. We think this is because the

Real Estate and Globalisation, First Edition. Richard Barkham.
© 2012 John Wiley & Sons, Ltd. Published 2012 by John Wiley & Sons, Ltd.

interest-rate effect predominates; in the longer term, it is the inflation effect that is stronger. Post GFC in the UK, inflation is unexpectedly high and real estate is performing well. This is because investors can see that the monetary authorities are constrained in their ability to raise interest rates, because of ongoing weakness in the banking sector. So even the short-term performance of real estate with respect to inflation is time-varying, because of the changing nature of economic policy.

As we noted above, real estate keeps pace with inflation, because lease contracts are reviewed or renewed relatively frequently and landlords are able to keep a relatively constant proportion of businesses' cash flows. In many countries, the link between property cash flows and inflation is even more direct, because contractual rent rises are linked directly to the percentage changes in specified indices of inflation. Our article of March 2008 shows that this is the case in France and other parts of continental Europe. The article also shows that problems can arise for tenants or landlords, because of imperfections in the ways in which inflation is measured. The general point is that property investors and tenants need good economic advice in constructing inflation-linked rental contracts, because indices of inflation do vary in their coverage and are never truly universal.

If index-linked rental contracts help real estate to preserve its real value in the long term, then depreciation retards this ability. There are three types of real estate obsolescence: technical (the building wears out); functional (the building is not fit for purpose); and locational (businesses prefer to locate elsewhere). All of these factors reduce the ability of real estate rents to rise over time and increase the amount of capital expenditure required to keep buildings operational and competitive. Our article of July 2008 deals with the difference between the ability of land, as opposed to buildings, to act as a capital preserver. Although land suffers from locational and functional obsolescence (through, for instance, contamination), it is less prone to these than the buildings themselves, particularly high-specification ones. So, other things being equal, investors should prefer low capital intensive buildings for capital preservation, because the land is a higher component of the overall value.

There are many other ways in which inflation affects real estate. In times of rising inflation, households tend to bring forward purchase decisions, so inflation can boost retail sales. Likewise deflation, which has been a specific concern in the period since the great financial crisis, can lead to deferred consumption and very weak retail sales. If inflation rises because of large rises in a specific sector, such as fuel, then households are deterred from making long shopping trips by car and 'out of town' retail centres can suffer. Where inflation takes hold in the real estate sector, as opposed to the economy as a whole, the results can be disastrous, because speculative investment and development booms can quickly develop, as has been seen most recently in the US housing market. We deal with this theme in more depth in the section on real estate crashes.

The point is, inflation is of vital importance to real estate, which is why we have spent so much time researching and analysing the short, medium and long-term inflation outlook. In analysing inflation, we pay great attention to three economic variables: the output gap; the rate of growth of the money supply; and inflation expectations. The output gap is the difference between the actual level of output and the maximum potential output of the economy. If output is above the maximum potential, then inflation develops quite quickly, because firms find themselves short of labour and start to pay higher and higher wages. So the output gap is key to inflation, but care is required, because it is not an easy variable to measure. In theory, the maximum potential output of an economy can be calculated by reference to the size of the labour force and the capital stock, but measurement issues make this difficult. Monetary authorities are often 'behind the curve' on inflation, because they do not correctly calculate the output gap. The relationship between inflation and money supply growth is more tenuous than that with the output gap, but it is still important, because the cost and availability of credit determines households' and businesses' desire to purchase goods. If the level of demand becomes too strong because credit is too easily available, prices start to rise. Finally, inflation becomes embedded in an economy when people expect prices to keep rising. Workers demand pay rises to keep pace with the price rises they expect to occur. Our article of June 2010 gives an example of the type of inflation analysis we regularly undertake.

In the past, the initial trigger for a period of inflation has come from a rise in the price of oil, commodities or other raw materials. Our articles of June 2004 and December 2007 deal with our assessment of whether oil price rises or food price rises will translate into more general inflation. Since the early 1980s, and particularly since the 1990s, monetary authorities in most OECD countries have shown themselves resolute in the battle against inflation. So, by raising interest rates when required, cost–push inflation has never been allowed to develop into general inflation. They have been aided in this by the general decline in the power of organised labour since the Reagan–Thatcher era and, more recently, the emergence of China, India and Brazil as low-cost centres of production. Now, OECD workers simply cannot force wage increases, for fear their jobs will be relocated to such low-cost production areas. So, rising fuel and food prices, mainly caused by the rise in demand from emerging markets, cannot be offset by rising wages. Our article of February 2011 shows how this is reducing the living standards of some OECD consumers quite dramatically. This, because it undermines consumption growth, is bad for real estate. As we said at the beginning of this chapter, a deep knowledge of inflation is essential for successful real-estate investment and occupation strategies.

Does property provide a hedge against inflation? (September 2009)

Although we are not concerned about inflation in the short and medium term, it is useful to review the case for property as a hedge against inflation. We know that in some countries, over the long term, property preserves and enhances real wealth. For example, UK IPD All Property returns have averaged 11.7% per annum since 1971, compared with inflation of 6.8% per annum. However, the term 'hedge' has a more specific meaning in financial economics. An asset is an inflation hedge if it protects investors from unexpected changes in inflation. In general, investors prefer assets that prevent the erosion of their purchasing power by increasing in value in line with unexpected surges in inflation. It is often asserted that property offers such a hedge.

Empirical evidence on the subject has been mixed. Fama & Schwert (1981)[1] find that property returns are negatively correlated with inflation. Hoesli (2006)[2] suggests that property provides a partial hedge against inflation: returns vary one for one with expected inflation, but not with unexpected inflation. The distinction between expected and unexpected inflation is important. In the last decade or so, investors have become used to a low and predictable rate of inflation. Nobody quite knows how quantitative easing will end, but it may be in a sudden jump in inflation.

The start point of our analysis was historic inflation, which we split into its two components, expected and unexpected inflation, using an ARIMA model. An ARIMA model is similar (but more sophisticated) to a moving average. The ARIMA model is used to forecast expected inflation in period 't' on the basis of the actual rates of inflation in the previous three or four periods. This is deducted from actual inflation in period 't' to reveal the unexpected inflation component in 't'. Figure 4.1 shows the unexpected component of inflation in four countries. In the long term, about 40% of the movement in the rate of inflation from period to period is unexpected.

---

[1] E. Fama and G. Schwert (1977), 'Asset Returns and Inflation', *Journal of Financial Economics*, 5.
[2] M. Hoesli, C. Lizieri and B MacGregor (2006), 'Inflation Hedging Characteristics of US and UK Investments', Working paper, Henley Business School, University of Reading.

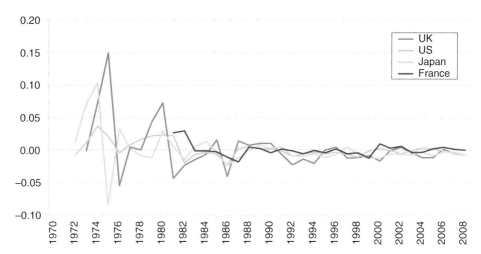

Figure 4.1: Unexpected inflation in selected countries
Source: Grosvenor

To test the inflation-hedging characteristics of property, we modelled property returns using GDP growth, construction growth (as a proxy for the growth rate of supply), expected inflation and unexpected inflation. We used data from the USA, the UK, France, Italy, Spain, Germany, Canada, Japan and Hong Kong. The precise relationship between returns and inflation across these countries was estimated using an econometric technique called 'panel estimation'. The results are shown in Table 4.1.

The positive coefficient on the expected inflation variable suggests that returns vary one for one with expected inflation. However, the negative coefficient on the unexpected components suggests that returns tend to fall where inflation turns out to be higher than investors expect. This suggests that returns do not systematically adjust to protect an investor against unexpected inflation in the system. One possibility is that property varies over time in its ability to hedge unexpected inflation. For instance, some have suggested that property is a better hedge in periods of high and persistent inflation than low and predictable inflation.

To test this hypothesis, a high inflation 'dummy variable' and a low inflation 'dummy variable' are included with the expected and unexpected inflation components of the model. The period of 1976 to 1985 is chosen as the high inflationary period and 1996 to 2005 as the low inflationary period. Although the data coverage is limited for the period 1976 to 1985, the results indicate that property returns do not vary with either expected or unexpected inflation. In contrast, during low inflationary periods, returns tend to move with expected but not unexpected inflation. This result

Table 4.1

Variable	Coefficient %	P-value
Constant	−0.02	0.14
GDP Growth	+3.21	0.00
Expected Inflation	+1.00	0.00
Unexpected Inflation	−1.21	0.07
Construction Growth (Lagged 3 Years)	−0.18	0.06
UK fixed effect	−0.01	
Japan fixed effect	+0.01	
USA fixed effect	−0.01	
Hong Kong fixed effect	−0.03	
France fixed effect	+0.05	
Canada fixed effect	+0.06	
Spain fixed effect	+0.00	
Germany fixed effect	+0.00	
Italy fixed effect	+0.06	

suggests that property does not improve as a hedge in periods of high inflation. In fact, property only provides a partial hedge against unexpected
inflation and only during low inflationary periods. To be absolutely certain
of this fact the research needs to be conducted on the basis of better data.

Given the amount of slack in the world economy, inflation should remain
in check in the short to medium term. However, if policymakers keep
expansionary policy in place for too long, then inflation will become a
concern as private demand begins to turn. The implication of this paper is
that, if policymakers attempt to inflate their way out of this recession, then
real property returns are likely to suffer. The only way that investors can
be sure to preserve and enhance their real wealth, at least in the short term,
is by holding their assets for a very long period of time.

Linking rents to construction cost
inflation – the French case (March 2008)

In a slowing economic environment, with yield compression a thing of the
past, where might investors turn to find some security? One factor that will
make some real estate markets more attractive than others is the nature of
the 'rental escalation mechanism' in occupational leases. By this we mean
the process by which the rent paid by the tenant is increased over the course
of the lease. In the UK, for instance, rents are reviewed to market every five

years. In France, by contrast, retail rents are indexed in line with the Construction Cost Index (CCI). As yields soften and economic growth eases, partly in response to inflation, markets in which rents move in line with price rises will prove attractive and defensive. In fact, most continental European retail markets operate with some form of rental indexation, but the French case is slightly different and currently in a state of flux.

The French indexation mechanism, which has prevailed until recently, has given investors good rental growth compared to other countries (see Figure 4.2). The Construction Cost Index (CCI), on which retail rents are escalated, has expanded at a fast pace (3.9% per annum since 2000). In Italy, rent indexation can be up to a ceiling of 75% of CPI, so with annual inflation around 2.4% p.a. since 2000 the indexation increases have been relatively modest, at around 1.8% on average. In Spain, the indexation mechanism has ensured rental growth increases of 3.2% on average since 2000, as rents are escalated by a 100% of CPI increase. In both Belgium and Germany rental values are also indexed on the CPI: in Germany, rents increased by 1.7%, compared with 2% in Belgium.

Now, it is important to recognise that these growth rates apply to passing rents on occupied properties: market rental values are quite different. In France, Spain and Italy, market rents have risen well above their indexation rates (CCI or CPI). In some ways this is bad for investors, but as the global economy sails into troubled waters, many will be very glad that they own 'under-rented' assets. In France, the degree of 'under-rentedness' is estimated to be very high. In 2002, 80% of French retail property was considered

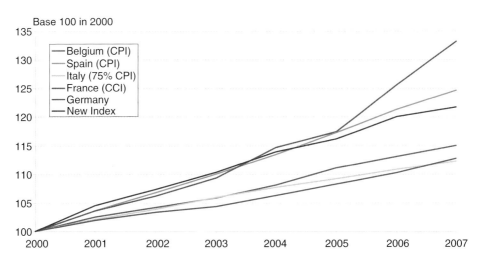

Figure 4.2: Indexation compared
Source: Grosvenor, CWHB

to be under-rented, which reduced to 60% in 2006. Research suggests that in France, even at the end of a lease, when rents could be reset to market levels, convention, politics and lack of market data mean that this is rarely the case.

Despite the fact that French occupiers would seem to be able to get a good deal almost as of right, they have been most unhappy in recent times. They believe that the rental indexation method of using the CCI has been detrimental to their business, saying that rents have risen much faster than turnover. For instance, French retailers assert that between 2000 and 2006, the CCI increased by 32%, while retailers' turnover rose by only 18%. Also, retailers have argued that the 'volatility' of CCI change is, on average, 'unfair'. They point out that the renewal of the lease in a specific quarter could lead to a huge increase, while in the next quarter the indexation mechanism may have been more moderate (Figure 4.3). Strong lobbying has brought changes to the indexation method.

Retailers have put forward a new index, called the ILC (Indice des Loyers Commerciaux), which is a weighted average of three series: CPI, CCI and a retailer turnover index called ICAV. We have back-tested this new index (Table 4.2 and Figure 4.3), and we see that, in the long run, the retailer turnover index has, in fact, produced the strongest growth per annum compared with the CCI, with a lower volatility. Potentially at least, French retailers would seem to be opting for a worse deal. The new ILC index is less volatile and potentially more predictable and, in the period 2002 to 2007, produced lower growth than the CCI, but in a period of high inflation

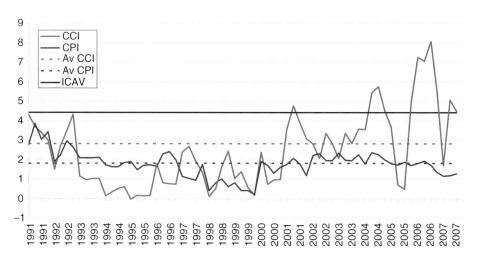

Figure 4.3:   Construction cost index vs. the consumption price index
Source: INSEE

Table 4.2: The alternative mechanisms compared

	ICAV	CPI	CCI	New Index
Period	Average per year (%) (*standard deviation*)			
1995–2007	4.4	1.8	2.8	
	1.4	0.7	2.1	
2002–2007	3.3	2.7	3.8	2.8
	0.9	*0.6*	*2.0*	*0.6*

and low economic growth might actually benefit landlords, rather than tenants.

The new ICL will be implemented in the retail sector voluntarily, based on negotiations between landlord and tenant: otherwise, the former CCI indexation will remain. In the recent buoyant past, the minutiae of such issues mattered less, but now, with returns harder to find, it will be detailed knowledge of the market alongside careful research that generates out-performance.

So much for the French case! Other markets in Europe have their own idiosyncrasies that need to be understood and monitored. The interesting general point is that markets that are under-rented, as they often are in continental Europe, are highly defensive. What investors lose in the up-swing, they gain in a down-market, as retailers, despite their protestations, have a buffer against declining turnover.

Oil prices, inflation and real estate (July 2008)

Motivated by the desire to find some 'good news' against mounting eco-nomic gloom, we examined the hypothesis that property is a good 'hedge' against inflation. As we move into a period of stagflation, can we advise investors to stick with real estate, or even choose it over other asset classes? This analysis is conducted within a broader programme: to understand the changing nature of inflationary pressures; in particular, the cost–push impulse from oil. The results presented here are based on UK data.

The relationship between oil prices and inflation is not quite as clearcut as might be expected. The left section of Figure 4.4 illustrates this point, by displaying a strong relationship between oil prices and inflation between 1970 and 1990. This is supported by econometric results, which indicate that a 1% rise in the price of oil leads to a 0.5% increase in RPI. In the right section of Figure 4.4, the period since 1990, the relationship is much less clear. It is tempting to suggest that this was the result of a new era of

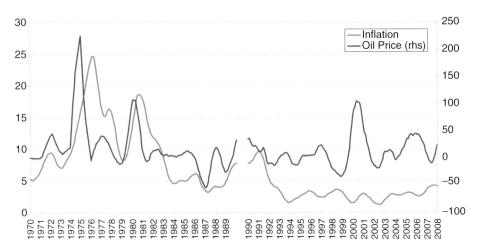

Figure 4.4:   Oil price and inflation
Source: Grosvenor; Global Insight

'inflation targeting' monetary policy, but the world of the 1990s was also blessed with extraordinarily low and stable oil prices. Our equation suggests that, over the 1990s, a 1% oil price rise was associated with only a 0.36% increase in inflation. Close inspection of Figure 4.4 suggests that, since 2002, the relationship between oil and inflation has reasserted itself, with analysis suggesting that a 1% increase in the price of oil is now associated with a 1.3% increase in inflation. The bad old days of 'wage-price spirals' have not returned, but the UK does have a very serious problem with inflation.

So how does UK real estate perform in relation to inflation? Figure 4.5 shows the results from a regression of inflation on real estate capital values as indicated by the IPD all-property index. Although there is a clear long-run relationship, indicating that real estate values keep up with prices, there are some worrying issues. First, in the equation, the fact that the coefficient on inflation is only around 0.7 suggests in that a 1% increase in inflation, in the long term, is only matched by a 0.7% increase in real estate values. Moreover, there are long periods in which real estate values lag the cumulative rise in prices. So real estate, as represented by the IPD index, appears to be a reasonable long term capital preserver, but not a 'sure-fire' short-term hedge. To check this result, a similar analysis was conducted on CB Richard Ellis 'prime property' data. The idea behind this analysis is that actual real estate values reflect both land prices and the value of the physical infrastructure/building. Buildings depreciate over time – sometimes, as in the case of offices, quite heavily. So heavy depreciation may obscure the capital-preserving characteristics of land. Since the CBRE index is of con-

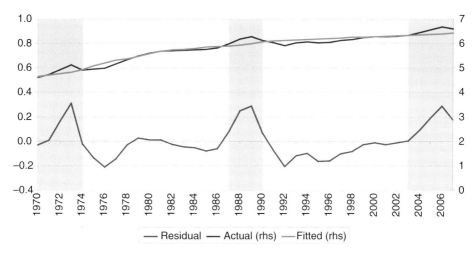

Figure 4.5:   Regression results: capital values on inflation
Source: Grosvenor; IPD

tinuously prime property, the effects of depreciation are removed. Here the
evidence is unequivocal: an equation coefficient of 1.2 suggests that land,
in the long term, more than maintains its real value. As with the IPD index,
however, the CBRE data shows that over certain periods, usually following a slump in values, even prime real estate does not keep pace with
inflation.

What are the implications of this analysis? Real estate, particularly the
sectors not prone to high levels of depreciation, such as land, industrial and
retail, is a good value-preserver, although a long holding period is required
to be sure of keeping pace with the cumulative rise in prices. This might
provide some comfort to investors contemplating the period of sustained
economic turbulence that is about to unfold. An interesting side issue is
what this says about yields; namely, that they are approximately the real
returns that investors can expect from real estate in the long run. So even
now, an investor buying and holding for ten years might expect to achieve
6% per annum real return.

So, what of the hunt for good news that motivated the study?
Notwithstanding the above, this was unsuccessful. Using monthly data
from IPD to understand something about the lead and lag relationships
between real estate and inflation, we discovered that, in the period from
1988, real estate capital values actually lead inflation. In other words, real
estate inflation precedes general inflation (see Figure 4.6). The recent pre-
cipitate decline in capital values actually suggests a relatively rapid decline
in inflation. With oil prices soaring, only a major recession would have this
effect. This seems to be what the property market and, somewhat late in

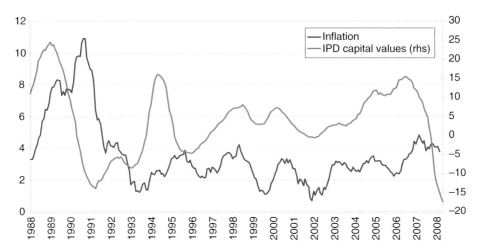

Figure 4.6:   Capital values and inflation
Source: Grosvenor; Global Insight, IPD

the day, the stock market, is signalling. It's time for investors to focus on the long-term (10 years plus), or get out of real estate.

Is inflation building up in the world economy? (June 2010)

Inflation is a perennial concern of this column. It is the key statistic in modern market economies. When inflation is low and on target, central banks have the ability to cut interest rates and stimulate production in response to negative economic shocks. This is what stabilised the global economy in the wake of the collapse of Lehman Brothers in 2008 and the onset of the credit crunch. Inflation also affects asset markets. During the high-inflation era of the 1970s, bond markets slumped, equities were highly volatile and capital sought the security of real-estate assets. Prompted by these thoughts and the strong theoretical link between quantitative easing and inflation, we have taken another look at global inflation.

   Figure 4.7 shows the rates of CPI inflation across a number of major economies in the industrialised world. Over the last nine months, as economic growth has resumed, inflation has bounced back sharply from its sharply negative trajectory at the height of the financial crisis in early 2009. This is a major success for policymakers. Even though the problems because of excess debt in the world economy rumble on, they would be much worse if deflation had set in.

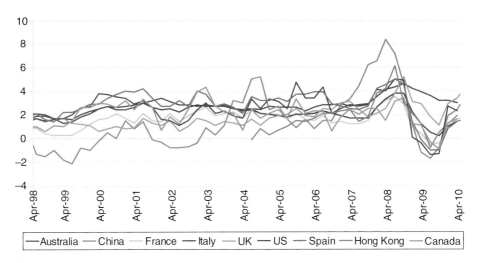

Figure 4.7:   Global inflation
Source: Global Insight

In saving the world from depression, have policymakers created the condi-tions necessary for inflation to accelerate? Output gap analysis, as in Figure 4.8, suggests not. The output gap indicates the difference between the pro-ductive capacity of the economy and the actual level of production. So a negative output gap indicates spare resources and downward pressure on wages. The large output gap that currently exists in the advanced economies suggests that there is no strong inflationary pressure in the advanced economies.

It is interesting to note that the advanced economies had built up a very positive output gap prior to the current crisis. There are two reasons why this did not show up in stronger advanced-country inflation. The first is that cheap manufactured products from China have helped to keep inflation down. Chinese products are cheap because of low production costs and an artificially low currency value. The second reason is that many advanced economies have benefited from an inflow of skilful migrant workers, who have kept wage rates down. Since these broader deflationary forces still exist, there is even more reason to think that inflation is not an important short- and medium-term concern.

Figure 4.9 completes the low-inflation thesis. It shows the rate of growth of broad money, across the industrialised world and some emerging markets. Although a precise causal link between growth of the money supply and inflation is difficult to prove, the growth of broad money does indicate the demand for credit from businesses and individuals. Where the private sector is de-gearing, broad money will be in decline. So Figure 4.9 indicates that there is no real inflation impulse from credit creation. The exception to this

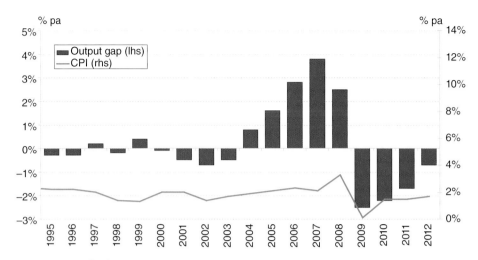

Figure 4.8:   OECD output gap
Source: Global Insight

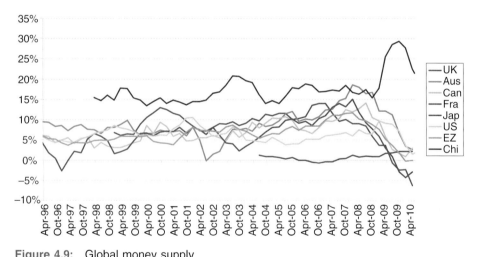

Figure 4.9:   Global money supply
Source: Global Insight

might be China, where the money supply has grown sharply since the crisis.
The rate of growth is now falling, but the legacy of aggressive expansion of
the money supply will be a period of inflation, or an unsustainable surge in
asset prices.

Are any other pro-inflation factors at work? Oil prices have bounced back
quite sharply since the middle of 2009. However, the reduction in oil inten-

sity of GDP in the advanced industrial nations has made oil prices much less of an inflation threat than they used to be. Of greater importance potentially is the trade-weighted value of the Chinese currency, the RMB. As the RMB rises against the currencies of the OECD nations, Chinese goods become more expensive. As OECD countries go through a painful period of restructuring, the Chinese will come under pressure to revalue their currency to relieve the pressure on OECD companies, but this is a longer-term issue.

Overall, a further rise in global inflation looks unlikely. In fact, deflation would seem to be a more important short- and medium-term worry. Nevertheless, in two years' time the global output gap will probably have closed and quantitative easing will still be feeding through into credit growth. Moreover, politicians faced with the need to deal with accumulated national debts have the motive to push central banks into a more inflation-tolerant stance. When we re-write this article in 18 months' time, there is likely to be a very different conclusion.

Can oil prices cause a global inflation problem? (June 2004)

The global economy seems to be facing an energy crisis once again, as strong demand combines with supply problems to drive oil prices back above $40 per barrel, 30–40% above prices at the end of Q3 last year. The demand side is driven by the same story as during the last oil spike of 1999 and 2000, when the accelerating Western economy reduced global oil reserves, but this time round the twist comes from booming China, which has become the world's second largest user of oil. On the supply side, OPEC's policy to restrict output to maintain the spot price last year has given way to attempts to increase production to calm markets rattled by the prospect of terrorist-induced supply disruptions in the Middle East. OPEC has relatively limited ability to lift production in the short term, though, so it may take some time to restore market balance.

Figure 4.10 shows that oil prices, in nominal terms, are back at the level of the second oil crisis in 1979–80, but in real terms prices – using US prices – are at much more moderate levels. Oil prices would have to increase by a further 185% to reach the same level (in real terms) as the worst point of the 1979 crisis. Even the most pessimistic of observers do not envisage crude oil prices increasing from $42 per barrel to $120 per barrel. But the level of oil prices is not the only concern. The disruption caused by higher prices will be greater if increases come sharply rather than gradually. During

Figure 4.10:   World oil price index 1970–2004
Source: Global Insight

the last oil crisis prices rose by 170% from the end of 1978 to the end of 1980. Even if such an increase were to occur now, the impact on final prices paid by companies and households would be much reduced. The reason is the tax wedge. Taxes levied on oil products now are much greater than they used to be and they work like reverse gearing. The higher the tax rate, the less a given proportionate rise in oil prices will generate a proportionate rise in final prices. For example, with duties equivalent to 10% of the oil price, a 50% price rise would cause a 45% increase in final prices, including duties. With duties equivalent to 50% of the oil price, the increase in final prices would fall to 33%.

So can oil prices cause a global inflation problem? Probably, but a crisis on the scale of past episodes is extremely unlikely. However, oil prices could be the spur that starts an inflationary spiral, so price data will be important to watch over the coming months as the hangover from the Fed's low interest rate policy begins to be felt.

Are food prices driving inflation up? (December 2007)

An important theme in recent press coverage of economics has been the impact of rising food prices on inflation. Articles have ranged from the implications of climate change for food production to the rising cost of a

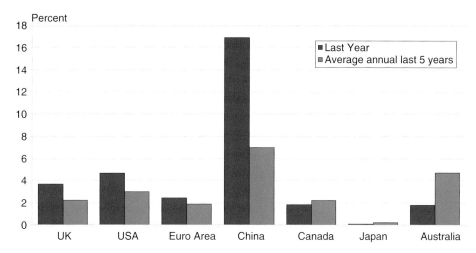

Figure 4.11: General (CPI) and food price inflation
Source: National Statistical Offices

Christmas lunch. We consider the potential implications for real estate. The world is in the grip of a credit crisis: the only respite in the offing is cuts in interest rates. If central banks consider inflationary pressures too pervasive, these cuts will be delayed.

Figure 4.11 shows the scale of the problem. The UK and the USA are suffering substantially higher food price inflation this year, compared with the last five. In Australia, following five years of high food inflation, recent trends appear improved, although the current drought may well bring problems next year. China is the country suffering the most rapid increases in food prices. In addition to the painful impact this has on low-income groups, there are substantive macroeconomic consequences.

Headline inflation is measured by calculating the price changes of a representative 'basket' of goods. The 'basket' is created from the results of surveys into how households spend their money. In countries with lower per-capita incomes, households spend a higher proportion of their income on food, so food has a higher weighting in measures of inflation. In the case of the UK, the USA and the Euro Area, the weighting is quite low (Table 4.1), so food-price growth only creates a small impetus to inflation. Australia's food weighting is low, but the persistent increase in food prices over the last few years will have had an impact. The country with the greatest potential feed-through from food to general inflation is China, where the CPI food weight is 35%. So far, the impact has been limited, because the prices of other goods in the CPI basket, such as clothing and footwear, are falling. However, China's inflation is at an 11-year high of 6.5%; and

Figure 4.12:   World wheat prices
Source: Global Insight

the issue has become a top concern for the Chinese government. Persistent inflationary pressures may feed into demands for higher wages, which would signal the end of the era of cheap goods for the rest of the world and, potentially, China's export-led expansion.

What are the causes of the hike in food prices? A variety of factors affect each food type, but we focus on wheat prices (Figure 4.12). As well as being a staple, wheat is also a major component of animal feed, so contributes significantly to the cost of producing eggs, meat and poultry. The correlation between wheat prices and those of eggs and feed is 0.6 and 0.7 respectively. The series is volatile, because, as with real estate, supply cannot respond to demand in the short term. The recent very substantial hike in prices has been linked, by some, to the transfer of production from food to bio-fuel. We think this unlikely: bio fuels currently cover 10 million hectares, compared with a total global cropped area of 1.5bn hectares. A series of weather-related bad harvests in the main producing countries are the real cause: the drought in Australia (the world's third biggest producer), wet weather in Canada and Europe, all reducing output by 10–20%. Figure 4.12 shows something of an upward trend in price changes since about 1998. This is likely to be driven by strong economic growth in previously poor countries. Is climate change an issue? It's probably too early to say, though some would draw the link between weather-related poor harvests and CO_2 emissions.

How will this impact on real estate? Inflation in China is a long-term worry, because low production costs are the basis of the current economic

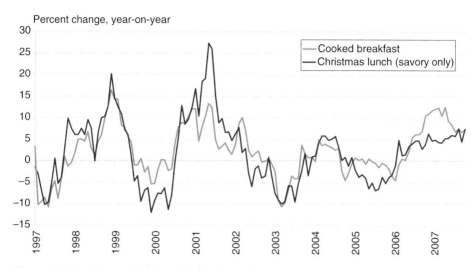

Figure 4.13:   The cost of breakfast and lunch
Source: ONS, Global Insight, Grosvenor Research

expansion in the region and elsewhere. Beyond this, food prices are making a contribution to general inflation in the West, but they are probably not sufficiently important on their own to derail imminent interest-rate cuts except in Europe, given the fear of some ECB members that inflation has become 'alarming', driven by energy, food prices and wages. Longer-term, there is likely to be an expansion of wheat production, leading to price falls next harvest.

In the UK, the immediate future may not be so comforting. Figure 4.13 shows an economic indicator created for the UK; but it applies, at least in general terms, to other Western countries: the 'Christmas lunch and full English breakfast' index. The cost of these two meals is rising much more quickly than general inflation. Since UK consumers are also feeling the pinch from increases in utility bills and mortgage rates, they may well decide that they cannot allocate as much to gifts, clothing and other household goods this festive period. This points, potentially, to a lean Christmas for high streets and malls.

Real wages and real estate in the UK (February 2011)

The economies of the industrialised world are emerging from a period of near deflation. By contrast, the UK has suffered above target inflation since

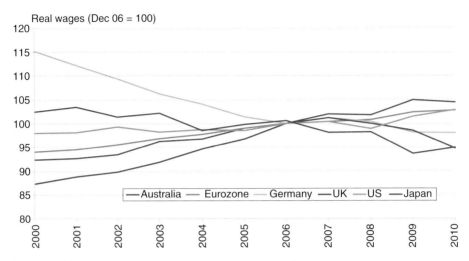

Figure 4.14:   Real wages in selected OECD economies
Source: EcoWin

the great financial crisis (GFC). Initially the fall in the value of sterling, induced by a combination of weak growth rates and extreme monetary easing, led to rising import prices. More recently inflation has been driven by the commodities boom and increasing indirect taxation. In previous eras, such a strong inflation impulse would have fed through into a 'wage-price' spiral and other 'second-round' inflation effects. It may still do that, but for the moment rising prices are eating away at households' real purchasing power.

Figure 4.14 shows that real earnings in the UK are now at the same level as they were in 2004. International comparisons suggest that periods of falling real wages are not uncommon. Real wages have trended down in Japan, despite persistent deflation, because of the long-term weakness of that economy. Germany has suffered a decade of falling real wages, because of the need to offset the negative effects of joining the Euro at an exchange rate which was too high. However, this painful period of economic adjustment has recently begun to pay off, as Germany's super-competitive export sector has driven a very robust economic recovery.

On the face of it, falling real wages would seem to be quite negative for real estate. Figure 4.15 shows why. In the long term, real wage growth is a major source of growth in retail sales. It is not the only influence: Australia has seen retail sales grow much faster than real earnings growth, because of strong population growth and the beneficial impact of a 'terms of trade shock'. The USA has also had strong population growth. The figures in Figure 4.15 may also be somewhat distorted by differences in the ways in

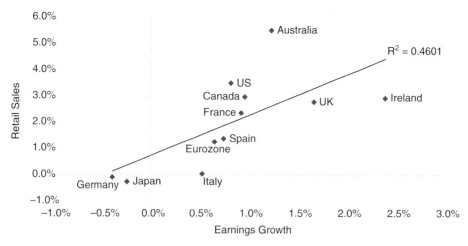

Figure 4.15:   Real earnings and retail sales growth
Source: EcoWin, Oxford Economics

which retail sales are calculated. However, in general, retail sales are fundamentally driven by real-wage growth. The period of falling real wages, which looks set to continue for a while, is negative for UK retailing. It is also negative for UK house prices, which are also affected by the real spending power of households.

Are there any benefits of falling real wages? One benefit is that unit labour costs fall, making British exports more competitive in world markets. When combined with the fall in the value of sterling, declining real wages make exports super-competitive. Some have argued that this gain in competitiveness will help the UK economy 'rebalance' away from consumption and the service sector towards exports and manufacturing. The manufacturing sector may well make strong gains, but the proponents of the 'rebalancing' view often miss the fact that the UK service sector, particularly that part of it located in London, is highly export-orientated, so London is also likely to outperform.

The fall in real wages over the course of the economic crisis is also due to the 'success' of British companies in holding down nominal wages and overall wage bills. As a result, it has not been necessary for companies to cut staff numbers as aggressively as they might have done, given the scale of the fall in GDP. Figure 4.16 shows our forecast of employment decline based on the correlation between employment and GDP in past recessions. The fall in employment has not been as bad as history would suggest it should have been. From a real estate perspective, higher levels of employment cquate to higher levels of occupation. Since occupied real estate is

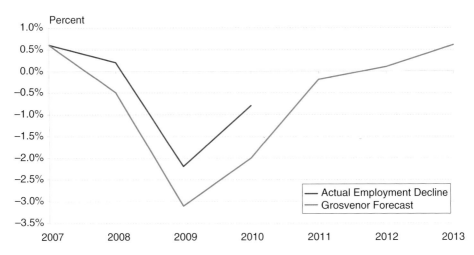

Figure 4.16: Forecast and actual employment change
Source: EcoWin, Grosvenor

more valuable than unoccupied, the fall in real wages partly explains the strong and somewhat unexpected bounceback in UK real estate values.

So, if falling real wages is painful for households but not all bad for the economy and real estate, where do we go from here? If the global economy keeps growing, we can only expect commodity prices to continue to rise, fuelling cost–push inflation. Ultimately, as the economy rebalances and labour markets tighten, this should feed through into nominal and real wage growth. However, in the longer term, rising living standards only come from innovation and entrepreneurship. The UK, and the rest of the OECD, urgently need to 'reinvent themselves' to counter market penetrations by emerging markets. This means creating new, high-value-adding businesses and industries. It can be done; it has been done before; but it will require a substantive change in social attitudes and taxation to achieve it.

5

Retailing and retail property

Over the last 30 years, retail property has been very attractive to institutional investors and REITs. In part, this is due to economic growth driving up consumers' incomes and spending ability. Furthermore, as Western societies have become wealthier, the overall share of consumer spending within overall GDP has risen. Both of these facts have given rise to a general sense that the 'fundamentals' of retail property are highly robust and that the demand for retail goods rises strongly in the long term. Investors have been keen to acquire the property assets that play a key role in the distribution of goods to acquisitive Western consumers. In order to enhance their returns, investors have become ever more skilful in managing their retail assets so that their appeal to consumers is maximised.

As consumer societies have evolved, skill in managing retail property has become ever more essential; consumers have a lot of choice about what they spend their money on. Although consumer spending is around 65% of most modern economies, only about 35% is spending on retail goods (see the article of November 2003). Non-retail consumer spending includes things such as cars, public transport, cinemas, sports clubs, pubs and restaurants, telephone bills, holidays, hairdressing and other personal services, rent and utility bills. Demographics play a part in what proportion of overall consumer spending goes to retailing. Older consumers prefer to spend on holidays, restaurants, travel and motoring, whilst younger consumers prefer physical goods. So owners of retail property have a vital part to play in

Real Estate and Globalisation, First Edition. Richard Barkham.
© 2012 John Wiley & Sons, Ltd. Published 2012 by John Wiley & Sons, Ltd.

promoting retail goods to consumers by making retail property as attractive and accessible as possible.

Skilful management of retail assets is important is also a response to intense competition within the sector. Traditional town centres, typically made up of shops in individual ownership, compete with purpose-built shopping centres, often in out-of-town locations which are more accessible to car-borne shoppers. In turn, purpose-built shopping centres compete with each other and other types of retail property, such as retail warehouses, supermarkets and hypermarkets. Recently, all physical retail assets have faced competition from the Internet (i.e. on-line shopping from home), the market share of which, as we discuss in our article of December 2006, is rapidly increasing.

Over the years, Grosvenor Research has devoted a lot of effort to understanding the drivers of retail performance, particularly rental value growth. As investment managers, it is important to be able to understand and predict periods of strong (or weak) rental growth in order to make the correct decisions about the acquisition and disposal of assets or major capital expenditures. In general, retail rental value growth is positively correlated with retail spending and negatively correlated with the construction of new shopping centres. Our article of January 2006 attempts to examine the relative importance of these supply and demand effects in generating rental growth. One finding from this research is that new supply, namely the construction of new shopping centres, does not always lead to a fall in rents as economic theory would suggest it should. In some markets, the latent demand from retailers for modern shopping space is high. So the construction of new assets actually causes rents to increase. This tends to happen in markets, like the UK, which are heavily regulated, or in 'immature' markets that are just developing as consumer economies.

If retail spending drives retail rents, what drives retail spending? First and foremost is the growth of consumer incomes. If unemployment is high, consumers' income growth will be weak and so also will be spending. We look at this in our articles of October 2001, June 2003 and August 2009. The state of the labour market – namely, the level of unemployment or its reciprocal, the rate of job creation – also affects the savings rate. Where households are in fear of their jobs, they will tend to reduce spending in order to build up a cash buffer. So when the economy is expanding and jobs are growing, retail spending is boosted not only by income growth but also by reduced saving. The articles of August 2004 and August 2009 look at the impact of unemployment on consumer spending.

When consumers are really confident, they will not only run down their savings but they will also borrow. Over the last 15 years, at least up until 2007, there has been an enormous increase in the level of consumer debt in many OECD countries, particularly the USA and the UK. This is partly related to strong economic growth accompanied by very low levels of unemployment, but it is also related to rising consumer wealth, particularly housing wealth. Our article of April 2005 looks specifically at the impact of house price growth on real spending, but it is also covered more generally in some of the other articles, such as January 2003 and June 2003.

The other key driver of retail spending is the level of interest rates. The precise transmission mechanism from interest rates and consumers varies over time and between economies. Often, the link is indirect. Stock markets and housing markets perform well when interest rates fall and this makes consumers confident enough to want to spend and to borrow to spend. Cheap money also drives banks and other financial institutions aggressively to promote themselves to the consumer sector, particularly in the area of lending secured on housing.

Interest rates are cyclical and impart cyclicality to retail spending. However, since the early 1990s nominal interest rates have also been in long-term decline. This is mainly due to the decline of inflation, but other factors have been involved, such as international capital flows from emerging and other 'high-savings' economies, such as China. As interest rates have fallen in the OECD, there has been a concomitant build-up of consumer debt in many economies. Too much debt, as we have found out in the period since the GFC. It is interesting to note that as early as 2004 (see article of August 2004), we were concerned about the dangerous build-up of consumer debt in the USA. Our fears were confirmed in the big retail downturn of 2009, which we cover in our article of May 2009.

One important trend over the last 15 years is the strong growth of 'luxury retailing'. Luxury retailing lacks a precise definition, but refers to very well-made items of clothing, footwear and accessories, which are expensive and heavily promoted by persuasive advertising. Bond Street exemplifies luxury retailing in the UK; in France it is Avenue Montaigne and in the USA, Rodeo Drive. The growth of luxury retailing is related to a growth in the number of 'high net worth individuals' (HNWIs) in Western societies and, oddly enough, to strong demand from newly rich consumers in emerging markets. Our article of June 2007 looks at this trend. Some authors have suggested that the growth of consumer debt and the rise of the HNWIs are related.[1] HNWIs are a product of rising inequality in society, which drives low net worth individuals (LNWIs) to borrow to keep up. It is further argued that government are complicit in this, because they fear social disruption arising from the growing wealth and income divide. In any case, from the property investment perspective, outlets selling luxury brands often pay premium rents.

---

[1] R.G. Rajan, *Fault Lines: How Hidden Fractures Still Threaten the World Economy*, Princeton University Press, 2010.

If retail property has been popular with real estate investors, this popularity has had some downsides. The most homogenous of all retail assets is the 'shopping centre' or 'shopping mall'. Perhaps the most successful business model in the Western world, shopping centres or malls, are springing up all across the emerging markets. Relatively cheap to construct, the shopping centre provides a comfortable and safe shopping environment, with units that are very productive for retailers. Shopping centres managed as a coherent whole have the ability to optimise pedestrian flow and to select the most appropriate mix of retailers for the catchment area. All of these advantages can be reinforced by a coordinated marketing effort. In societies where car ownership levels are high, shopping centres are generally purpose-built with car parks, which provides a powerful secondary advantage over more constrained traditional centres.

The popularity of shopping centres with investors means that the market for these assets is deep and liquid and cuts across international boundaries. As a result, when economic troubles develop, the shopping-centre market tends to react like the stock markets, with steep and immediate falls in value affecting all assets, almost regardless of local fundamentals. Our article of October 2009 shows how this happened in Europe in the wake of the GFC. It shows that real estate markets, particularly those for standardised assets, can overshoot in the same way that stock markets do. Interestingly, the values of traditional shops in town and city centres do not seem as sentiment-driven as shopping centres, presumably because they have a more diverse shopper and investor base.

Splitting retail property into food and non-food can increase portfolio performance (November 2003)

The main economic driver for retail property is the value of retail sales, which generally makes up between a third and two-thirds of overall consumer spending and is driven by income, employment prospects and wealth. Total retail sales, though, are the sum of two different components. Non-food sales are generally the larger component and tend to dominate food sales in more developed retail markets. In the USA, food sales are particularly low and make up around 13% of total sales and 18% of sales excluding autos. Food sales tend to grow more steadily than non-food sales, but not necessarily with lower growth rates. In the USA and Spain, food sales have underperformed, but in the UK and France there is little difference and in Germany, food outperforms.

In theory, non-food sales should have a tighter relationship with the overall economy, because the economic cycle will have a more direct effect on discretionary spending than on necessities like food. Our research in Spain shows that the food sales there have no relationship with the classic economic drivers of consumer spending. Food sales tend to run to their own dynamic and feature large spikes, which are out of line with the rest of the consumer sector. Looking at the relationship between food and non-food sales and overall consumer spending in other countries, the correlation between overall consumer spending and the non-food element of sales is higher than the correlation with the food element in the USA and Germany – but not in the UK or France (Figure 5.1). Interestingly, though, the correlation of total retail sales with consumer spending is consistently higher still, suggesting that the components of retail sales diverge from overall consumer spending for specific reasons, but that these divergences tend to compensate each other once the components are combined to give total sales. Therefore, if retail property is being included in a portfolio as a diversifier to the local economy or as a growth element, investors should investigate the relationships between food and non-food separately before making a decision, because no general pattern exists across countries (Figure 5.2). But investors should include both food and non-food if they want to increase the portfolio's exposure to particular national economies.

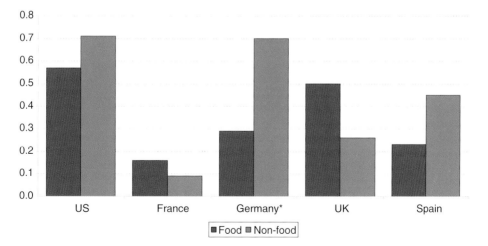

Figure 5.1:   Correlation of retail sales with consumer spending
* *Total retail sales used instead of non-food*

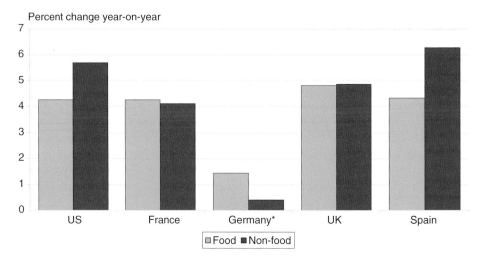

Figure 5.2:   Average growth of retail sales values since 1996
* *Total retail sales used instead of non-food*

A prosperous future for UK shopping places? (December 2006)

One story that is likely to dominate the business headlines this Christmas, at least in the UK, is the squeeze put on store-based retailers by the internet. It is not a new story, but anecdotal evidence suggests that internet retailing has achieved some sort of breakthrough in consumer acceptance this year that will allow it to make a step change in capturing the vital seasonal trade. There are many implications for real estate and society, if this is true. Figure 5.3 shows historic retail development completions and those projected for the next five years. The supply pipeline is higher in the next five years than at any time in the last ten years. Most of this is being built on the expectation of growth in retail rents that may be more difficult to achieve than planned; too bad for retail developers, but there are also consequences for society. Since the mid-1990s, the UK's planning policy has been increasingly prohibitive of 'out-of-town' developments. There are many reasons for this, including the desire to preserve the vitality of towns and cities. The British Council of Shopping Centres (BCSC) has recently published research, in its 'Future of Retail Property Series', that documents the success of this policy. In the mid-1990s, in-town retail completions were 14% of total completions; in the 2000s it has risen to 40%.[2] Thus the success of retail

---

[2] Michael Bach and Mark Thurstain Goodwin, In Town or Out of Town, BCSC Future of Retail Property, London 2006.

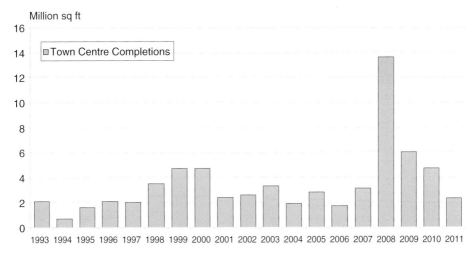

Figure 5.3: Large levels of new supply in the UK
Source: Verdict

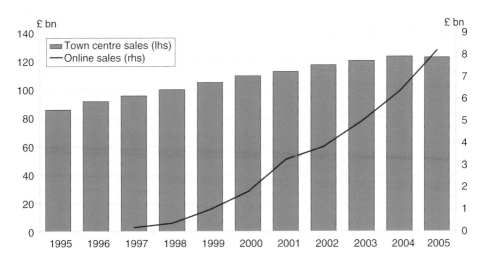

Figure 5.4: Rapid growth in internet retailing in the UK
Source: Verdict

developments has profound implications for Britain's urban areas. Figure 5.4, however, shows that, 'new schemes' notwithstanding, Britain's town centres have a fight on their hands. Moreover, town centres are facing strong competition from the UK's large grocery chains. These operators, with networks of large, highly accessible stores, are increasingly generating revenue from non-food sales (see Figure 5.5).

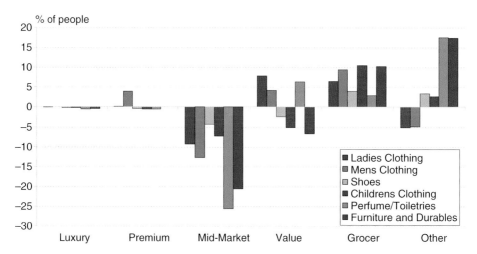

Figure 5.5: Large swing in sales towards grocers
Source: TGI Survey

All this said, further research by the BCSC indicates that the idea that shoppers are deserting physical space, in particular the high street, is not quite right. The relationship between on-line shopping and store-based shopping is far more complex than currently imagined.[3] First, retailers that are doing well on the internet are often the ones that have a strong high street presence and brand. In other words, the high street complements the internet. Second, consumers are adopting complex 'multi-channel' shopping strategies: for instance, browsing on the web, to refine choice and minimise search costs and buying in the store for instant gratification. Third, a large proportion of web shoppers recognise that the web is not quite as stimulating or interesting as 'real world' shopping. Web-shopping is a somewhat 'clinical' process, motivated primarily by convenience.

A tempting conclusion from the BCSC (and other) research is that the internet will always have the edge on convenience, so convenience-type goods should be left to the internet retailers, whilst stores concentrate on highly differentiated comparison goods that need to be seen to be bought. This conclusion may be wrong. Shopping places should use the internet to improve their own convenience. One area that is 'crying out' for better, quicker and more usable information is in the area of transportation and access.[4] A common theme, running through the eight reports on the future

---

[3] Yvonne Court, *Online Retailing: The Impact of Click on Brick*, BCSC Future of Retail Property, London, 2006.
[4] Derek Halden, *Future of Retail Transport: Access, Information and Flexibility*, BCSC Future of Retail Property, London, 2006.

of retail being produced by the BCSC is the disincentive to store-based shopping from poor access and bad transport experience.[5] This is particularly true of older shoppers, the fastest-growing retail market. If store-based retailers or shopping-centre owners can respond creatively in the transport market, then market share can be won back for physical retailers. For the time being, using the internet to drive solutions in public transport would be difficult to achieve, given the parlous state of UK public infrastructure. However, internet-based solutions in private transport offer real opportunities for shopping-place managers to add to their offer. One area that could be developed further is 'personalised travel plans'. Shoppers contact the centre of choice with a range of goods they are interested in and the times they can shop: the centre emails back the best route to the centre, the parking options and the most efficient route round the centre. Real-time information on parking options and prices offers the opportunity to address the weakest link in the 'physical retailing' value proposition: the transport experience. Without this creative response, shopping places will face many more bleak Christmases.

Examining European retail rents (January 2006)

This month we investigate the drivers of rental growth in a number of European retail markets. Rents change for many reasons, but there is an argument that introducing modern stock (such as shopping centres) into traditional town centres often provides an upward rental shift. The aim of this preliminary research is to shed some light on the relationship between rents, economic drivers and additions to stock in selected European retail markets.

Rental data from Cushman Wakefield Healy and Baker (CWHB) (now Cushman and Wakefield), for locations in Portugal, Spain, Italy, France and Belgium were used. However, Gross Lettable Area (GLA) data was only available at the country level. Household consumption and population, for NUTS2 areas relevant to the shopping location, were obtained from Experian Business Strategies.

Our expectation was that retail rents would be influenced by local factors (for which we have no data), along with the two macro-level variables that

---

[5] But see, in particular, Hayley Myers and Margaret Lumbers, *Consumers over 55: Silver Shoppers Provide a Golden Opportunity*, BCSC Future of Retail Property, London 2006.

we had: consumption and GLA per capita. With missing information we estimated using fixed-effects, which allows the intercept to vary and corrects for biases caused by missing variables. Potentially, this allows for factors, such as the demographics of the catchment population in each location, which may explain higher or lower rental levels, but which we were not able to include in our equation. With these caveats in place, what did we find?

An equation, with real rents being explained by GLA per capita and consumption, was estimated. The results from the equation indicate that a 1% increase in consumption will add 2% to real rental growth. Similarly, a 1% increase in GLA per head will cause a 1% decline in rental growth.

Do individual countries behave differently? Figure 5.6 suggests they might. Spain, with high GLA growth and high consumption, has high rental growth. Italy had strong GLA growth and modest consumption growth, but had similar rental growth to France. In France, GLA growth was modest and consumption growth was strong, as shown in Figure 5.6.

Separately estimated equations for each country implied that consumption had positive and significant explanatory power in France and Belgium, but was perversely negative and significant in Italy. The GLA variable was negative for all high street locations, except for Spain, where it was insignificant. These results add support to localised responses and market conditions. For example, the more mature retail markets of France and Belgium appear to behave in line with normal demand and supply conditions, whereas the Italian and Spanish retail markets are still maturing; rental

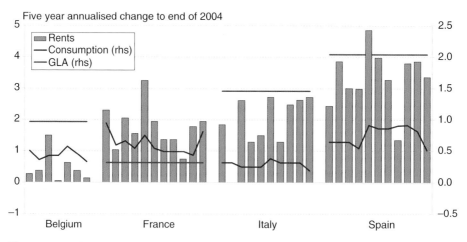

Figure 5.6: High street shops

pressure may be driven by international brands looking for space and retailers looking to upgrade their stock, rather than just from consumption growth.

An equation was also estimated for shopping centres. In this case, we found: a 1% increase in consumption implying a 1% increase in real rental growth and a 1% increase in GLA per head, implying a 0.5% decrease in real rental growth. The coefficient, on GLA per head, in the shopping centre equation is lower than in the high street equation. This result concurs with new space in shopping centres impacting negatively on high street rental performance.

Separately estimated country equations show that only in Italy is the GLA per head variable negative and significant, but with a similar negative impact to that found on the high street. The other locations had either positive signs or statistically insignificant results. Figure 5.7, showing shopping-centre data, offers some support to these perverse results. Portugal has seen the largest increase in GLA per head, the lowest consumption growth, and yet has displayed rental growth over the four years.

In aggregate, these results fit with prior expectations of increased consumption being positive on rents and increased space dampening rental growth. Nevertheless, the idiosyncrasies of the retail markets (rent controls; consolidations of retailers; influx of foreign multinational brands) will impact on rents in ways that contradict what would be expected from macro-level indicators. Also, our results suggest that the same level of consumption growth would produce a much larger impact on shopping-centre rental growth than on high-street rental growth, potentially, as shopping

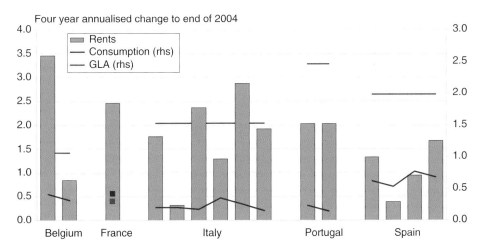

Figure 5.7:   Shopping centres

centres take an increased share of consumption growth. As well, space impacts were found to be greater on high-street rental growth than on shopping centre rents: potentially, as demand and customers move their business to shopping centres.

Perspective on international retail (October 2001)

The outlook for the international retail sector has been changing over the last few months in response to the global slowdown, but as with other parts of the economy, some markets are doing much better than others. The most obvious fundamental to look at is the retail sales data (Figure 5.8). From this it is clear that activity in North America in general, and the USA in particular, has slowed down, but definitely not ground to a halt. The results over the third quarter were consistent with overall consumption, growing half way between 'new economy' estimates of trend growth (c. 3.5%) and the more conservative estimates we lived with over the last 30 years. The most recent number, though, is for August – before 11 September and also before the bad economic news from August and September had been released. Since then, consumer confidence looks weaker, unemployment has risen strongly and the stock market has fallen further. The combined impact and the expected further worsening in the unemployment and consumer confidence situation, will worsen US fundamentals over the coming months, putting pressure on the retail industry.

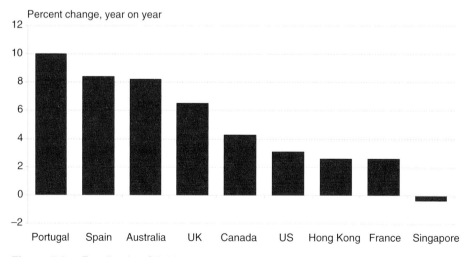

Figure 5.8:   Retail sales Q3 2001

A further potential pitfall is the savings rate. The official data points to an extremely low, perhaps unsustainably low, savings rate in the USA throughout the recent growth run. This gives ammunition to those who project a rebound to a more sustainable level that would imply a significant weakening of consumption. In fact, the calculation used in the USA for the savings rate produces an artificially low figure, so it is not as unsustainable as it appears at first glance. But, even if savings are not below equilibrium currently, they should definitely rise in a period of rising unemployment and erratic stock market valuations – not to mention a possible prolonged conflict – so increasing downside risk.

In Europe, the picture is more varied. In the UK and Spain, retail sales have raced away this year and by the third quarter were recording some of the strongest results of the last few years. This is despite a moderate easing of consumer confidence in both countries and reflects the impact of interest-rate cuts on a consumer sector already seeing employment increases and unemployment decreases. With the full effect of the recent cuts still to be felt, and more cuts to come in Spain at least, underlying retail activity should remain very strong until the end of the year. In Portugal, the expansion in sales volumes has been on a gradual downward trend for some time, but the early summer showed that activity is still increasing after signs in the spring that the retail sector could be going into recession. Consumer confidence has been falling heavily, though, and was down to a four-year low in July (Figure 5.9), despite continuing low unemployment, faster employment growth, falling interest rates and reduced inflation that should boost household income growth. In our main European retail markets, then,

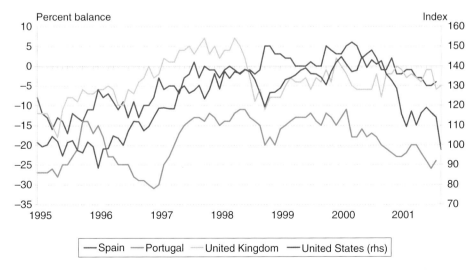

Figure 5.9: Consumer confidence – worse than '98 but not at recession levels yet

confidence remains a problem, but the sector fundamentals suggest a fairly upbeat performance in the months ahead.

What could derail this is a negative confidence reaction to a period of sustained conflict. This sort of uncertainty is impossible to quantify, but barring an all-out war, any drop in confidence should be reversed after a relatively short time. This would reduce the impact across the sector, but implies that markets where the turnover rent element is more important would be most vulnerable.

In Singapore, retail activity is suffering more than in any other of our other retail markets. Growth in sales volumes has collapsed from close to 30% year-on-year in December to –3% in July. This is not too surprising, given that unemployment has risen phenomenally over the year so far (Figure 5.10). The total is up 50–75% this year, depending on whether data is seasonally adjusted or not. With overall output in the economy under increasing pressure from the electronics industry recession, retail activity looks set to worsen over the remainder of the year.

In Australia, the economy picked up well over the first half of the year and this was reflected in reasonable retail sales figures – although the impact of the new sales tax means that volumes were rising more slowly than the total sales figures suggest. Consumer sentiment picked up over the summer, though, and employment growth has been gaining momentum, so activity looks relatively secure in the shorter term. That is, of course, barring a strongly negative reaction in consumer sentiment to 11 September and the subsequent reprisals.

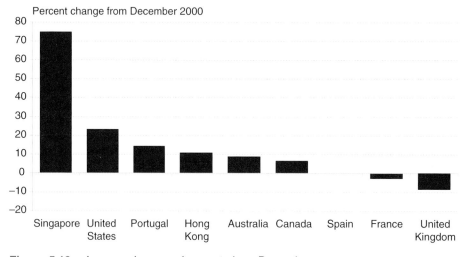

Figure 5.10:   Increase in unemployment since December

Consumer confidence and consumer spending (June 2003)

Consumer confidence numbers are regularly used by economic commentators to make short-term predictions about the path of consumer spending in general and retail spending in particular. This is despite the body of economic theory that points to the level of household income as the real driver of spending. The level of consumption is the product of the level of disposable income and the proportion of that income that is spent. This proportion is called the savings rate and should be affected by the same factors that are usually used in the construction of consumer confidence indices, such as job insecurity and concerns about the future financial situation. But changes in the savings rate are generally rather small and, while a long-term trend can have a significant impact on spending levels, as happened in the USA in the late 1990s, in general only a small proportion of the variation in spending can be attributed to the variation in the savings rate.

Figure 5.11 shows that the correlation between confidence and consumer spending is usually much weaker than the correlation between income and spending and in some cases, notably Australia, the confidence indicator has little relationship with movements in consumer spending. Looking further at the correlation between confidence and the savings rate across countries, we find that this relationship is weaker still and that the negative relationship we expect does not always hold.

One of the problems is undoubtedly the nature of the survey data. Confidence data come from frequent surveys of people, who are asked to

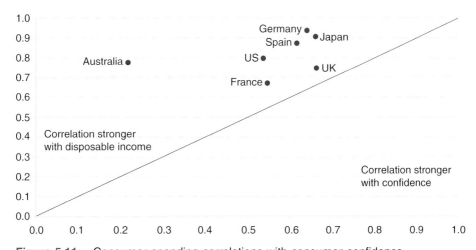

Figure 5.11:   Consumer spending correlations with consumer confidence

rate how favourable or unfavourable they feel about a set of issues. These responses are aggregated into summary indices. But survey responses tend to exaggerate underlying sentiment changes in the household sector, just as in the corporate sector. Thus confidence data tends to swing much more dramatically than spending patterns. In addition, short-term changes in sentiment are often transitory and can be reversed before they have had any real impact on spending. A second problem is that the bulk of consumer spending is on non-durables – products that households use up, such as food. Purchases in this area are little affected by changing sentiment. Durables, on the other hand, such as cars and electronic goods, are more likely to be affected by sentiment, but they make up a relatively small proportion of overall consumption.

So, while changing consumer sentiment numbers make good copy for commentators in the media and financial markets who need to produce stories, they are not the most useful indicators of actual consumer trends.

The outlook for UK retail (August 2009)

According to the Royal Bank of Scotland, the UK household debt to disposable income ratio stabilised during Q1 2009, at a high of 168%. This compares with an average ratio of c.100% during the 1990s. Recent income transfers from the government to private households and significantly reduced debt servicing costs have been major contributing factors to averting a complete collapse in consumer demand during this current downturn so far.

UK retail overall has shown an element of resilience, albeit sales have been driven by heavy discounting and performance varies greatly by operator, sub-sector and region. With the threat of pending increases in the cost of debt servicing, the current onerous level of UK household debt clearly represents a significant burden to UK consumers and a headwind to UK retail in the short to medium term (Figure 5.12).

Supermarket retailers are performing well as they continue to grow their market share of non-food items, whilst 'value-orientated' fashion brands are also capitalising on increasing consumer austerity. Whilst few are immune to the current downturn, some are taking the opportunity to capitalise upon recent more favourable occupancy costs and are stepping up their expansion plans, including recent new market entrants to the UK from the USA and Scandinavia.

The consumer flight to both quality and value has, however, placed pressure on the middle market offer and this has resulted in a large number of

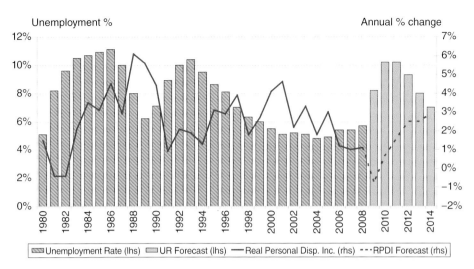

Figure 5.12: Consumer headwinds
Source: Global Insight

retail failures. A number of these were overdue, with recent years of buoyant consumer spending keeping a number of sub-optimal retailers 'artificially alive'. On the upside, these recent retail failures have resulted in increased available market share for remaining competitors.

A flurry of pre-pack administrations (retailers going into administration and emerging under new ownership without onerous liabilities) has contributed to further polarisation in the UK retail landscape, with underperforming stores in poor locations closing, whilst strong performers in strong locations continuing to trade (albeit at a renegotiated rent).

According to CBRE (the firm of property consultants), just 85 UK retail locations currently attract 50% of comparison goods spend, versus 200 forty years ago. Both consumer and occupier demands have contributed to this trend and we are likely to see further polarisation as a result of this downturn, with much tertiary retail location stock becoming obsolete. Vacancy rates in some UK locations are currently in excess of 50% and are rising. By comparison, a recent study by DTZ highlights that vacancy rates in the top 20 UK retail shopping centres are running at about 5%. This is clear evidence of polarisation, which is being perpetuated by the current downturn.

The consensus is that the UK has too many shops, but this view doesn't deal with the issue of quality versus quantity. In a market where there is also an occupier flight to quality, meeting modern occupier needs is paramount to averting functional obsolescence. Having just seen this recent record year of pipeline schemes delivered in the UK (less than 8m sq.ft. in

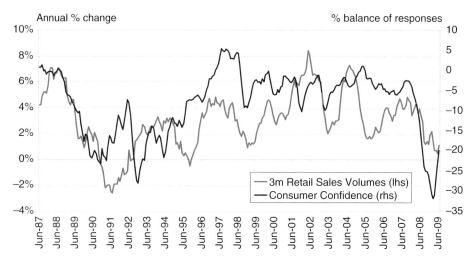

Figure 5.13:   Rebounding consumer confidence
Source: Reuters EcoWin

2008), with the exception of Westfield Stratford and St David's Cardiff, the UK prime retail development pipeline has effectively come to a standstill. The prospects for new supply in the medium term look very weak.

Retail sales volumes, according to national statistics, grew by +0.7% in Q2 2009, +1.1% higher over the year – this is up from an annual growth of +0.7% in Q1 2009. In June 2009 consumer confidence, which in the UK is mainly in negative territory even in times of strong economic growth, registered its highest growth since May 2008 (Figure 5.13). This is likely to have been partly driven by consumers' steadily improving expectations over the UK economy and partly by good weather during June 2009 versus June 2008. UK retail has shown resilience so far, but still remains fragile.

Key asset prices now appear to be stabilising and households are beginning to rebuild savings and pay down debt. Based upon the household savings ratio at only 3%, versus LT trend of about 6.5%, however, deleveraging still has some way to go. With rising unemployment into early 2011, reduced earnings growth, the gradually rising cost of debt and the prospect of broad-based tax increases over the short to medium term, headwinds facing UK consumers appear plentiful.

Faced with this, consumer demand is likely to be subdued for some time to come and the short-term outlook for UK retail, on the whole, looks anaemic. Competition from the large 'grocers' such as Tesco in non-food merchandise, the success of online retailing (now accounting for about 7% of all UK retail sales), plus further polarisation of the retail offer, will continue to contribute to changing the UK retail landscape.

Large-scale retail developments are created for the long term and ride the economic cycles. The majority of the premium schemes that were recently delivered were well conceived and are well let. These developments and their occupiers, in addition to already established well-tenanted and managed prime locations, look well placed to ride out the downturn and to capitalise upon the upturn, when it arrives.

Within retail and retail property, winners will continue to exist and those that emerge from this downturn will be more efficient. Mindful of a changing consumer, the looming headwinds and the changing dynamics of retail and retail property, both are, arguably, facing a challenging period of further structural, rather than cyclical, change. The gap between winners and losers is growing.

USA retail outlook (August 2004)

The tax cuts delivered by the Bush administration provided a sharp kick-start to the consumer sector last year and both retail spending and overall consumer spending (including spending on personal and household services not sold in shops) surged in the second half. But total consumer spending fell back dramatically in Q2 (according to preliminary data), raising concerns that the retail property sector can continue to rely on persistently strong underlying spending growth. A slowdown in total consumer spending in Q2 was inevitable after the unsustainable pace reached last year, but few economists were predicting annualised growth to drop to 1.0% from 4.1% in Q1 and 5.0% in Q3 last year. Initial explanations have pointed to the increase in oil prices eroding the purchasing power of household income, but a higher CPI does not explain all the slowdown, because nominal spending also eased back. Part of the slowdown was probably due to the end of the boost from federal tax rebates and may have also been a reaction to consumer spending having grown more quickly than disposable income in the six months to March. The slowdown has not found its way into quarterly retail spending data yet, but June's monthly data does show a fallback in nominal spending growth from May's record levels.

Looking forward, the mainstream of economic forecasters view the consumer sector as fundamentally sound, based on an improving labour market and buoyant wealth levels. Although debt levels are extremely high, with total debt having moved well above 100% of household disposable income, US households are relatively insulated from an increasing Fed Funds rate because most of the debt, and most of the increase in debt, has come through mortgages held at long-term rates that do not move in line with the official Fed Funds rate. Non-mortgage debt has been stable, as a share of disposable income.

But employment growth could be much less robust than the mainstream forecasters expect. The recent downturn was extremely shallow and hardly a recession at all, using the revised GDP data, but the employment contraction was as big as in the 1982 and 1991 recessions. In those earlier recessions, the percentage drop in employment almost exactly matched the drop in real GDP. In the recent recession, the percentage contraction in employment was 3.4 times greater than the percentage drop in real GDP, as the corporate sector exploited the gains in productivity to rationalise its work force and reduce the demand for labour. This may well lead to disappointing employment growth throughout the rest of the recovery, while the economy continues to adjust to higher productivity levels.

A more familiar risk comes from household savings behaviour. The revised national accounts data show that savings rates have once again fallen below 2%, despite the spending cutbacks of Q2, and there is a clear risk that they could rebound up and reduce spending further. One of the key determinants of savings behaviour is the probability of becoming unemployed, which is proxied by the unemployment rate (Figure 5.14). This relationship has been changing, as the developing financial market has increased the supply and appetite for debt products, so that the level of savings associated with a given unemployment rate has fallen. But since 2000, the savings rate has fallen below even this new relationship, suggesting that savings rates are unsustainably low – probably as a result of extremely low interest rates that encourage households to borrow rather than save. A higher Fed Funds rate will begin to reverse this incentive.

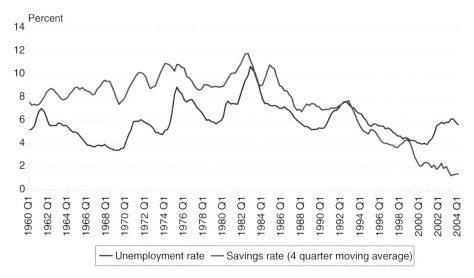

Figure 5.14:   Savings rates look low given the risk of unemployment

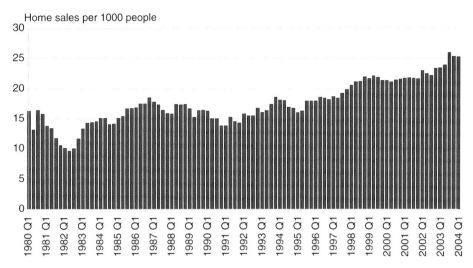

Figure 5.15:   Stronger home sales have underpinned consumer spending growth

If short-term factors point to a more modest path of consumer spending than many forecasters are predicting, medium-term structural factors from the housing market and demographics are giving mixed messages. Taking the housing market first, it is important to look not just at house value but also at the impact of housing turnover on spending, via expenditure associated with buying a new house – new carpets, curtains, furniture and so on. The pace of housing transactions per person in the USA has more than doubled over the last 20 years (Figure 5.15) and this can't continue indefinitely. When house sales per person begin to plateau, an important structural prop to the retail sector's growth will disappear. Demographics point to continuing strong growth in the overall population, which should keep home sales increasing (if at a slower rate), but the age mix of the population will change. Those close to retirement age will become increasingly important and that is a negative factor for most multiple retailers. But the 20–35 age group, the prime customers for fashion multiples, will grow much more rapidly than they have over the last 10 years (Figure 5.16). Retailers and retail centres that can successfully target these two age groups stand to benefit most in the medium term.

What will an end to the run-up in house prices mean for consumer spending? (April 2005)

In recent years, retail property has been bolstered by healthy consumer spending and strong investor demand. The growth of consumer credit

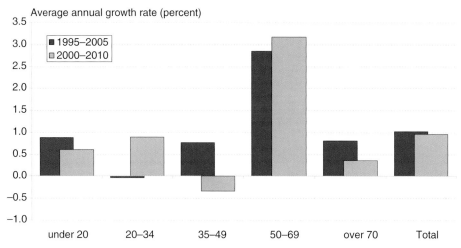

Figure 5.16: Changing USA age distribution poses risks and opportunities for the retail sector

(through credit cards and home equity loans) has been a key driver in retail spending growth. These products have given consumers greater control over spending, so that consumer spending remained healthy during the economic slowdown that started in 2002. The strong appreciation of house prices, via retail credit, has been a key factor enabling consumers to finance their consumption. The benign interest rate environment has made financing even more advantageous. However, academic research has been somewhat ambiguous about the house-price/consumption relationship and the Bank of England wrote recently that the relationship in the UK may have broken down. We looked at the interaction between house prices and retail sales to establish our own view.

Housing prices and consumer spending

In recent years, house price appreciation has arguably been the most significant driver of consumer spending, via home equity loans and mortgage refinancing. While consumers have used some loan proceeds to pay off higher-interest loans, most of the money has been used for consumer spending, much of it on items for the house itself. In the USA between 2002 and 2004, those that refinanced mortgages took $400 billion in extra cash out of their homes; two-thirds of it was put directly back into the economy through spending. In the Netherlands, released housing equity provided the Dutch economy with an additional 1% GDP growth in 1999 and 2000, years when house prices appreciated dramatically. In 2001, when released equity-related spending halved, the direct result was a reduction of GDP by 0.5%,

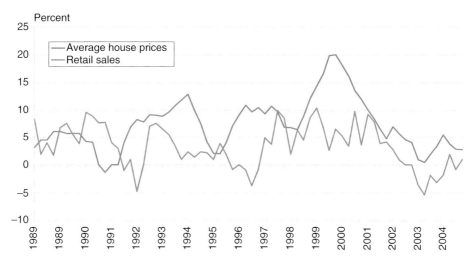

Figure 5.17: Housing and retail sales in the Netherlands
Source: Global Insight

according to the Netherlands' central bank. The experience of the Netherlands is interesting, because it was the first country in our analysis to see both a significant rise and subsequent slowdown in house-price appreciation. As a result of the country's 2001 slowdown (due to a global slowdown and factors unique to the Netherlands), there was a deterioration of the financial position of Dutch households. The slowdown in house-price appreciation, in particular, had spillover effects to other parts of the economy, including the consumer sector. Approximately nine months after house price growth slowed significantly, retail sales growth was negative, despite the still-benign interest rate environment (Figure 5.17). In the event that interest rates were to rise significantly, the balance sheets of debt-laden Dutch households would deteriorate further.

What about the longer-run relationship between housing and consumer spending?

We ran two analyses to measure the significance of the long-run relationship between house prices and consumer spending (in the form of retail sales). The first employed a regression framework for nine countries, using a standard set of explanatory variables (employment growth, disposable income, interest rates, stock-market performance, inflation and house prices), over a 9–18-year timeframe. These drivers, by definition or intuition, filter into consumption. In eight of the nine countries, changes in

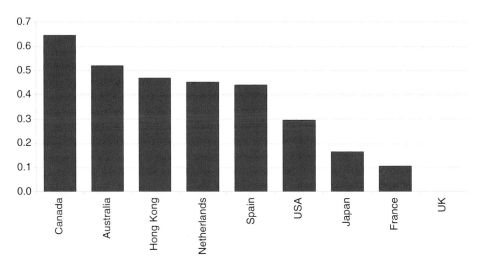

Figure 5.18:   The coefficient of the elasticity of house prices as an explanatory variable of retail sales
Source: Global Insight, Grosvenor

house prices were a statistically significant contributor to retail sales, with the surprising exception of the United Kingdom (Figure 5.18). Among the remaining eight countries, house prices were the most significant factor in explaining retail sales performance in half of them. While not necessarily a definitive result, it means that house prices have played an important role. For the UK economy, touted as a paragon of housing-fuelled consumption, the relationship may have broken down.

The second analysis used a Granger test to establish the direct causality between housing and retail sales (Table 5.1). If introducing house prices to the model improved its explanatory power, causality is established. Among the nine countries, there were six instances of causality between house prices and retail sales. Included among those six countries is the UK. It seems, then, that more analysis is required before a definitive conclusion can be made about the country.

The Bank of England suggests that the relationship between house prices and consumption may have recently broken down. Consumers' use of leverage to exploit the run-up in house prices in the latter half of the 1990s might have already run its course by the end of the millennium, so that recent house-price rises are now having a statistically insignificant impact on consumption. Another explanation is that house prices and retail sales are not both driven by a common factor, such as expectations of personal income growth. If this were the case, households might have cut back on their consumption in anticipation of slower income growth, despite a

Table 5.1: Granger Causality

	House prices Granger cause Retail Sales	Retail Sales Granger cause House prices
Australia	2 lags	–
Canada	–	1, 3 lags
France	–	–
Hong Kong	1 lag	–
Japan	–	–
Netherlands	1, 2, 3 lags	1, 2, 3 lags
Spain	1, 2, 3 lags	1, 2, 3 lags
UK	3 lags	–
USA	2, 3 lags	–

housing market that continued to appreciate. In any event, an unbinding of the relationship will be a relief to investors of retail properties and those convinced of a house-price correction.

Retail fundamentals (January 2003)

The state of the retail sector was the factor most associated with the divergence of economic performance in 2002 between those economies that survived the global downturn relatively well and those that did not (Figure 5.19). The UK and Australia, notably, produced trend growth for much of the period, largely on the back of extremely solid consumer spending. In the USA, consumer spending was not as strong, relatively speaking, but was solid enough to allow the economy to deliver a marked return to growth. By contrast, the weakness in the Euro zone was not the result of particularly bad net exports or investment spending, but rather because Euro zone consumers did not take up the slack in 2002 in the same way. One of the main drivers of the consumer in the high-growth economies was the fall in interest rates. Households in the UK, USA, Canada and Australia are typically much more sensitive to interest-rate changes than consumers in the Euro zone or in many parts of Asia. With savings levels much higher in these areas and debt much lower, interest-rate cuts have a weaker effect. In some countries, notably Italy, households are actually net savers and so interest-rate cuts may actually depress consumer spending. There was also a clear second-round effect from the housing market. Lower interest rates stimulated much stronger house-price growth in interest-sensitive countries,[6] so

---

[6] In Australia, the house-price boom was more the result of specific changes to housing-market policy.

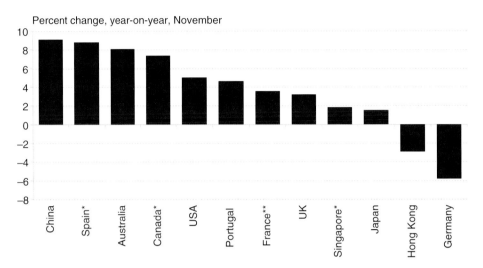

Figure 5.19: Growth of retail sales values had diverged significantly by the end of 2002
* 2002–10; ** 2002–8

the interest-rate cuts of 2001 put in place an offsetting increase in personal wealth that offset the falls in stock-market wealth. The regional differences were not completely clear, though. Some of the Euro zone economies produced solid retail spending, reflecting the failure of the global slowdown to produce widespread recessionary conditions in Europe.

The retail property sector thus emerged from 2001 as one of the most defensive sectors. Activity levels held up well, keeping the occupier market reasonably strong. Retailers remained under considerable margin pressure in many countries, however, so rental growth was not as strong as might have been expected in such strong trading conditions. But the stability achieved helped keep yields low, as institutions searched for positive returns. But signs of moderation are beginning to emerge. This should come as no surprise. Volume growth of up to 7% in the UK, for example, is not sustainable and could only continue whilst interest-rate cuts were still boosting the economy. But interest rates in the UK have been on hold for over a year now, while they have fallen only marginally in the USA and even risen in Canada and Australia. Hence, the months ahead should see more moderate spending in these higher-growth economies, but this should not be interpreted as the start of a consumer recession. Such a recession is highly unlikely without sharp increases in both interest rates and unemployment rates, and neither are in any major forecasters' baseline scenarios. The retail sector should therefore continue at reasonable activity levels, particularly compared with the more distressed office market.

US retailing in recession (May 2009)

We already know that consumer spending is down significantly from its peak, but what items are consumers buying and what stores will they continue to visit? The rash of retail bankruptcies has accelerated and, at least in the short run, it is clear that America is 'over-retailed'. In this game of retail musical chairs, where there are too many retailers and not enough consumers, stores will continue to 'go dark'. Consumers are buying fewer automobiles and they are also driving less, even with lower gasoline prices. So we can expect fewer automobile dealerships and possibly automobile manufacturers and gas stations, to survive. Consumers have also cut back on business and personal travel, as evidenced by layoffs at Disney, hotel occupancy and spending declines in Las Vegas, but they are flocking to the movies as a low-cost substitute. Clearly, Americans will still be purchasing milk, clothing and other essentials and they still want to be entertained.

What appears to be happening is a classic economic response to such situations. Confronted with growing uncertainty, shrinking credit availability and decreased wealth, Americans are saving more if they can and, when they do spend, they are more concerned about quantity rather than quality. That is, they are substituting 'inferior' goods for 'superior' goods, such as hamburger for steak, dyeing their own hair rather than visiting a salon, paying more attention to the price tag than the logo embroidered on the front of the shirt and buying their groceries from the lowest-cost provider, regardless of their market niche. When they do splurge, they expect deep discounts and are more likely to pay cash, or at least pay off their credit card that month (see Figure 5.20).

By living beyond their means for so many years, American consumers gave retailers and retail property investors a false sense of unlimited prosperity that has now come to a crashing halt. In response, investors and retailers did what good capitalists do; they opened more stores to meet consumer demand. According to estimates from F.W. Dodge, total US retail square footage grew by almost 20% between the beginning of 2000 and the end of 2008. In contrast, real median household income fell slightly during the same time period and the absolute number of households grew by approximately 10%. Furthermore, this does not adjust for other factors, such as the ongoing shift in consumption away from non-auto durable and non-durable to services of approximately 2%; the emergence of internet shopping (many of the same stores and brands at the mall cannibalise their own sales on their web sites); the continued redistribution and concentration of wealth and income; the physical downsizing of consumer goods and

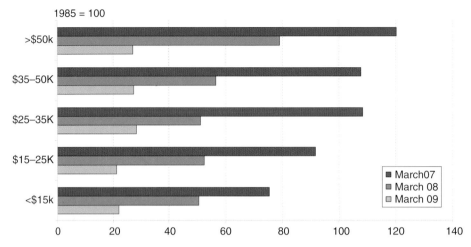

1985 = 100

Figure 5.20: Consumer confidence by income class

packaging; and an 18% loss in household wealth in 2008. Unfortunately, long-term demographic projections will only reinforce these trends. These trends suggest that an ageing population will be downsizing their homes and spending more on medicine and personal services than on furniture and the latest fashions. In the short run, savings not spending will dominate the headlines. Even though retail construction starts have started to recede, there are still enough projects in the development stage that are coming online at precisely the wrong time.

So what's in store – no pun intended – for investors? The futures market expects a sharp drop in private equity retail returns over the next 18 to 24 months, akin to what retail REITs have already experienced. Some, such as General Growth Properties, are in dire straits because of refinancing issues, while other owners will find it difficult to replace tenants or cover their debt service as cash flows erode. Especially hard hit will be owners needing to replace big-box retailers, as well as those whose income is highly depend-ent on 'Mom and Pop' retailers. Also vulnerable will be newer projects located at the epicentre of the housing crisis in cities such as Tampa, Las Vegas and Phoenix and those purchased during the past 36 months that depend on aggressive rental growth and occupancy assumptions. Many of these properties may already be in technical default, depending on their leverage levels. Certainly, many highly levered properties bought in the last 18 months are likely to be worth less than the outstanding debt, and these owners will need to find ways to renegotiate with their lenders or obtain additional equity injections to maintain their ownership positions.

Luxury retailers, once thought to be immune, have seen slowing sales. With the recession spreading across the globe and the surprising strength of the dollar, foreign tourists who were flocking to the United States in 2007

Table 5.2: Household spending moving away from retailers – Consumption by category

	2000	2008
Durables ex-auto & parts	7%	6%
Auto & parts	6%	4%
Non-durables ex gas & fuel	26%	25%
Gas & fuel	3%	4%
Services	58%	60%

Source: Global Insight

and early 2008 are now staying at home. For example, Tiffany's has been bruised by the decline in luxury spending by US consumers. Reporting a 21% reduction in global holiday sales and 30% in the USA, the high-end jeweller is cutting costs and closing its Iridesse chain, which specializes in pearls. However, because most luxury retailers did not expand as aggressively as other price points and have higher margins, high-end retailers are likely to weather this storm better than most.

But not every owner is doomed to suffer the same fate. Retailers will continue to covet their prime locations and do everything to maintain their presence in these key spots. For the handful of retailers who are expanding or the few new retailers who are starting up, these central locations remain desirable. Also grocery/drug-anchored centres in well established neighbourhoods are apt to be relatively stable, since they provide basic core items that will continue to be purchased. The trade-off for these retail formats will be the volatility of cash flow from 'in-line' non-credit tenants.

Grosvenor Research believes that investors should abandon their traditional horizontal perspective and adopt a more vertical one. That is: higher-density locations in or contiguous to urban areas will probably be best positioned in the long run, because they provide the greatest number of potential shoppers within the shortest distance from any given location. In addition, when the economy begins its recovery, real energy prices will once again spike, putting a premium on minimising time and distance travelled. Aggressive and proactive property management may also help mitigate some of the risk, but even the best asset management cannot overcome a strong cyclical downturn. Therefore, there will be little reason to celebrate anytime soon.

Luxury retailing in Europe (June 2007)

Since 1998, rental values on French high streets have increased an average of 60% in real terms. In both Italy and Spain, high street rents have more

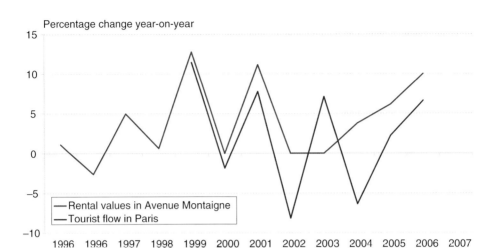

Percentage change year-on-year

Legend:
— Rental values in Avenue Montaigne
— Tourist flow in Paris

X-axis: 1996 1996 1997 1998 1999 2000 2001 2002 2003 2004 2005 2006 2007

Figure 5.21:   Rental values in luxury districts and tourist flow in Paris (t-1)
Source: CW, Insee, Grosvenor Research

than doubled over the past eight years. This performance is the result of a strong rise in income per capita, and in some cases, town centre regeneration. More surprising, perhaps, is the growth of rental values in prime luxury streets, such as the golden triangle in Paris (Figure 5.21) or the Golden Quad in Milan. Rents here have increased by 6.3% and 10.1% per annum respectively, outperforming any other kind of retail property assets in their domestic markets.

In Continental Europe, particularly France and Italy, the traditional key macroeconomic variables do not seem to explain the rebound in luxury retailing, as they do in emerging countries. What other factors explain the apparent disconnect between luxury brand performance and general indigenous economic activity? The question is crucial for assessing rental growth potential and sustained performance over the medium term of city centre retail locations.

The world market for luxury goods amounts to €159 billion and has risen by 7.5% per annum over the past three years, with shares of 36% in the Americas, 34% in Europe, 16% in Japan, 10% in the Asia-Pacific region and 4% elsewhere. Furthermore, the turnover of luxury brands has increased by 9% in the Americas, 7% in Europe, 11% in Japan, and 16% elsewhere. In emerging economies the luxury market has expanded at a fast pace, in line with the huge increase in High Net Worth Individuals (HNWI). According to Merrill Lynch, the number of HNWI in emerging countries has doubled or tripled, compared with their national output growth figures.

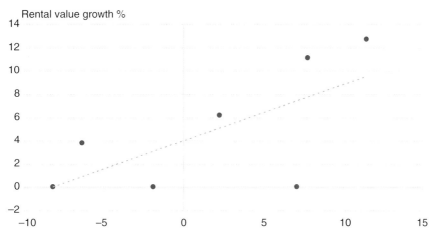

Figure 5.22:   Increasing relationship between rental values in luxury districts and tourist flow
Source: Grosvenor Research

In the developed economies, other factors are at work. Regression analysis shows tourist numbers to be a strong explanatory variable of rental value growth in luxury retail locations (Figure 5.22). France is the world's biggest tourist destination, with over 78 million tourists (6.5% of GDP), so the power of tourist spend is very great. Obviously, Paris keeps the lion's share, taking €15.1 bn out of the €37 bn tourist revenues. Italy is fifth as a destination, with 40 million tourists, who are attracted to cities such as Rome, Venice, Florence and Milan. In Paris, a 1% increase in tourist flow is associated with 4.5% increase in rents, on average, in Avenue Montaigne. The relationship in Italy is slightly stronger, with a 5.5% increase in rents on luxury streets like Via Montenapoleone in Milan and Via del Corso in Rome.

Total returns in luxury streets have outperformed (Figure 5.23), with the exception of the Rue du Faubourg Saint Honoré in 2003. Located near the American Embassy, the district has been subject to stringent security measures which forbid car parking. The less friendly environment has dampened the footfall of the luxury street and hampered rental growth potential; as a result, yields have shifted outward. This demonstrates how 'historical accident' – a random event – can change the popularity of a location, even one of the most prestigious, making it attractive to luxury tenants or not.

The number of HNWI tourists visiting Paris and Italy from Brazil, Russia, India and China (the BRICs countries) has been accelerating over the past few years. Further investigation shows that many HNWI from BRICs prefer to buy abroad, because of the prevalence of counterfeits and higher prices

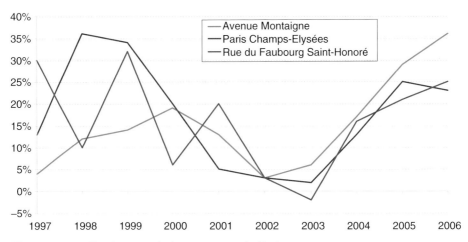

Figure 5.23:   Total returns in luxury streets in Paris

(up to 30%, due to import and consumption taxes) at home, plus the enjoy-able ambience that enhances the value of luxury goods. The demographics of BRICs mean that HNWI represent a large set of potential travellers and spenders. The World Tourism Organisation's long-term forecast keeps Paris and Italian cities as the main destinations for luxury tourism. On this basis, the niche market of luxury retail is likely to continue outperforming in the long term in Continental Europe.

State of health in the retail market in continental Europe (October 2009)

Traditionally, retail property has been seen as more defensive than the office sector in Europe, but recently the sector has lost its sparkle as capital values have fallen across the whole continent. The differences in the magnitudes in movement between the different countries suggest that the re-pricing has been a function of domestic market fundamentals and capital market changes. The latter captures broad risk aversion towards the countries and sectors. Strong and quick adjustments were made to values at the end of 2008 across all countries, despite there being no real transaction evidence. Valuers, evidently, were looking for more coherence across submarkets, compared with past downward cycles. The consolidation of the European retail landscape, mainly in the shopping centre and retail warehousing sub-markets, has driven this convergence in valuation. As of today, the largest outward yield shift was seen in shopping centres, while both the high street

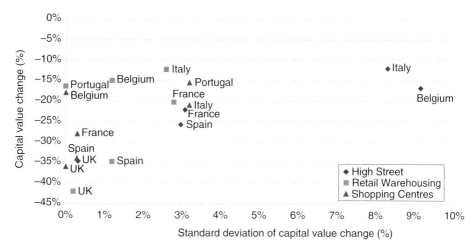

Figure 5.24: Capital values re-pricing by sector[7]
Source: Grosvenor

and the retail warehousing submarkets, where supply is more regulated, have shown stronger resilience (see Figure 5.24). In this article a cross-sectional analysis of the French, Spanish, Italian, Portuguese and Belgian markets is used, to understand how the re-pricing has taken place.

Within the countries we look at, in various cities and in the different retail sub-sectors, the scale of the drop in values has been very uneven. The re-pricing of shopping centres has been the least variable of the retail sub-sectors, with no real discrimination among cities, except in Italy. Values have fallen between −18% in Belgium and −34% in Spain, while values have fallen by −36% in the UK since the end of 2007. In France, values have dropped by −28%, while in Italy the fall has been −21% in the wealthiest locations. As might be expected, there is a strong correlation between outward yield shifts and past inward yield shifts ($R^2 = 0.82$).

In the retail warehousing submarket, capital values have fallen between −12% and −42%. The volatility of the downward adjustment – captured by the standard deviation – has been higher than in the shopping-centre market. Quantitative analysis suggests that the higher heterogeneity in the capital value downward adjustment is: (i) higher in markets with a high level of supply; and (ii) lower in the wealthiest regions with the highest rental

---

[7] Average capital value movements refers to the average of the main retail locations within each country. The standard deviation of capital value movements refers to the spread of capital value movements within each country. So a country like the UK, in the bottom left of Figure 5.24, has a large and uniform drop in values. A country in the bottom right would have a highly variable fall in values that was, on average, large, and so on.

values. As an example, in Spain, Madrid is suffering slightly more than Barcelona, in the wake of the ongoing cannibalisation effect initiated by a high level of supply in this area. In Italy, huge discrepancies exist between the downward adjustments seen in the North – the wealthiest area – compared with the economically weak South, where rental values are forecast to continue dropping for a while. Finally, the correlation between past inward yield shift and outward yield shift is lower than in the shopping centre case, as there is more heterogeneity within countries ($R^2 = 0.64$ in France; $R^2 = 0.55$ in Italy), but also within the retail warehousing submarket itself.

Finally, in the high-street shop submarket in Europe, capital values have fallen between –11% and –25%, compared with a drop of over –35% in the UK. Yields in this submarket have stabilised much more quickly than in the other submarkets. More interestingly, the dispersion of capital value falls within a country is much higher than the retail-warehousing and shopping-centre submarkets. The volatility reflects the heterogeneity of the high-street submarket between core and secondary cities. More explicitly, in continental Europe, core cities have a competitive edge in terms of wealth per capita, as well as having modern retail formats, which definitely justify either the minor outward yield movement, or the limited fall in rental values. Conversely, lots of secondary cities have caught up too quickly in the recent past, justifying the higher outward yield shift.

Digging deeper, in terms of countries, Spain has been hit harder, on the back of the hard landing of the housing market and a highly depressed macro environment. In France, capital value falls have been minor, in line with the rationale of the market and a more favourable macro environment going forward. It seems that macroeconomic expectations were fed into global values, as there has been a strong positive relationship between Sovereign Credit Default Swaps (CDS) spreads, which captures risk aversion toward a country, and capital value falls. Drops in capital values have been the steepest where the CDS prices have been the highest. The current easing in the CDS prices for some countries has coincided with a stabilisation in yields, notably in Spain and Italy. Nonetheless, as the macroeconomic background is set to remain gloomy in Spain and Italy and CDS prices could well rise again in the medium term. As consumption is likely to contract in 2009 and 2010, the gradual drop in turnover will continue pushing retailer's effort ratio (turnover to rent payable) upwards, putting further downward pressure on rental values and potentially pushing yields further out. In Spain and Italy at least, it is too early to call the bottom of the market.

6

Property companies and REITs

Property companies and REITs (Real Estate Investment Trusts) are entities whose assets almost or entirely comprise real estate. Often they will undertake some real estate development activity, in which case their assets may include land or partially constructed buildings. Property companies and REITs are typically financed by a mixture of debt and equity. The level of gearing, or leverage, varies between companies, and in the sector as a whole, over the course of the cycle.

REITs differ from property companies in that they are fiscally transparent, so that if they distribute a minimum level of their rental income (typically around 85%, but dependable on specific country rules), then they are not subject to taxation on the rental income or capital receipts from property disposals. In effect, the investors in a REIT are deemed to have a direct interest in the underlying real estate investment of the REIT. In return for this favourable tax status, REITs accept certain limitations on the proportion of their assets that can be devoted to development and their level of gearing. Around the world, the REIT regime seems to be taking over from the structures that were traditionally used by property companies. One of the main purposes of REITs is to allow – even encourage – small investors to be able to diversify into commercial real estate. The last 20 years has seen something of a 'REIT revolution', with the numbers of countries with

Real Estate and Globalisation, First Edition. Richard Barkham.
© 2012 John Wiley & Sons, Ltd. Published 2012 by John Wiley & Sons, Ltd.

REITs growing from 5 to over 20.[1] It has been estimated that approximately 15% of the 'stock' of investment grade real estate around the world, is in the hand of property companies, especially REITs. One of the benefits that REITs or property companies bring to the economy is specialisation in property management. For instance, certain REITs specialise in the management of health care facilities, others in offices or retail.

REITs and property companies may be private, but the ones that are of most interest from the perspective of property research are those that are traded on public exchanges. Public markets are densely traded, liquid and monitored by many thousands of informed investors, which means they incorporate new information about risk and prospective cash flows very quickly. In other words, public equity markets are generally thought to be 'informationally efficient'. By contrast, the private real estate market is fragmented, relatively infrequently traded and not subject to the same level of overall scrutiny as public markets. Moreover, potential dealing prices are not quoted daily, but are estimated from time to time by professional valuers (appraisers). So, it is likely that the share price changes of REITs, individually or collectively, contain important and useful signals about future price movements in the unsecuritised real estate market.

Our article of January 2007 examines the level of correlation between price movements in the 'direct property market' and price movements in the public markets in the UK. The article was motivated by the then recent adoption in the UK of legislation permitting the formation of REITs. The article describes the level of correlation between listed and unlisted real estate but also tackles some broader themes, for instance, that listed markets can drift a long way from fundamentals due to positive or negative sentiment alone. This 'bubble tendency' can cause REIT prices to diverge substantially from the value of the underlying real estate. The article notes, with some prescience, that the UK REIT market was probably in a 'bubble phase' and that small investors, perhaps taken in by the 'hype' that surrounded the launch of REITs in the UK, could get badly hurt. It also argues that the 'price signal' that the listed market offers about the direct market is 'noisy' and variable over time.

Our article of November 2008 looks at the relationship between REIT prices and property prices in the case of Spain, which, at the time, was beginning to feel the full effects of the GFC. As in the UK, there is a link between the two markets with the impact of the looming recession being

---

[1] USA (1960); New Zealand (1969); Netherlands (1969); Australia (1971); Canada (1993); Belgium (1995); Turkey (1995); Singapore (1999); Japan (2000); South Korea (2001); France (2003); Hong Kong (2003); Taiwan (2003); Bulgaria (2005); Malaysia (2005); Thailand (2005); Israel (2006); Dubai (2006); UK (2007); Germany (2007); Italy (2007); Pakistan (2008); Finland (2009); Spain (2009); Mexico (2010); Philippines (2010).

seen most immediately in the public markets. The article also suggests that one of the transmission mechanisms from monetary policy to stock markets is via the real estate holdings of listed companies.

One of the most established REIT markets in the world is that of Australia. REITs (or Limited Property Trusts as they are locally known) have been in existence since 1971 and are a favoured sector of institutional investors. LPTs have developed over the years, specialised and built up formidable real estate expertise. Westfield, for instance, is a world-renowned expert in the development and management of shopping centres. The article describes the changes that were taking place in the LPT sector at the time, such as consolidation and internationalisation, which were raising the risk profile of the LPTs. Although it was not noted at the time, by the author, some of these changes were clearly being driven by strong economic growth and monetary expansion (the factors that to some extent created the GFC). Post-financial crisis, some LPTs have struggled under the weight of their debt and poorly performing assets though the very rapid, post-crisis bounce-back of the Australian economy prevented a serious crisis developing in the LPT sector.

One benefit the listed sector provides is the ability to calculate the real estate cost of capital using the capital asset pricing model (CAPM). It is quite hard to apply CAPM to real estate directly, because indices created from appraised values do not capture the true level of market volatility. It has been reasonably well established by academic research that real estate valuations are subject to cross-sectional and time series averaging, because of the valuation process. Since the cost of capital to a company or a sector is directly linked to the volatility of the company or sector valuation based indices are unsuitable for use in the CAPM. This is where property company or REIT prices are useful. They are the product of daily trading in a liquid, public, stock market and, as such, they provide a more accurate picture of real estate risk. One of the problems with using REIT prices to estimate the real estate costs of capital is that REITs operate on different portions of the risk curve. Our article of May 2008 shows how we have used econometric methods to 'filter out' some of the impact of differences in REIT business models in order to gain a clear picture of real estate risk and cost of capital.

Small investors should wait for the REIT moment to invest in property securities! (January 2007)

The arrival in the UK of Real Estate Investment Trusts (REITs) is a signifi-cant moment for the UK property market. Not, perhaps, as significant as

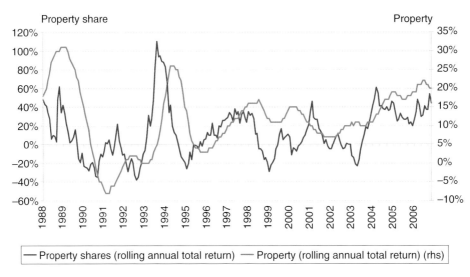

Figure 6.1:   Property and property share over 20 years

some have made out, since it has been possible to invest in listed UK property companies for at least 50 years. It's true that UK property companies have lacked transparency in taxation, financial reporting and strategy, making many of them unattractive to non-specialist investors, but the option has been there. It is possible to use property company returns, with some caveats, to make some predictions about REIT performance. In particular, to answer the question: 'is investing in REITs the same thing as investing in a diversified portfolio of UK commercial property?'

Figure 6.1 shows monthly (rolling annual total return) for property (IPD Monthly Index) and property shares (UK component of GPR 250 index). Whilst both series have the same mean of 12% the standard deviation of the property shares series is 26% as opposed to 9% for the direct property series. Property shares are more volatile than property but this is to be expected. First, property shares are based on geared property company asset values. Very approximately, every 10 percentage points of balance sheet gearing raises net asset volatility above the volatility of the underlying market. Second, property companies engage in development. Assets in the course of development, except where pre-let, are fully exposed to the spot rental market and are, as a result far more volatile than 'stabilised' investments. Third, 'valuation smoothing' artificially reduces the standard deviation of real estate indices, below the real volatility of the market. Add to this, the fact that the general stock market movements affect all listed stocks to a greater or lesser extent and it is not really surprising that property shares have been more volatile than direct property. Since REITs are allowed to gear and undertake property development it is not clear that REITs will be any the less volatile than property companies.

If it is accepted that volatility in property shares is a price worth paying for greater liquidity and management expertise, is it possible to say that, in the longer term property shares move in line with the property market? The fact that the long-term average return of property is the same as property shares gives some indication that this might be the case. So does econometric analysis. Regression analysis provides strong evidence that property shares and property move together in the long term. Technically speaking, the two series are 'cointegrated', meaning if one moves away from the other in the short term, it will, over time, catch up with the other. The key thing, for practical investing purposes, is: how long the 'catch up period' is.

A less technical way of examining this is in Figure 6.2, which shows rolling correlations between property and property shares. Over the whole period, the contemporaneous (i.e. the period's return in both series) correlation is fairly low, at 0.35. However, a rolling five-year correlation coefficient shows that, at times, the correlation between the two series is much higher than 0.35 and much lower. Interestingly, the correlation seems to be lowest in the period of the 'tech-boom', when property was very much out-of-fashion 'old economy'. Since about 2002, when real estate roared back into the investment universe, the correlations have become much higher. It's as if property shares are priced more efficiently in periods when property is in fashion than when it's not. Based on the idea that public securities markets

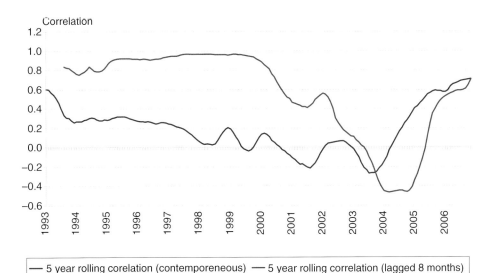

Figure 6.2: Correlation between property and property shares

impound new information more quickly than private markets, Figure 6.2 also shows the rolling correlation between property shares and property lagged by 8 months. As well as providing quite strong evidence that property shares lead property, the lagged correlation also shows strong variations over time. It is unlikely that REITs will be immune from these vagaries.

One final point can be made by returning to Figure 6.1. Property has put in a stellar performance since 2003, posting 19% compound annual total return. Property shares have done better, showing a compound annual return of 35%. Leaving aside the thorny issue of whether the direct property market is overvalued, property shares look to have overshot fundamentals. Indeed, this pattern of overshoot and undershoot can be seen over the whole period since 2001. One other indicator of this is the discount to Net Asset Value (NAV). UBS and Merrill Lynch have both shown the sector discount closing from around 40% in 2003 to around 0% in 2006. That the long-run sector discount is around 15% and 'mean reverting', suggests a degree of overvaluation in property shares. Furthermore, Grosvenor research suggests that UK leading property companies may be trading at a substantial premium to NAV.

The advantages for the UK of a REIT regime include better managed and more transparent property investment companies, lower cost of capital and opportunities for small investors to gain exposure to commercial property. However, small investors need to be advised that REITs only resemble direct property in the long term, tend to overshoot and undershoot the direct market and are certainly more volatile than real property. Moreover, after three years of blistering performance, the sector seems set for a period in the doldrums. Small investors need to wait for the sector to adjust to more normal valuation levels before taking a position in REITs. The industry could suffer irreparable damage to its reputation if it does not point to the risks as well as the advantages of investing in REITs.

Listed real estate in a 'perfect storm' – the case of Spain (November 2008)

The listed real estate market in Spain was one of the first to register the onset of the credit crisis. In this piece we look at how it is now faring. Spain, as other nations, is suffering a very hard landing, with falling house prices, reduced industrial production and contracting retail sales. The negative wealth effect echoes the UK and Irish situations. The unemployment rate jumped recently to more than 11%. Interestingly, the Spanish banking system has not shown any sign of chaos: the Top Three domestic banks are in good shape. This said, Spain failed to launch a bond last week, which clearly suggests continued worldwide risk aversion towards the country.

Given the global and domestic backdrop, how has real estate in Spain performed? The listed property sector has been more resilient compared with the IBEX-35, the main index, until recently. However, the financial turmoil has increased the risk associated with listed property companies in the wake of tougher credit conditions. Over the long term, the correlation coefficient between the two indices has been low, at 0.39, but it has jumped to 0.93 since August 2007. The Pearson coefficient shows that the volatility of the Spanish EPRA index has been explained by 87%, compared with 16% over the long term. Clearly, the real estate index is being affected by the general volatility of the main index. However, the big fall of the Spanish EPRA index is probably also justified by the exposure of these companies to the beleaguered residential sector, as well as quality of assets and balance sheets.

It is widely accepted that the listed real estate market is a leading indicator of direct investment market and there is a strong inverse relationship (r = –0.76) over the long run, which strengthens to –0.93 after 2000. The volatility of the prime yield profile is explained by 98% by the volatility of the EPRA index. Data suggests that there is a linear relationship between both variables, with a high negative elasticity (see Figure 6.3). Therefore, the level of the re-pricing seen in direct investment has been fairly in line with the overshooting seen in the listed property market. However, there

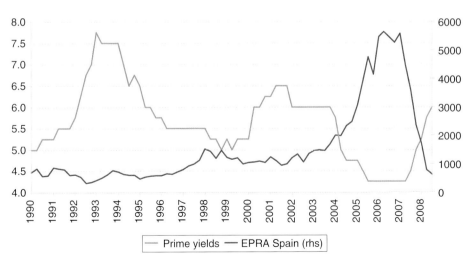

Figure 6.3: EPRA Spain and prime yields: strong inverse relationship after 2000
Source: EPRA, CBRE, and Grosvenor Research

will be more adjustment to be seen in the months ahead: the Spanish EPRA
index has fallen by 90% compared with H1 2007, while yields have shifted
outward by 150 basis points.

Underlying both property share movements and yields has been the monetary expansion of the last eight years. Increasing credit volumes have been
a cornerstone of yield compression, probably more in Spain than anywhere
else, with cheap credit being a driver of the huge inward yield shift observed
over the past few years. Credit was particularly important to the entrepreneurs who have dominated the market over the past ten years. Figure 6.4
shows the strong negative relationship between the change in the credit
volume and prime yields. Again, regression analysis shows a strong elasticity between the yield level and changes in credit volumes related to the
property sector. The correlation coefficient stands at −0.76 over the long
run. More interestingly, the volatility of the yield profile has been largely
explained by the volatility of credit changes: from 0.51 in the long run to
0.85 over the past three years.

As credit dries, there seems only one direction for real estate yields and
property share prices. The banking environment, despite its basic sound-
ness, is now more reluctant to lend and investors have continued to 'sell
off' companies characterised by: high leverage, low dividend yields, low cash
flow, as well as companies with heavy investment in the residential sector,
land loans and developments.

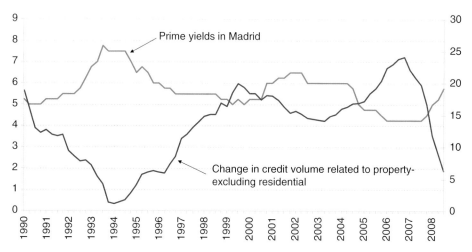

Figure 6.4: Yield compression has been explained mainly by the cheap cost of
domestic credit
Source: CBRE and Grosvenor Research

Disturbingly, the total valuation of the top 10 Spanish listed real estate companies is pointing to only a minor loss of 10% (total GAV moved from €69.9 billion in 2007 to €63.4 billion in 2008). However, this is probably due to substantial lags in the valuation process. As Spanish companies only need to value their portfolio once a year, they will not have fully captured the recent downturn, which helps to explain the reluctance of banks to lend. Given this deteriorating environment and the loan to value cornerstone, banks have pressured blue-chips to reappraise either their portfolio or key assets, with some companies having to sell assets to roll over a part of their debt. There are prospects that commercial properties could be valued at less than the loans on the property, putting further pressure on listed companies in the months ahead. Yield spreads may widen even more, because investors may anticipate falling valuations and build a risk premium into the capitalisation rates.

Because of the turbulence, some banks have been swapping debt for real estate and others have switched debt for equity. Residential portfolios are not favoured, as the market is not expected to recover soon; commercial properties have, it is thought, more chance of becoming profitable in the medium term. Investors are watching from the sidelines, waiting for opportunities to buy distressed properties, portfolios or bad loans across sectors at discount prices. Listed companies continue to fight against the headwinds, with banks unwilling to gain exposure.

Beta and the cost of equity capital to the UK property sector (May 2008)

The Capital Asset Pricing Model (CAPM) provides a relatively easy method of estimating the cost of equity capital to an industry or sector:

$$\text{Required Return} = \text{Risk Free Rate} + (\text{Beta} \times \text{Equity Risk Premium})$$

The 'risk free rate' and the 'equity risk premium' are fairly well understood. Beta, which measures the sensitivity of an individual company's, or sector's, performance to changes in the economy, is less well understood, especially in property. To be better able to estimate the cost of capital, not only to property as a whole, but to different aspects of property business, such as investment and development, retail and offices, we have undertaken some econometric analysis of property company betas in the UK. Our database is far from perfect, but the initial results, though tentative, are interesting.

Based on the idea that beta reflects the security of the fundamental cash flows of a business, we strongly suspect that the following are some of the factors that drive individual company betas:

- **Gearing:** the more highly geared a property (or any) company is, the more sensitive profits are to changes in turnover;
- **Yield on property assets:** low-yielding property is traditionally considered low risk, because it is well located or let on a long lease to a secure tenant. However, a low yield also means that a higher proportion of the total return has to come from growth, which is highly sensitive to the state of the economy. We thought yields would affect beta, but were not sure in which way.
- **Development as % of net assets:** property developments are highly exposed to market movements in construction cost and tenant demand (unless they are pre-let). We thought that more development would mean a higher beta.
- **Freehold ownership:** cash flow from a freehold is more secure than cash from property held on a long leasehold basis, because, in the case of the latter, in many cases, rents are payable to the freeholder whether the property is let or not.
- **Time period:** cash flows from property tend to be much more secure in times of falling interest rates, partly because of enhanced economic growth, but also because tenants are less stressed. We think that property company betas vary over time in response to the interest-rate environment.

To test our hypotheses, we used betas calculated for a sample of 40 British property companies and regressed these betas on the data extracted from each company's report and accounts. Panel estimation techniques were used on data that stretched back five years. Table 6.1 summarises the results.

As expected, the results show that as gearing increases so also does beta. Figure 6.5 shows financial gearing and beta and Figure 6.6 shows the related issue of interest cover. The results also indicate that higher yields on a company's property assets are weakly associated with higher beta. Clearly the risks associated with high yielding property such as short leases and poor covenants dominate the cash flow benefits of yield. Completely against expectations, higher levels of development seem to be associated with lower betas. It is possible that, higher levels of development are being undertaken by the bigger and more substantive companies and the regression is insufficiently well specified to isolate this effect. Proportion of freeholds in the portfolio is not related to beta at all.

Table 6.1: Regression Results

Driver Variable	Statistical Significance	Direction	Strength
Gearing	Strong	Positive (1)	High
Yield	Strong	Positive	Low
Development	Strong	Negative	Low
Freehold	Nil	Unclear	Nil
2002	Strong	Negative	High
2003	Strong	Negative	High
2004	Strong	Negative	High
2005	Strong	Positive	High
2006	Strong	Positive	High

(1) Increase in variable leads to increase in beta

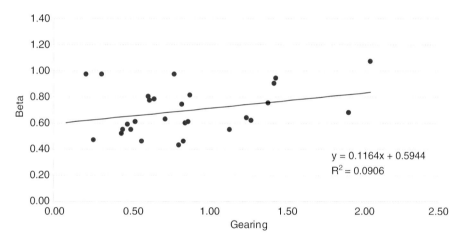

Figure 6.5: Gearing and beta
Source: London Business School Risk Management Service, Datastream, various Reports and Accounts

Possibly the most interesting finding in the analysis is the importance of time period on beta. Between 2002 and 2004, as interest rates fell, so also did average property company betas. In effect, the real estate industry got a two-pronged boost to its cost of equity capital: the first from falling interest rates, the second from falling betas. As can be seen, the reverse has been true since around 2005; as rates have been rising, so have betas. It was only a matter of time before this fed through into values. We expect property

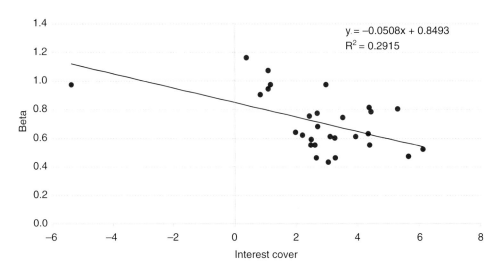

Figure 6.6:   Interest cover and beta
Source: London Business School Risk Management Service, Datastream, various Reports and Accounts

company betas to continue to rise, as the impact of higher interest rates on the credit quality of tenants is felt in the property market. Although the research is somewhat inconclusive on the issue of property activity and beta, it highlights the danger of relying on historic betas (that reflect more benign monetary conditions) to estimate forward cost of capital.

7

Real estate and construction

The construction sector is one of the most important 'transmission mechanisms' between real estate prices and the wider economy. Booming real estate markets send price signals that encourage resources into the construction sector which, in turn, boosts GDP growth. Because construction is a relatively low-skill, low-barrier to entry industry, it can expand very rapidly to become a relatively large share of GDP. When the construction sector grows to more than 10% of GDP, a national economy becomes acutely vulnerable to a downturn in real estate prices. This is why the economics of Spain, Ireland and even the United States have struggled to pull themselves out of recession in the period between 2009 and 2011. In the period leading up to the GFC, because of booming real estate markets, they become overly dependent on construction activity as a source of GDP growth. Probably the most important weakness in China's current breakneck expansion is that it is too heavily based on construction activity.

The articles of March 2006 and April 2007, particularly the latter, indicate that the build-up of construction activity in the world economy was increasingly worrying the Grosvenor research team in the period prior to the GFC, even if they did not specifically 'call' the peak of the boom. The April 2007 article makes a number of points that are worth highlighting with the benefit of hindsight. The first is that there is a 'natural choke' for the construction sector which comes from rising input prices. Rising materials and labour prices depresses the profitability of real estate development and

Real Estate and Globalisation, First Edition. Richard Barkham.
© 2012 John Wiley & Sons, Ltd. Published 2012 by John Wiley & Sons, Ltd.

slows construction. However, if input prices are themselves suppressed, as they appear to have been in the period prior to the GFC in some markets, then there is no 'natural choke' in operation and construction gets out of hand.

One of the key factors that suppressed rising input cost was international migration. As the real estate markets of the USA, Spain, Ireland and the UK boomed, the construction sector attracted a huge influx of migrant labour. The UK would have suffered a much greater oversupply of real estate, had the extremely tight land use planning system not prevented the rapid construction of new homes, as in the USA and Spain. It is also clear that the globalisation of construction supply chains also acted to suppress the rise in construction costs that would otherwise have taken place.

An interesting finding of the April 2007 article is that, in aggregate, housing market movements have more impact on overall construction output than commercial real estate markets. The reason for this is that the bulk of land use and real estate value is in the housing sector. As is mentioned elsewhere, approximately 90% of urban land is housing land.

The articles of March 2006 and March 2009 are both concerned with the outlook for construction costs. Both of these articles were motivated by the needs of Grosvenor's operating companies, which in normal conditions deploy a proportion of their net assets in development projects, to have some guidance as to likely future movements in development costs. The earlier article would have been based on the sense that costs were rising quite quickly and could threaten development profitability. The latter article was testing the idea that the downturn in the global economy would provide good 'contra-cyclical' development opportunities for those with the foresight to see through the acute economic difficulties of the time. In the event, the extremely rapid rebound in emerging market growth, particularly in China, has meant that construction prices did not fall by as much as was expected. Thus in the OECD, in the period 2010 to 2012, developers are facing depressed real estate markets and relatively high construction costs, so little private-sector construction is taking place. In emerging markets, at least at the time of writing (mid-2011), the construction boom continues; where it will end is the subject of debate. On one hand the long term trends of urbanisation and rising GDP per capita provide robust fundamental demand for real estate. People need to be housed and community infrastructure created. On the other hand, all development booms end: the bigger the boom the bigger the crash. For the time being the scale of emerging market growth continues to put upward pressure on development costs despite economic weakness in the OECD.

The articles in this section have attempted to show that there is a natural link between the real estate sector and the construction sector. The price signals which govern construction sector activity are generated by demand

and supply in real estate markets. However, in the press and even amongst professional economists and analysts, the two sectors are treated as separate and distinct. Real estate economists often relegate construction output to 'new supply' or 'additions to stock'. Certainly, new supply has a major impact on real estate prices and can, to an extent, be studied in isolation. However, the elasticity of new supply with regard to changes in input or output prices is determined by the structure and operation of the construction sector. A holistic approach to real estate research needs to take this into account.

What factors determine construction costs? (March 2006)

This month we look at construction costs and some of the factors that influence costs: labour, materials and industry structure. Specific projects have their own idiosyncratic cost issues, which are difficult (if not impossible) to predict beforehand. However, maintaining a watching brief on macro factors to ascertain how they could impact construction costs can reduce uncertainty.

Labour costs account for a significant proportion of all construction costs. UK earnings data, from the annual survey of household earnings (ASHE), shows that in 2005 there were year-on-year earnings increases for steel erectors (8.6%), bricklayers (7.5%), roofers (5.6%) and glaziers (7.2%), but plumbers saw a decline of 1.9% (Figure 7.1). Although these official figures

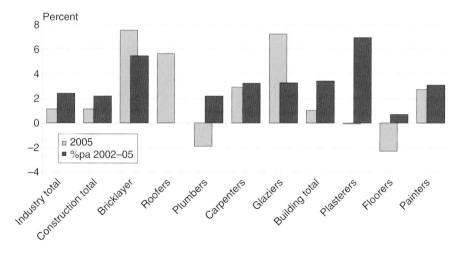

Figure 7.1:   Construction labour cost change
Source: Annual Survey Household Earnings, Grosvenor

do not count any 'unreported' earnings, they should pick up general trends and be indicative of the premiums available for scarce skills.

Shortages of quality tradespeople in the UK seem to persist, but an inflow of overseas workers is often cited as keeping labour costs down. Research by the National Institute of Economic and Social Research (NIESR) on net migration concludes that in-migration to the UK has kept inflation lower and boosted GDP growth. This supports the hypothesis that inflows are easing supply shortages and reducing construction cost increases and moderating the earnings growth of tradespeople.

However, an inflow of migrant workers may not be the panacea for the construction industry and may bring its own issues: health and safety and potential quality concerns. In the longer term, migrant workers may return to their country of origin or move to alternative countries. Skills shortages within the construction sector are now receiving government attention and, in the long term, this may help to alleviate labour problems.

Raw building materials can experience wide variations in price, because of localised extraction issues, wars or competitive demand from elsewhere. However, the impact of such swings in price depends on how much is used in the building and if there is a substitute. Currently, copper prices are increasing strongly: 39% year-on-year in January, but the relatively small proportions used in construction mean this will have less impact than the hike in steel prices in 2004–5.

Oil prices impact on building costs in two ways: production of materials and transportation costs. Also, it has been estimated by a cost engineering practice that approximately one barrel of oil is used in the construction of one metre of building.

Cement is a particularly energy-intensive material and the impact of increases in energy prices are now showing up in cement prices (see Figure 7.2). Historically, spikes in oil prices have been associated with similar, but smaller, moves in cement prices. In the current cycle there is a lag; earlier oil price increases are still feeding through into this year's cement price spike.

There are a relatively small number of large players in the construction sector. In such a situation, economic theory suggests that non-price competition is preferable for the players, as price competition will leave all participants worse off and no one better off, if they all undercut to win contracts. Therefore, rational participants will try to maintain an 'industry inflation rate' and compete by non-price means.

Game theory also suggests that firms benefit from cooperation: to build partnerships and maintain a continued source of work. Individual firms will perform better within a cooperative framework, if it is assumed they are all intending to participate in numerous developments. Also, partnerships can

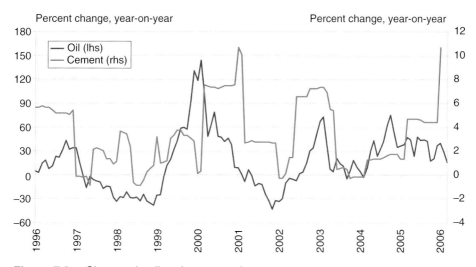

Figure 7.2:   Changes in oil and cement prices
Source: Global Insight, Grosvenor

reduce the risk of the 'winner's curse', where the contract winner has under-priced to gain the contract.

A specific project's final costs are determined by so many factors that to estimate them *ex ante* is almost impossible. Entrepreneurship is about making judgements in uncertain cost and revenue situations. Volatility in costs is one reason property development remains a highly entrepreneurial activity.

Is there a global construction boom? (April 2007)

Many of the world's great cities have begun to feel a little bit like building sites, with new offices and shopping malls being built on every block. This casual observation has prompted the Grosvenor research team to investigate whether there is a global construction boom taking place? If there is, what are the causes and the potential consequences? Of course, there is a serious motivation for the research: most real estate cycles end with huge numbers of glistening new buildings standing empty. Is this what the world is heading for?

There are some difficulties in assessing the extent of global construction output, because of data inconsistencies, so Figure 7.3 is indicative. It shows construction output in the seven largest developed economies (the USA, the UK, France, Spain, Italy, Germany and Japan). Construction growth is

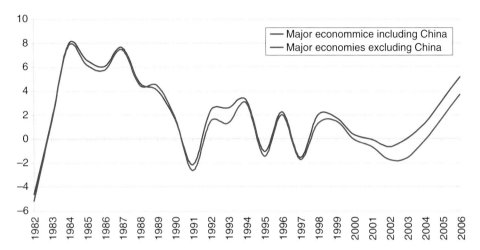

Figure 7.3: Construction output in the major economies
Source: Global Insight, Grosvenor

stronger than it has been at any time since the late 1980s. If construction output in China is added to the series, then it is clear that the world is in a period of very significant construction activity, if not quite a boom.

What has stimulated this level of activity? It is tempting to think that broad macroeconomic factors, such as GDP growth and low interest rates (via cost of capital) are the key influences. Econometric modelling, however, suggests that this is not the case – at least, not in any direct sense. The model that best explains construction activity at global and country level contains, as explanatory variables: house price growth; government fixed capital investment; and labour earnings growth (as a proxy for construction cost inflation).

The impact of house-price growth is positive in all countries: as prices rise, profitable opportunities are created and developers respond by increasing construction activity. The same is probably true of commercial construction, although this is difficult to prove in the econometric models because of data limitations. In any case, the fact that 90% of urban land is housing land strongly suggests that housing markets have the dominant impact on construction activity. One of the key themes of the current economic expansion, stimulated as it has been by ultra-low interest rates, has been strong growth in house prices in most countries. So, macroeconomic factors impact on construction activity strongly, but indirectly. As interest rates rise across the OECD and beyond, we expect house-price growth to slow and this will feed back into lower levels of construction.

Our econometric model also reveals, in line with expectation, that fixed capital spending by governments strongly boosts construction activity.

Invariably, governments have responsibility for building schools, roads and hospitals and so directly control the level of construction activity. It is probable that government spending on buildings is related as much to the electoral cycle as the economic cycle, so it is not easy to predict how this component of global construction activity will behave in the next few years, except to say that the OECD nations are collectively running strong deficits and these will need to be addressed by higher taxes or lower spending in the medium term.

If rising real estate values create development opportunities, then rising costs choke them off. In fact, when costs rise faster than values it is usually taken as a sign that the top of the cycle is near. It is almost impossible to get internationally comparable long-run data on construction costs, so, on the assumption that a large proportion of construction costs are payments to workers, we tested the impact of earnings growth on construction activity. As we expected, the impact was, in general, negative: as wage rates rise, construction activity falls. We suspect that construction activity in the OECD has received a boost in the last five years from migration. Western Europe has received workers from the EU accession countries. The USA has high levels of immigration over the long run. Migration keeps wage rates down and boosts development profitability. It is even possible to argue that the inflow of labour to cities in China from rural areas has had a similar effect.

What are the consequences of a global surge in construction? As we have said, data on overall construction price inflation is very difficult to obtain. Figure 7.4 contrasts construction inflation with overall inflation for the countries where such data are available. We know that construction cost data reacts slowly to real market activity and so understates true inflation. In any case, we can see that construction prices are rising strongly. This will make life very difficult for developers and will act as a brake on construction activity in the next two years. On the plus side, it will begin to be possible for homeowners to locate that elusive tradesman for much-needed repairs. Those active in real estate do not want to see serious over-supply develop, so a downturn in construction is to be welcomed. On the downside, construction is an important sector in the global economy: as it slows, so will GDP growth.

UK construction costs and the recession (March 2006)

With the fall in commercial and residential values across the world, the outlook for property development is bleak. However, history shows that input prices fall sharply during recessions. When this happens, development

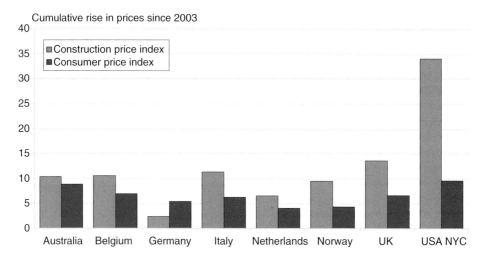

Figure 7.4:   Construction cost inflation
Source: Davis Langdon & Everest, Global Insight

will begin to look attractive once again. In this article we consider what might happen to construction costs in this current recession.

The construction sector of most advanced countries represents 5 6% of total output (Figure 7.5). The percentage has gradually fallen from over 7% in the early 80s, as industrialised countries have moved towards service-based economies. By contrast, Spain and Ireland have seen significant construction booms over the last 10 years, fuelled by large credit inflows from excess saving countries. Construction, as a share of GDP, increased from 7% and 5.5% in Spain and Ireland in 1998 to a peak of 12.2% and 9.9%. Since the 2007 peak, the construction industry in these countries has collapsed, as residential and commercial property prices plummeted and credit dried up.

The growth of most advanced economies has not been fuelled by a construction boom. Although UK construction, as a share of GDP, drifted up from around 5% 10 years ago to 6.5% in 2008, this has occurred at the expense of the manufacturing sector. The UK construction sector has grown by 2.8% per annum, which is in line with GDP growth. The USA, Germany and Japan have seen their construction sectors shrink as a share of GDP. Nonetheless, despite the absence of a boom, UK construction costs increased by 6.0% per annum in nominal terms and 3.5% per annum in real terms over the last ten years (Figure 7.6). This compares with real construction cost growth of 1.2% per annum in the 10 years to Sep 1988, a time of intense development activity.

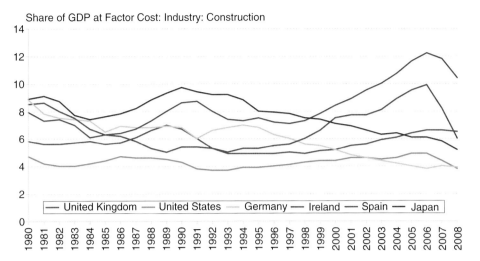

Figure 7.5:   Construction as share of GDP
Source: Global Insight

Figure 7.6:   UK Tender Price Index deflated by GDP deflator
Source: BCIS; Ecowin; Grosvenor Research

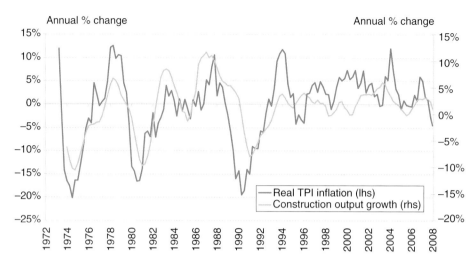

Figure 7.7: UK Tender Price Index Inflation and UK Construction
Source: Global Insight; BCIS; Grosvenor Research

Previous surges in UK construction costs have largely been driven by domestic factors (Figure 7.7). The increase in energy prices also played a role in driving up construction costs in the mid-1970s. As the demand for construction work increased, wages and building materials costs shot up, thereby pushing up the cost of development. In contrast, the increase in construction costs over the last 10 years has more to do with global factors.

The increase in construction costs over the last decade has coincided with the emergence of the BRICs (Brazil, Russia, India and China). Industrialisation in emerging markets has pushed commodity prices up sharply, forcing up input costs. In addition, the global construction boom has meant that contractors have diverted resources to booming markets, forcing domestic developers to pay higher prices for work.

The credit crunch and the global downturn has resulted in a significant number of development schemes being delayed or shelved. As a result, the global construction boom has come to a sudden halt and commodity prices have fallen back sharply. This will feed into significantly lower building material costs. In addition, as the world economy slows the increase in the supply of labour will push down wages. The combined impact of weaker demand, lower commodity prices and increased competition for a shrinking amount of work will force down construction costs.

To what extent will construction prices fall? Figure 7.8 shows a strong relationship between world GDP growth and the real growth of UK construction costs. Construction costs fell by 30% in real terms in each of the

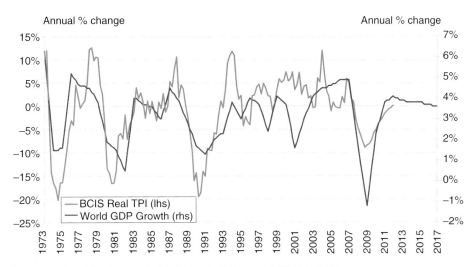

Figure 7.8: UK Tender Price Index inflation and World GDP
Source: Global Insight; BCIS; Grosvenor Research

previous three postwar global downturns. Given that the current global downturn will be worse than each of the previous downturns, then construction costs are likely to fall even more sharply over the next two years. The extent of the fall in UK construction costs will be tempered somewhat by the fall in the pound against all major currencies. Roughly, a sustained 1% depreciation of the pound results in TPI inflation increasing by 0.5–0.6%. In addition, public spending on construction projects will also mitigate the decline in prices. Nonetheless, forecasts of TPI deflation by leading UK Quantity Surveyors of only 2 6% per annum over the next two years seems optimistic in this environment (source: BCIS). Recession economics suggests that construction costs will fall around 10% pa over the next two years, possibly more.

So things seem very tough right now in property and they will be for another two–three years. But the process of resetting prices and restoring profitability to development has started. Far-sighted developers will have recognised this and will be taking advantage of the recession to work up schemes for the future.

8

Asia

The 'rise of China' is the defining event of our time. It is wrong to use the word 'event', of course, to encapsulate political, social and economic developments which are complex and take place over many years. However, the industrialisation of China seems to have taken place so quickly and left Western policy-makers so completely wrong-footed that the word 'event' probably conveys the right meaning. As well as other things, the rise of China has major implications for real estate markets, not just in Asia but elsewhere in the world.

Within China, economic growth is driving a massive rural-to-urban migration, with new cities being created – if not overnight – then easily within the space of a decade. The need to provide homes, offices, factories, social infrastructure and shopping malls is creating a huge real estate development boom. This boom is mainly being exploited by local entrepreneurs, but real estate companies from other, more developed parts of Asia, such as Hong Kong, Taiwan, Singapore and Japan are also involved in creating new real estate assets. Many of the shiny new buildings springing up in China's burgeoning cities have not been built to Western safety standards or with the necessary local permits, leaving a legacy of risk for users and investors.

In some ways the creation of new user demand for modern real estate in a country that was communist and poverty-stricken a mere 20 years ago is the least interesting part of the China story. The world has seen rapid economic development before and urbanisation, even if not on quite the same

Real Estate and Globalisation, First Edition. Richard Barkham.
© 2012 John Wiley & Sons, Ltd. Published 2012 by John Wiley & Sons, Ltd.

scale as in China at present. The more interesting part of the story, at least from the perspective of global real estate investing, is the impact of the rise of China on OECD economies and real estate markets.

China's rapid growth dates from the late 1970s, when the 'doors were opened' to foreign direct investment. A step-change came in 2001, when China joined the World Trade Organisation and gained greater access to the world's major markets. We commented on this development at the time in the article of January 2002, perhaps failing to see its full significance. The key issue, from a global perspective, was and is that a huge new pool of labour was opened up to the world trading system. Manufacturing firms previously located in Asia, the USA and Europe have moved to China 'en masse', to take advantage of the low-cost environment it offers. These cost advantages are not only due to low wage rates, but also powerful scale and agglomeration economies in the manufacturing process. The resulting export of cheap manufactured goods to OECD countries is one of the factors that created an 'epoch' of stable low-inflation economic growth: broadly, the period from 1992 to 2007.

Low inflation and stable economic growth allowed OECD interest rates to trend down from the mid-1990s onwards. In turn, falling interest rates led to a long period of real-estate capital appreciation and strong positive total returns in most OECD countries. Falling interest rates over the period were also partially to blame for repeated stock-market booms and slumps, as we argue in the opening chapter.

If low inflation provided the impetus for low short-term interest rates, the outflow of capital from China into the US bond market brought rates down at the long end of the market. China has maintained a persistently high trade surplus, as it has exported its way to economic growth. Foreign currency has flooded into the country and promptly been reinvested in US bonds and China has become the world's largest creditor nation. The significance of this, from a real estate perspective, is huge: as US and OECD bond yields have fallen, so have real estate yields. As a direct consequence of falling bond and property yields, those investing in global real estate markets, including the banks, got so used to rising real estate prices they thought they would do so for ever. When interest rates peaked in 2007 and the party came to an end, the GFC ensued. Currently, China is trying to diversify its holding of foreign assets away from US bonds and has created a very well-capitalised Sovereign Wealth Fund. This fund is, amongst other things, targeting the build-up of OECD real estate assets. It is the biggest SWF in the world.

As a means of fostering and sustaining its export-led growth, China holds the value of its currency below its true market level. This currency manipulation is highly controversial and could lead to protectionist tariff barriers being created in the countries, such as the USA, which are losing manufacturing jobs. We look at the prospects for currency reform in China in our article of December 2004. Any rapid change to the value of China's currency would have a major impact on the global economy, which is why we take such a close interest in the matter. It would increase inflation in the OECD, which might be quite good for real estate, but it would badly impact China's rate of growth and social stability.

We follow developments in China not only as we favour China as a long term investment location but also because the world economy is becoming ever more dependent on China's growth. There was a feeling, prior to the GFC, that a slowdown in OECD consumer markets would quickly trigger a slump in China. However, it was highly notable that during the recession China was able to stimulate enough domestic activity to replace that lost from the slump in exports quite quickly. The article of June 2009, with something of a sense of relief, explores the way in which China was able to survive the crisis. Where there is continued worry about China's economic performance, it concerns inflationary pressures, which we look at in the articles of June 2008 and March 2011.

If China, over the last 15 years, has provided a 'text-book' case study of market-driven economic development, then Japan has been the global exemplar of deflation and long-term recession. In fact, many of the policies that have been used with success in the USA, the UK and elsewhere to counter the deflationary effects of the GFC were pioneered in Japan. These policies include zero interest rates and quantitative easing. Japan experienced the same sort of rapid economic growth as China in the period from the early 1960s to the late 1980s. At the end of this period, Japan had emerged as the second largest economy in the world, with a manufacturing sector that was feared by all other industrialised nations. As with China, Japan's export boom was stimulated by the low value of the currency. In the mid-1980s the USA put pressure on Japan to revalue, just as it is putting pressure on China to do so now. Japan revalued the Yen and the long boom came to an end. The monetary expansion that was initiated to boost domestic demand and offset the decline in export growth stimulated the world's biggest-ever real estate and lending boom. As world interest rates rose at the end of the 1980s, this boom came to an end and Japan slipped into a decade-long recession, from which it has not yet fully emerged.

Over the years we have taken a great interest in the Japanese economic experience. Markets which are slumped or depressed provide the opportunity to purchase cheaply and hold until a long-term recovery in the economy and asset markets takes place. Also, reflecting Japan's continued importance in the global economy, its real estate should always feature in a 'neutral' global real estate portfolio. In an interesting precursor of the current economic debate, the article of March 2004 reviews the impact of the then 'new' economic policy of quantitative easing on Japan's economic performance. The article of September 2004 looks at the prospects for a recovery in land values and concludes that, because of the widespread prevalence of 'false-value accounting', further value declines were likely, despite a turnaround in the economy. Given the tendency in post-bubble Japan for policy mistakes to derail nascent recoveries, the article of April 2006 examines the likely impact of winding down quantitative easing.

Our article of November 2007 gives a brief overview of Asia's rapidly mounting real estate markets. Currently, Asia represents 30% of the global real estate universe and it has the potential to be a much higher proportion. The largest and most liquid market in Asia is Japan, which offers plenty of core product with low returns. China offers high returns, but also high risk. At the moment, because the China 'growth story' is so well trumpeted in the Western media, it is China that attracts most attention from investors. However, Asia is much more than just China and provides a much wider set of opportunities.

China/WTO (January 2002)

China's much-heralded WTO entry finally took place in November 2001 and signals a major next phase along the path to full integration with the global, capitalist economy. China remains an incredibly poor country, and even the richer coastal regions lag some way behind the West, but WTO entry will undoubtedly accelerate the catch-up process. In the short term, though, we can expect a considerable amount of economic pain at a time when Chinese growth is very high, but slowing. WTO entry will lower tariffs and shift demand towards imports hitting domestic producers and causing price cuts that could intensify deflation. This will increase the pressure on highly inefficient state-owned enterprises and one of the reasons for the government's acceptance of some very dramatic concessions during WTO entry negotiations was probably to increase foreign competition in China and so force these SOEs (State Owned Enterprises) to restructure. Any large-scale restructuring will increase urban unemployment and reduce the growth of consumer spending. Urban unemployment is officially recorded at a very low 3.3%, but is more realistically estimated at around 8% (once account has been taken of official overstatement and the large numbers of employees who have been effectively laid-off but have been kept on the payroll at nominal salaries) and significantly higher unemployment will reduce the dynamism of the domestic economy.

These negative effects should be fairly short-lived, though. WTO entry will also increase the competitiveness of Chinese exporters and underline the inflow of foreign capital into the economy. The levels of foreign direct investment in China remain very high and show no signs of dropping off sharply, despite the uncertain global economic environment. This inflow of capital and external labour should help support asset prices through the initial economic turbulence and set the scene for impressive growth in the years to come.

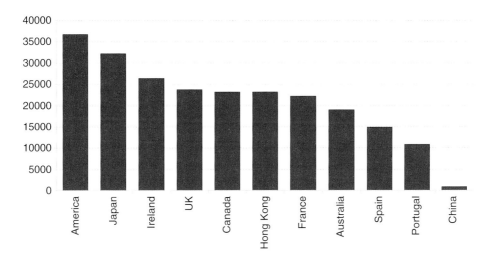

Figure 8.1: GDP per capita – 2001 estimate

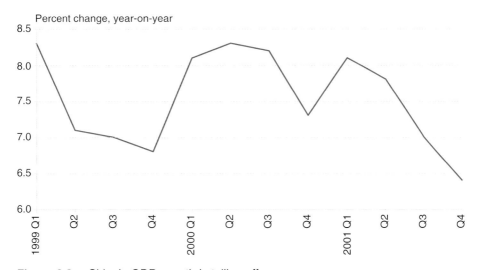

Figure 8.2: China's GDP growth is tailing off

Chinese currency reform (December 2004)

Recent speculation on what is likely to happen in the Chinese currency market has confused currency revaluation with currency reform. Beijing wants a flexible currency regime, not necessarily a revaluation. But, under the current balance of payments surplus, the currency will rise if Beijing relaxes control. Some also speculate that the Hong Kong dollar would follow the RMB to revalue against the US dollar, because of the close economic ties between Hong Kong and China. However, despite market speculation of an imminent move, odds for any major policy shift are low in the short term.

First, China's financial market infrastructure remains insufficient for a big change in the policy regime, because of the lack of depth of the derivative market and the unavailability of hedging products. Second, Beijing must have better control of other monetary tools, notably interest rates, to avoid economic chaos when freeing the currency. It also needs deeper money markets to run effective interest rate policy. Third, Beijing wants any change to currency policy to bring minimal disruption to the economy. But the current rampant speculation will create significant economic disruption (Figure 8.3).

Investment banks estimate that a 30% rise in the RMB, as many in the market see, would not only hurt China's economy and cut GDP growth by two percentage points a year; it would also prompt those overseas Chinese

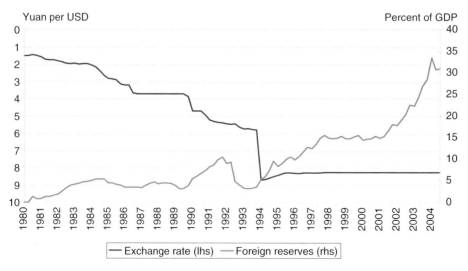

Figure 8.3:   Chinese USD exchange rates and foreign exchange reserves
Source: Global Insight

speculators who had parked money in Chinese banks to take profit and withdraw their funds. Because of the huge positions built up, the withdrawal would depress money supply and hurt the economy. The impact would go further, as Asia and the world commodity market have grown dependent on China's import demand for sustaining their own growth.

International pressure cannot push Beijing to revalue. China has won kudos and earned foreign confidence by resisting enormous international pressure to devalue the RMB after the 1997–1998 Asian crisis. It is more likely to resist this revaluation pressure because the RMB is undervalued, which is more manageable than an overvalued one.

If speculation recedes and Beijing's measures to cool the economic hot spots succeed, a policy shift may come in the next year. Beijing has already ruled out a large one-off revaluation because the resultant negative economic shock would be unbearable. A small revaluation would lack credibility and invite more speculations on further revaluations. A likely option would be a wider RMB trading band, in the range of 3–5% above and below the central rate set by the PBoC. Over the longer run, China is likely to follow a 'crawling peg' regime like that in Taiwan and Singapore, where the authorities intervene in the market to control the pace and magnitude of the exchange rate movement to give the economy time to adjust to changes.

HKD will not have to follow the RMB, even if the latter were revalued. Hong Kong's economy is tied closely to those Chinese sectors (foreign trade-related) that are US-dollar denominated. There is no particular reason for the HKD to follow the RMB move. Overall, any shocks on the regional markets from an RMB policy shift should be contained.

What's the outlook for the Chinese economy? (June 2009)

Recovery has started

The widespread fear that gripped China late last year has been replaced by relief or even subdued optimism. After stalling in the final quarter of 2008, the economy grew by 6.0% annual rate in the first three months of this year. The impressive turnaround follows a resolute and coordinated intervention by the government to boost domestic demand following the export slump caused by the global downturn.

First, monetary easing was swift and credit expansion robust. The PBoC cut the policy rate to its 2004 level in a matter of four months. Loan growth accelerated sharply and by March had reached 90% of last year's level. Second, a massive stimulus programme worth RMB 4 trillion ($2.3trn) was also set in motion. As a result, while foreign direct investment slowed sharply, because of the credit crunch, the pace of fixed asset investment growth quickened, as major public infrastructure works and housing construction were front-loaded.

The current leg of this recovery still has room to run, when the secondary effects of the stimulus kick in. The lift-off in public sector investment from the government's aggressive infrastructure plans will persist as more large-scale projects were reported to have been launched over the past quarter. That and loose credit conditions will continue to drive a narrowly-based recovery in construction-related industries, such as steel and cement. Consequently, the drag from inventory correction will also be less pronounced. Corroborating this general improvement in industry is the ongoing uptick in the Purchasing Managers Index (Figure 8.4). While further interest rate cuts are unlikely, there is room for the reserve requirement ratio to be eased as the pace of credit expansion slows. The government has also promised additional supplementary stimulus, should signs of a renewed slow-down emerge.

Premature to pronounce sustained upturn

Despite some healing and more positive undertones, the Chinese economy remains fractured and sizable downside risks prevail. The recovery so far is narrowly based and mainly underpinned by massive public spending and opening of the credit floodgates.

True, the global financial and economic landscape is slowly turning around, but 2010 world growth is expected to stay weak, uneven and

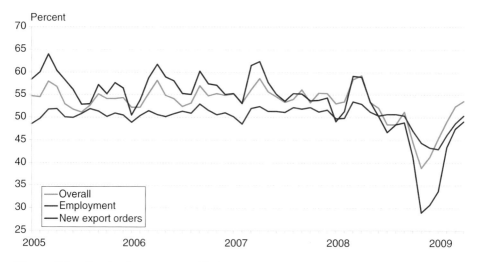

Figure 8.4:   Purchasing managers' index
Source: National Bureau of Statistics

disorderly. As a result, private investment growth in China – which has continued to lag behind government spending in this cycle – will stay moribund from excess manufacturing capacity, significant pressure on corporate margins and sluggish global demand.

Against this backdrop, it looks unlikely that labour market conditions can recover well enough to drive domestic consumption, the perennial Achilles' heel of the economy. So far, household consumption has stayed relatively resilient from the boost to purchasing power from lower prices, wealth effect from rising equity prices and reduced deflation expectations. But urban joblessness is creeping higher and private sector jobs are still lacking. It is estimated that about 25% of fresh graduates will be unemployed this year, adding to the 15 million migrant workers who have already lost their jobs.

Finally, strong credit creation at a time of declining industrial profits raises concerns over the quality of loans and the long-term risk to the banking system. Indeed, early warning signals that asset quality could be deteriorating are surfacing, with the increase in loan–loss provisions and special mention loans.

All said, the immediate term outlook is positive, but over the longer run, the ingredients for broad-based growth have not yet fallen into place. The economy is likely to grow at slightly below trend pace this year, with risks of a renewed downturn in 2010 once the multiple effects of stimulus start to fade. Widespread pessimism at the depth of the crisis is not without cause. The reality is not as bad as feared, but the Chinese economy still has some problems.

Housing market running ahead of the economy

The residential property market continues to recover alongside steadily improving economic sentiment. Sales of existing and newly constructed residential property have risen by more than 40% from a year ago in April, sustaining the renewed momentum from the January bottom. The run-up in transaction activities not only underlies the positive impact from cuts in interest rates, down payments, taxes and property prices but, importantly, it reinforces the strong fundamental demand for housing outside of the high-end sector.

Prices, too, have bottomed and are slowly on the uptick. The rebound in prices is most visible in Shenzhen, where the correction had been the steepest, but in April more than 50 cities registered prices rises. It is unclear, however, if the price support level can be sustained. While there is a serious medium-term mismatch between high-end supply and significant demand in the low-mid-market segment at the national level, the unbalanced and fragile recovery and strong pace of new completed supply point to still-significant downward pressure on prices.

The Chinese economy is still frayed at the edges, as is the housing market, but there is a better than evens chance of a sustained recovery in the medium term.

Will China's problematic inflation subside? (June 2008)

China is facing an inflation quagmire and consumer price inflation is turning out to be the biggest economic issue for mainland China in 2008. From historically low rates, price rises soared to 8.5% in April. This has grabbed the full attention of policy-makers, global investors and observers alike. In a global context China's inflation matters, given that much of the 'new economic paradigm' of strong growth and low inflation was based on cheap Chinese products.

China is not alone in grappling with the rising threat of inflation to economic stability. Over the past five years, a powerful set of reflationary forces entered the global economy, in the form of Asian demand and policy dynamics. Global resource utilisation and commodity prices have now reached levels that are producing a sustained upward push on inflation. Even though the global reverberations of tight credit markets and the weak US economy are likely to lead to below-trend world growth this year, which should help take some steam off the inflation engine. However, there is some danger that this cyclical dynamic will reaffirm itself when financial market stress reduces in the USA.

In China, structural forces have been at play, too. Since 2004, consumers have been largely shielded from the purchasing-power squeeze of rising energy prices, because of the improvement in terms of trade and government subsidies. On average, inflation rose at an annual pace of slightly above 2%, through to 2006. But the tide began to turn in early 2007, when a combination of rising core inflation and reduced energy subsidies intensified price pressures alongside longer-term structural drivers including rising labour costs, commodity and energy prices and liquidity growth.

So there are long-term structural and cyclical reasons for China's current inflation spike, but these reasons alone are not enough to explain recent inflation increases. China's present inflation problem stems largely from a more 'mundane' but no less important driver; the sharp price rise in food (Figure 8.5), where temporary supply shocks have pushed prices. Natural disasters, in the form of February's unprecedented snowstorms and last month's Sichuan earthquake, are likely to prolong the inflation problem. Although the snowstorm impact is fading, the earthquake is generating new

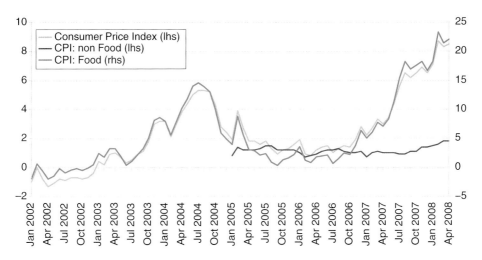

Figure 8.5:   The impact of food prices on inflation
Source: CEIC

inflation concerns, as Sichuan is a major agricultural area. Food CPI has soared by double digits since mid-2007 and by more than 20% this year, accounting for more than 80% of overall price increases. In contrast, non-food 'core' prices have risen at a relatively benign 2% pace. China does not have a broad inflation problem; instead, it has a food price problem. Food prices are volatile, which means the food price issue could resolve equally rapidly and, going forward, food (and pork) prices should ease.

Concerns about domestic banking liquidity during the recent inflation spiral are also unwarranted. Whilst inflation is a monetary phenomenon and monetary expansion is a fundamental force driving inflation over the long term in China (Figure 8.6), there is a reasonable correlation between broad money M2 and CPI inflation over time, with some notable periods when the relationship breaks down. During the deflationary period 1998–2003, M2 growth was around 16%. More recently, broad money grew by 17.5% in 2007, but this does not correspond to the 8%-plus inflation today. Further, bank credit growth – the transmission mechanism from money growth to inflation – has stayed consistently well below M2 over the past four years, suggesting that sterilisation operations have actually forced a contraction in loan-to-deposit ratios recently.

China's problematic inflation should begin to subside, as 'one-off' price rises move out of the figures. These fading impulses will lower headline inflation incrementally over the remaining course of the year. However, for China, the days of easy macro policy-making are over. To stabilise inflation and the slowly overheating economy, the government will allow faster RMB appreciation in order to address supply-side inflationary pressures. In concert, the PBoC is likely to keep its focus on managing liquidity and

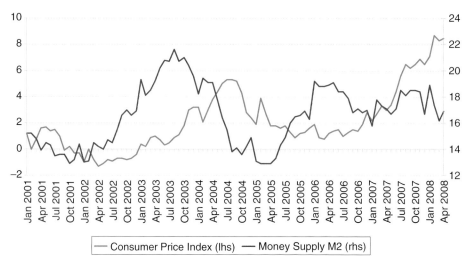

Figure 8.6:   Money supply and inflation
Source: CEIC

credit conditions by raising the reserve requirement ratio to 17% later this year. Interest rate hikes are less likely, given the spreading consensus that they are not an effective approach to controlling Chinese inflation.

Is real estate in China heading for a hard landing? (March 2011)

The fear of a real estate bubble in China is a recurring theme in the Western press. Such concerns are fuelled by the persistent house-price increases of recent years and the fact that the measures put in place to cool the market have not been fully effective. Nor is the real estate market the only source of anxiety. Worries persist about the general price environment, because of monetary expansion and structural wage inflation. In our view, a key reason for these lingering fears is China's constrained monetary management.

Runaway inflation concerns are exaggerated

The recent surge in consumer prices is a 'hot button' issue at the moment, in China as well as the West. In the long run, inflation is a monetary phenomenon and it should be a real concern for China. However, the recent acceleration in the headline inflation, to 4.9% in January from 1.5% a year back, mainly reflects the impact of rising food prices. Driven by a weather-related demand and supply imbalance, food-price inflation jumped to 10.3% in January and has averaged around 9.5% in the past six months. Barring unexpected disruption to the food supply chain in the coming months, the impact of food price increases will begin to ease soon.

In addition, the government has taken steps to curb rising consumer prices by increasing the import of selected food products, abolishing tax rebates on some agricultural exports and releasing national reserves of key staples. Producer prices have also started to ease for raw materials and industrial goods, notably agricultural input. With the sequential monetary tightening in the past few months, money supply growth has started to slow. Figure 8.7 suggests a more benign inflation environment ahead. We expect the rate of price increase to slow in the second half of the year and average around 4.5% by the end of 2011 (4% in 2012).

Nevertheless, long-term trend inflation will step up, to 4–5% from around 2% before the financial crisis. The drivers of this 'structural inflation' will be tighter labour markets, alongside resource and utility price adjustments. Concerning the labour market, the working-age population will start to decline from 2015 and this shrinking employment pool, amid robust economic growth, implies that wages will trend up, because of increasing competition for both skilled and unskilled labour. Also, general production costs are expected to rise (despite excess capacity in some manufacturing sectors), because of upward wage pressure from rural migrants wanting a better standard of living.

A real estate market collapse is not imminent

Unlike the recent worries over runaway inflation, a real estate bubble has been a long-standing concern. China's real estate 'bears' have consistently based their fears on falling housing affordability and excessive construction. On the face of it, these fears seem justified. Housing has become increasingly unaffordable to the 'average' citizen. On the basis of the ratio of average home price to household disposable income, the most recent data suggest that it would take nine years to pay off a very modest home in China. However, households that buy homes are not households with an average income. Housing still remains highly affordable to the top 20–30 percentile of the population, whose income is 2.2 times that of the average earner. Grey or non-wage income, cash down-payments of 50% loan-to-value and inter-generational transfers from parents to grown children are also not captured in the household surveys.

Similarly, over-building fears miss the point that, despite the long construction boom, private home ownership only started in 1997. Nationwide

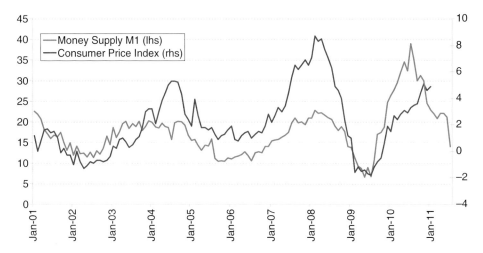

Figure 8.7: Correlation between CPI and M1 growth
Source: CEIC, Grosvenor Research 2011

completion of residential space between 1997 and 2009 totalled 7.8 billion sq.m., or some 78 million units (assuming average home size of 100 sq.m.). By comparison, there are 215 million urban households in China. Demand from those wishing to upgrade from state-owned apartments built prior to the housing reform further suggests that the housing penetration rate is low by most counts. Finally, China, like so many countries in the West, is experiencing falling household size.

In our view, the important fundamental drivers of strong income and urban population growth, alongside widespread upgrading, will continue to drive demand for modern housing over the next 10 years. Figure 8.8 shows that continued rural to urban migration will provide secure long-run demand for housing. We do not dispute the idea that the housing market has witnessed some highly localised bubbles in the past two years. Prices have risen too fast in some areas, despite repeated measures to cool the market. However, the latest tightening measures implemented in January[1] will have the intended impact, which is to slow price growth. In Shanghai, residential property sales have already fallen and prices have started to stabilise, a trend which we believe will persist.

---

[1] Recent measures to curb property prices:
- Increase in the minimum down-payment requirement for second home mortgages to 60% (from 50%);
- Extension of home purchase restrictions to more cities with overheated markets;
- Decree that city governments must establish a real-estate price target in 2011.

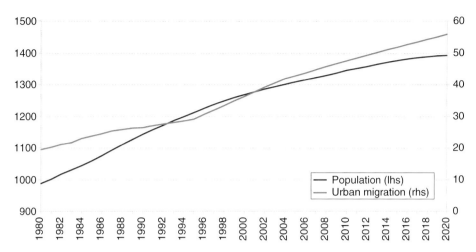

Figure 8.8: Rising urban migration rate
Source: CEIC, Grosvenor Research 2011

A hard landing in the long term?

How the Chinese real estate market evolves over the next 10 years depends crucially on the 'tug of war' between strong fundamental demand and much-needed financial and land reforms.

China has made good progress in monetary management over the past decade, even within the framework of a centrally planned economy. Nevertheless, the state still plays a significant role in holding and allocating resources. Within this context, while money-market and bond rates are market-determined, commercial benchmark rates remain artificially bound through a ceiling on deposit rates and a floor on lending rates. This heavily distorts relative asset pricing. With savings running at more than 50% of GDP, a historically underweight position in financial assets, and lack of alternative investment channels because of capital controls, artificially low real deposit rates are likely to continue to drive funds into the real estate market.

China's quasi-fixed exchange rate and large balance of payments surplus also pose a substantial financial risk. In order to keep the RMB from appreciating too much, the People's Bank of China (PBoC) has been buying up excess dollars, thus increasing money supply in the banking system. Sterilisation, through central bank bill issuance or increased reserve requirement ratio, together with binding capital controls, has so far helped to contain base money and credit growth. However, sterilisation costs to the PBoC and the commercial banks may end up delaying the necessary monetary tightening and interest rate hikes, leaving the banking system awash with too much liquidity. In due course, leaving monetary policy too loose will create runaway inflation for both goods and assets.

On the demand side, shallow financial markets, lack of alternative investment channels and artificially low interest rates are reasons why households have been allocating a disproportionate amount of wealth to real estate assets. In addition, the cheap carrying costs of property (with a low effective tax rate) makes people more accepting of low or non-existent rental yields and pushes down the effective supply of rental properties. In turn, this further raises demand for owner-occupied housing, even at the increasing risk of equity loss.

On the supply side, risks stem from the monopoly control of urban land by local governments, which have an interest in maximising revenue and, in turn, artificially pushing up land and housing prices. The recent emphasis on providing more social housing is a positive start, but greater urgency is needed to reform the land supply system, change local governments' incentives and levy a nationwide property tax. A trial scheme is currently under way in Shanghai and Chongqing.

The risk of Chinese real estate heading for a hard landing is low in the coming two years. Economic growth is projected to slow from 2010, as is bank lending. Tight housing control measures will bite on speculative demand. However, if the government continues to run a large external surplus and leave ample liquidity in the economy, allowing real interest rates to remain negative, the struggle to contain the incipient boom in the real estate market will remain intense. Further reform of the land market to ensure increased supply of housing is also essential. We believe in the long-term attractiveness of the Chinese real estate market, but recognise the constant danger of constrained price pressures and stop–go policy measures. Perhaps more than anywhere else in the world right now, successful investment in Chinese real estate requires skilful and well-informed local expertise.

What's happening to Japan? (March 2004)

After a year of above-trend growth, Q4 GDP data for Japan, released in mid-February, showed the expansion accelerating to a 7.0% annualised growth rate from the third quarter; the fastest pace since Q2 1990 (Figure 8.9). Has a real turning point arrived, following progress on restructuring and the Bank of Japan's innovative policies to boost the money supply, or is this just another false dawn?

Looking through the Q4 data, fixed investment spending was a major driver; this augurs well for future production levels. However, almost half

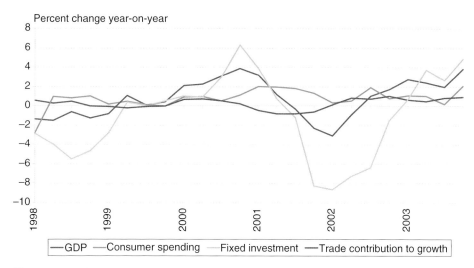

Figure 8.9:   Real economic growth in Japan since 1998
Source: Global Insight

of the reported growth was accounted for by inventory accumulation and an improvement in net trade. Inventory accumulation, or stock-building, is output that has not been sold and, as such, it is one of the weakest forms of growth, because it can actually reduce future output levels. The net trade contribution is a much more solid form of growth, but the big problem for Japan over the last decade has been that it can only generate growth when the highly efficient, but relatively small, export sector responds to a recovery in global trade conditions. It is true that Japanese exports now target China, as well as the USA and that continued extremely rapid growth in that market should support further robust net trade results, but Japan will not achieve sustainable growth until the domestic sector can translate export growth into higher employment and domestic demand.

A key uncertainty, then, is whether the Q4 investment numbers are the start of a trend. More important, however, is consumer spending and Japan has produced a run of reasonable consumer spending numbers over the last few quarters. Together with the resurgence in investment spending and the Bank of Japan's (BoJ) commitment to monetary expansion, this is taken by many to indicate a turning point in economic prospects. Pessimists, however, point out that incomes have remained weak and spending growth has only come about because Japanese households have been spending their stock of savings. Savings rates fell from 11% in 1999 to 6% in 2002 and cannot fall much further (they might even reverse), so further strong consumer spending will depend on a resurgent labour market. But there are still no signs of this: the unemployment rate has only stabilised because the potential unemployed are leaving the labour market rather than registering as unemployed; the total number of employed is falling; average hours worked by those in employment is on a trend decline.

It is not clear, then, that Japan has returned to sustained growth. Paradoxically, that may turn out to be a good thing. If growth were to return and deflation were to end, bond yields would undoubtedly rise and with outstanding government debt now around 150% of GDP, higher bond yields could make debt service costs uncontrollable.

Japan capital values (September 2004)

Since the collapse of the last property bubble at the end of the 1980s, a feature of the Japanese market has been that the bubble did not burst, but rather has been slowly deflating. Capital values declined sharply at first, but then the decline slowed to a much more controlled pace than is typical in more open markets. In fact, capital values in most sectors of the Japanese markets are still falling (as measured by the official land price index) after 12 years of decline. Here, we compare the Japanese market with the UK market, because both are underpinned by rich economies where land is scarce and the capital city holds a dominant position. In fact, land scarcity is more of an issue in Japan (340 people per square kilometre) than in the UK (247 people per square kilometre), although they look similar in this respect when compared to a country like the USA (32 people per square kilometre). The density numbers help explain why real estate always seems expensive in Japan and the UK, when compared with other countries.

During the 1980s, UK office sector capital values and Japanese commercial land prices followed similar growth paths, as their economies expanded. In the UK, however, the peak in values in 1989 was followed by a sharp decline and then a slump, before a resumption of growth in 1993, rather than the extended negative period seen in Japan (Figure 8.10). The UK market lost 62% of its peak value (using annual IPD data) from peak to trough, which compared to a 48% peak-to-trough loss in the aggregate US market in the same cycle (1988–1995), using National Council of Real Estate Fiduciaries (NCREIF) data. The Japanese market peaked in 1991 and had fallen further than the US market by 1994 and matched the UK market decline by 1995. It kept falling, though, and by the end of 2003 was 85% down on its peak.

There is no simple explanation for the decline. Certainly, Japanese asset prices had reached such levels in the bubble period that a particularly large downward correction was required. That correction has been frustrated by

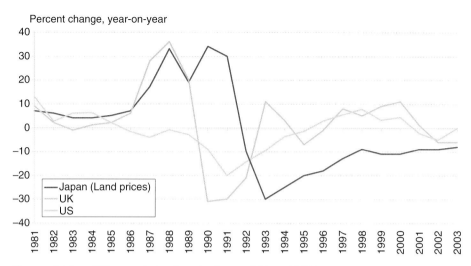

Percent change, year-on-year

Figure 8.10: Office capital values in Japan, UK and USA

accountancy rules that have allowed real estate assets to remain booked at cost rather than market value. This meant that reported capital assets of banks and corporates were much higher than market value, which prevented sales of badly-performing assets by owners who wished to avoid a sharp write-down in their balance sheets. In the banking sector this was particularly serious, because sales of overvalued real estate assets would have threatened some banks' required capital ratios. The result is that the adjustment process was extended and may continue, while historic cost accounting is in place.

The secular downward trend contributed to a breakdown of the relationship between land prices and overall economic activity (Figure 8.11). Using real GDP as a measure of overall activity, this relationship in Japan was strong from 1980 to 2003, with a correlation coefficient of 0.76. But from 1992 onwards, the correlation coefficient is very small and negative, suggesting that the relationship had changed and become much less certain (Table 8.1). The relationship between GDP change and value change remained much more constant in the UK and the USA over the two decades, with the UK registering a slightly weaker relationship than Japan over the entire period, but the USA showing a significantly weaker relationship. This weakening in the relationship in Japan between GDP and land prices argues against the resurgence in the Japanese economy in 2003 translating into a real estate market recovery, unless the structural shift that occurred during the 1990s has reversed.

The reforms to implement mark-to-market accounting are a key part of reversing that structural shift. By reducing the recorded capital value of assets, the policy change should greatly reduce the incentive for banks and

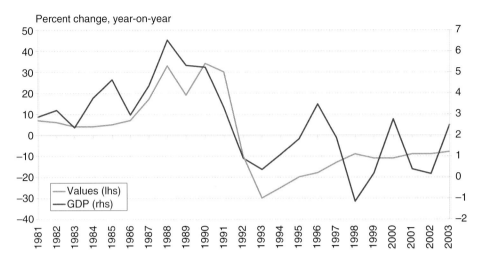

Figure 8.11:   GDP growth and land prices diverged in the 1990s

Table 8.1:   Correlations between GDP and capital values

	Japan	UK	USA
1980–2003	0.76	0.63	0.28
1980–1992	0.77	0.67	0.22
1993–2003	−0.01	0.42	0.48

corporates to hold on to overvalued property assets. However, the implementation of the reforms is being controlled tightly by the Japanese authorities to limit the negative impact on asset markets and mark-to-market for fixed assets such as real estate is still not required, two years after the new regime officially went into operation. A minority of firms are using mark-to-market (HSBC estimate the proportion is somewhere below one-third), but until the practice becomes the convention (loosely pencilled in for 2006), real estate capital values will still be vulnerable to a potential negative price correction.

Without mark-to-market, renewed confidence in a return to capital growth in the Japanese office sector requires a belief that the overvaluation from the bubble period has been clearly corrected. The Japanese market has fallen by so much more than other rich-country markets since the late-1980s bubble that it is reasonable to expect that a floor has been reached. In addition, the trend in Tokyo land prices is towards stabilisation and, although the market remains expensive, it is not as expensive as it used to be. It takes an average person in Japan just over one year and one week to earn enough disposable income to buy a square metre of Tokyo office space. In the USA, it takes just under three months to earn enough disposable income to buy one square metre of mid-town Manhattan office space. This difference is huge but is to be expected, given the much greater land scarcity in Japan. In the UK, it takes an average person around 11 months and two weeks to buy a square metre of central London office space, which suggests that London is slightly more expensive than Tokyo, given relative land scarcity.

But the declines of the national land price series show no sign of slowing (which questions the sustainability of Tokyo's moves towards stabilisation) and mark-to-market accounting is not yet in place. Together, these imply that, although Tokyo is probably close to a turning point, the risks of further capital value decline are still significant.

Bank of Japan ends quantitative easing – the impact on property will be neutral (April 2006)

To combat weak economic growth and falling prices, the BoJ has aggressively pursued a policy of easy money for the last five years: interest rates at zero percent and a massive liquidity injection called quantitative easing (QE). Under QE, the BoJ kept aggregate bank reserves at JPY30–35 trillion.

With the economy emerging from 15 years of stagnation (the recovery is 14 quarters long) and the end of falling prices, the BoJ ended QE in March of this year. The move signals the normalisation of Japan's monetary environment. Forward indicators point to GDP growth of about 2.5% a year in the medium term. Confidence in the property market is returning, reflecting a general sense that the outlook is positive.

By ending QE, the BoJ shifts its focus back to the zero interest rate policy (ZIRP) it introduced in 1999. This will allow aggregate banking sector reserves to fall to JPY6 trillion; this is the amount needed to keep the short-term interest rate at 0%. The BoJ will also continue to buy government bonds at a rate of JPY1.2 trillion a month (to help keep long-term rates low and stable) and indicated its medium-term inflation reference range to be between 0% and 2%.

We expect the end of QE to have only a limited impact on the property market. Although the introduction of QE in 2001 appears to have caused some initial capital value growth in the residential sector, after the rate of bank reserve accumulation peaked (in early 2002), the growth rate of property capital appreciation flattened (Figure 8.12). So, even though QE injected cash balances well in excess of what was needed to keep the interest rate at 0%, the banks did not make use of the added liquidity, so that there was only a limited multiplier effect on growth and the property market.

We also think the impact of QE on asset prices is somewhat illusory, because it coincided with the Japanese economy's 'false recovery' of 2000

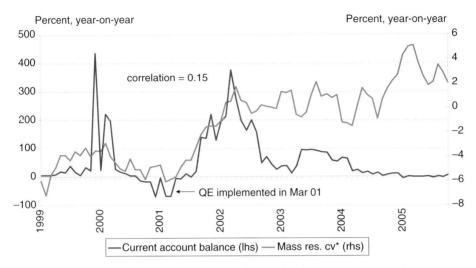

Figure 8.12: Quantitative easing in Japan has had little impact on property
* *Tokyo 23 wards; both series in 3mma*
Source: CIEC, Recruit, IPD

and 2001. This short-lived recovery was reflected in improved corporate profits and a recovery in investment; the introduction of QE could have added some power to this brief recovery and to a slight improvement in property prices. However, the economic recovery faded, as the banking sector's non-performing loans continued to rise and structural changes within the corporate sector were not yet in full force.

The BoJ implemented ZIRP in February 1999 (two years before the introduction of QE). However, Tokyo's property prices only began to recover in late 2004, when structural reforms began to revive the economy and restore confidence; this boosted borrowing, investment and consumption. Liquidity *per se*, as manifested by QE and ZIRP, was helpful, but not a sufficient condition for turning the economy and the property market around. Although the end of QE will result in a reduction in liquidity, the fact that banks made limited use of the extra balances when they were available, suggests that they will not be missed when they are gone.

Given we are moving to tighter monetary policy as indicated by the end of QE, when will the BoJ raise rates? The risk of a sharp rate hike is small this year, as the broad macro environment still requires low interest rates. The risk of falling prices in Japan is not quite eliminated and the BoJ's 0% to 2% inflation reference range may be too low, given that structural reforms (in the postal saving system and labour market, for example) are best conducted with some inflation as a facilitating factor.

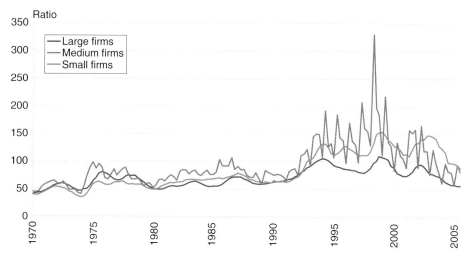

Figure 8.13: Total debt-to-profit ratio
Source: CIEC

Hence, the positive spread that has existed between property yields and interest rates should be maintained; the overnight call rate is expected to rise only gradually, to 0.25% this year and to 0.8% in 2007. The 10-year government bond yield is expected to rise to 2% by the end of 2006 (currently 1.4%) and 2.5% next year. Japanese borrowers are in a much stronger position today, as most firms have de-leveraged (debt levels are at levels last seen in the early 1980s) and restructured. As a result, they are cash-rich (Figure 8.13).

The growing significance of Asia-Pacific real estate (November 2007)

The value of the investible[2] commercial property stock in the Asia-Pacific region was estimated by DTZ (a firm of international real estate consultants) to be around US$4.4 trillion at the end of 2005. Since the total global stock of investible commercial property is approximately $15 trillion, it follows that the Asia-Pacific region accounts for 30% of the universe. The sector make-up of Asia-Pacific is different from elsewhere. While both

---

[2] Investible stock refers to real estate that is owned and traded for the income and capital growth it yields, rather than that in owner-occupation. Investible stock and stock in owner-occupation constitute total stock.

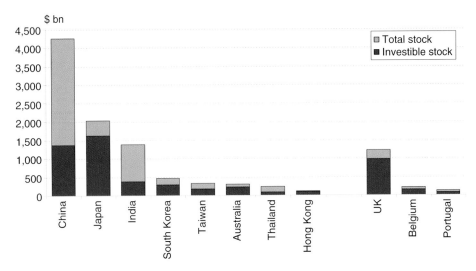

Figure 8.14: Estimated Asian property market size
Source: Grosvenor on DTZ data, 2007

Europe and the Americas are dominated by the office and retail sectors, the industrial sector in Asia-Pacific represents the largest share of stock, at around 53% (against 28% in Europe).

Although China is the largest property market in Asia-Pacific, based on total stock levels, Japan is the biggest in terms of investible stock, followed by China, India and South Korea (Figure 8.14). Overall, China and India have the lowest ratio of investible to total stock, given their relatively recent transition into free-market economies. This said, interestingly, investible stock in Taiwan and Thailand is larger than in Belgium and Portugal, respectively. Stock invested by professional investors is again dominated by Japan, while other sizeable markets are China and Australia.

The implied owner-occupation ratio is defined as non-invested stock as a share of total stock. As a result, more developed markets with a higher degree of investor activity will show a lower owner-occupation ratio than less developed markets. Indeed, owner-occupation is highest in the Asia-Pacific region, averaging around 76%, while it is lowest in the USA, at 53%. Owner-occupation ratios in Asia-Pacific are lowest in Singapore (25%), Hong Kong (27%) and Australia (28%), reflecting the significantly more developed service sectors and capital markets – levels which are compatible with advanced Western economies. Conversely, India, (99%), Thailand (87%) and China (85%) have the highest rates of owner-occupation in the continent, at around 90%, reflecting both the lack of professional investor markets and of a developed services sector.

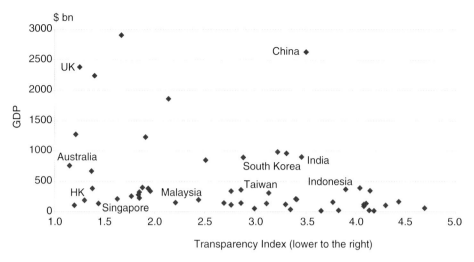

Figure 8.15:   Transparency vs. GDP
Source: Grosvenor on JLL and Global Insight data, 2007
N.B.: Japan is excluded from the analysis

The Asian property market is undergoing a rapid transformation. Investors' appetite for Asian property has increased markedly over the past few years and foreign investors are now very active in the region. As a result, it is expected that institutional property investors and developers will replace government and corporates – as had happened in Australia, Hong Kong and Singapore – as key players and drivers of the market. Also, most Asian markets are characterised by relatively low levels of transparency, unrelated to their level of economic development, which, for many investors, enhances the region's attractiveness in terms of the opportunities arising from mispricing (Figure 8.15). IPD has been present in Australia from 1984 and in New Zealand from 1989 but, in the main Asian countries, an IPD Index exists only in Japan (from 2002) and Korea (from 2007). This sums up the transparency problems relating to property investments in Asia and highlights the importance of local knowledge and on-the-ground participation.

The total volume of commercial property investment transactions across Asia-Pacific reached $42 bn in 2006 (up 182%, against 2003) while the volume of cross-border investments rose to $10 bn in 2006 (up 226% from 2003), around 24% of total investments (Figure 8.16). Although data for the second quarter are not yet available, survey evidence suggests that investment demand in Asia-Pacific is still quite high. Offices are the most sought-after type of property, representing more than 60% of acquisitions. The dominance of this type of investment may be explained by the relative liquidity and transparency, compared with other sectors in Asia-Pacific. Japan saw about 45% of total transactions, mirroring the relative size of the

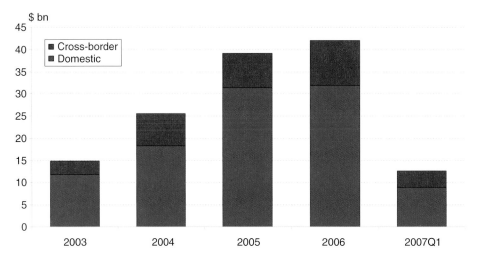

Figure 8.16: Direct property investment in Asia
Source: Grosvenor on DTZ data, 2007

market, but also the renewed strength of the economy. Singapore and Hong Kong were the next most dynamic markets, having the highest ratio of turnover compared with property stock. While Asian investors still dominate cross-border transactions in Asia-Pacific, American, European and Middle Eastern investors are also showing increasing interest in the Asia-Pacific region.

A final point is that the currency conversions to the US dollar have been undertaken at current exchange rates. It is well-known that the Chinese currency is held at an 'artificially' low rate by the monetary authorities. The value of the Chinese market could be 27%[3] higher than stated. This is another reason to expect savvy investors to build long-term portfolios in the region.

---

[3] Estimates of the Equilibrium Exchange Rate of the Renminbi: *Is There a Consensus and, If Not, Why Not?* William R. Cline and John Williamson Peterson Institute for International Economics, October 2007.

9

Real estate returns

The purpose of commercial real estate research, it might be argued, is to enable the businesses that fund it to generate higher, or more stable, returns. Companies may choose to measure the returns from investing in real estate in any of several ways. The most common measure is the Internal Rate of Return (IRR), but Net Present Value (NPV), return on capital employed (ROCE), profit on cost and average annual total return are all used. Within the real-estate fund management industry, average annual total returns is the measure that is most commonly used. The annual total return from a real estate investment is the change in capital value over a defined time period, usually a year, plus the net income from the property as a percentage of the initial value. This approach to measuring returns is popular because it facilitates comparisons within real estate, say between a portfolio and a benchmark, and between real estate and other asset classes, for instance between real estate, stock and bonds. The annual total return measure also facilitates the statistical and economic analysis of macro- and micro-economic factors that generate high returns. The articles in this chapter explain some of the research that we have carried out in this area.

The *annual* total return, described above, is a very convenient unit in investment analysis, because it corresponds to the normal period over which companies and other organisations report their activities to their shareholders and to the general public. However, businesses and investors have very different perspectives on the time period in which they are

Real Estate and Globalisation, First Edition. Richard Barkham.
© 2012 John Wiley & Sons, Ltd. Published 2012 by John Wiley & Sons, Ltd.

prepared to hold an investment in order to gain the returns they require. Some investors require each year's total return to be above a certain benchmark, such as the market average return or a fixed absolute return target. Other investors are much less concerned with any single year's return or the volatility of these returns over the investment period, so long as the average total return in the longer term meets their expectations. Indeed, it is sometimes argued that real estate investors should – and do – ignore annual volatility, as measured by standard deviation, because rents rise by at least the rate of inflation and, due to the high income returns, real estate always produces a strong positive average real return in the long term.

Nevertheless, a central contention of modern financial economics is that investors are never indifferent to loss of income or loss of capital value, even for only a short period. The notion behind this is that investors, no matter how wealthy or secure, never quite know when they will need to have ready access to their wealth. So, if they need to realise their assets, and the market is in a short-term trough, a financial problem could arise. So investors protect themselves against the volatility of annual returns by holding diversified portfolios and, more importantly from our perspective, require a higher average or prospective return from investments that are more volatile. Thus, the greater the volatility of an investment, the higher the average rate of return that will be required by investors in advance of making those investments. Our article of July 2009 presents some evidence that real estate risk, as defined as the annual standard deviation of returns actually delivered by the market, is somewhat related to average total return. The results, however, as in other studies, are not clear-cut. The real estate market is prone to periods of boom and bust, which creates periods of extreme volatility which is not, apparently, priced by investors. It could be that investors simply do not, *ex ante*, expect these events to occur, perhaps because there is insufficient long-term data to draw inferences with any degree of confidence. Or, as property-market anecdote suggests, investors know that, on average in the long term, despite even violent cyclical swings, investors are confident that real estate produces a positive real rate of return.

Explaining real estate returns in terms of risk is interesting from an analytical perspective, but from a business viewpoint, predicting them is better. Our articles of August 2006 and May 2007 take two quite different approaches to this task. The first article makes the very simple point that the average returns on a portfolio over, say, a five-year holding period, are largely determined by the going in capitalisation rate. Those who buy when capitalisation rates are high do well and those that buy at low capitalisation rates do badly. The reason for this, as we explore further in the chapter on yields, is that capitalisation rates are somewhat mean-reverting. Put another way, this article states that, where possible, investors should stay out of overheated markets, despite the temptation of rising prices. Interestingly, the article is quite prescient as to the real-estate crash that was looming in 2006.

In the article of May 2007, we attempt to quantify the impact of GDP growth on real estate returns. We find that the link is very strong. This is not surprising, since GDP growth creates demand from businesses for real estate and, more generally, the confidence that underpins asset values. However, we also find that there are country-specific effects, apart from demand and supply, that affect returns in the long term. These are not well understood, but could include population density or tax legislation or land use planning. In the long term, real estate investors can generate out-performance from a detailed knowledge of these local market effects.

Another way in which investors have traditionally sought to generate out-performance is through gearing or leverage. The use of debt to finance the purchase of assets reached a historic pinnacle in the period before the great financial crisis. Financial theory suggests that gearing enhances returns because it acts as a tax shelter. Our research, in the article of October 2010, indicates that, because of the nature of the property cycle, gearing on its own actually detracts from investment performance. Gearing, in fact, only works when it is carefully managed over the property cycle. Perhaps this hints at a more general lesson; good returns only flow from detailed knowledge of the market and very careful management. There are no free lunches, even in real estate.

Do investors care about the standard deviation of property investment returns? (July 2009)

This financial crisis presents us with a good opportunity to reflect on the property industry's approach to assessing risk. This paper asks if the standard deviation of returns is a good proxy for risk, or whether there are other risk measures which are more important to investors.

To assess whether the standard deviation of returns and other risk measures are important to investors, we need to introduce to concept of the 'hurdle rate'. A hurdle rate is the minimum return that investors require to invest in a project. If the expected return is below the hurdle rate, then the net present value is less than zero and the investor doesn't proceed with the project. A hurdle rate allows investors to decide amongst alternative investments in a capital-constrained environment, including keeping the capital in cash or returning it to shareholders. Some companies choose to be very transparent in assessing risk by calculating an explicit hurdle rate. Others are less structured in their approach, relying instead on intuition and investor preferences. Whichever is the case, a hurdle rate always exists.

A hurdle rate is constructed so that an investor is sufficiently compensated for the opportunity cost of capital, taking into account the time value of money, inflation risk and volatility. The yield on 10-year government bonds is typically used to capture the time value of money and the inflation elements of the required return. The additional return above the government yield is required to compensate investors for the additional chance of losing money associated with riskier investments. This premium is a linear function of the riskiness of the project (the higher the risk, the higher the premium).

The standard deviation of returns is most often used to proxy the riskiness of an investment. Standard deviation is the statistical term for volatility. This is calculated from historical returns. However, the exclusion of other risk measures (skewness and kurtosis risk) assumes that investors are only concerned about the average spread of returns around the mean in arriving at their required return for an investment. The sharp decline in property values witnessed since the middle of 2007 might suggest that investors should be more concerned about the probability of earning an extreme negative return, rather than just the long-term volatility around the mean.

Skewness risk is the possibility that property returns are not spread symmetrically around the average. Rational investors would prefer positive skewness, since this increases the chance of obtaining higher returns. Kurtosis risk is the possibility of extreme events occurring (e.g. the current financial crisis). Investors would have a preference for returns to be concentrated around the mean (lower kurtosis), since this increases the chance of achieving a return close to the average. If these risks were important, then investors would demand higher returns, as the likelihood of a lower return increases (skewness becomes more negative) and as the probability of extreme events increases (high kurtosis).

The IPD UK Key Centres data set for the period 1981–2008 is used to test whether the standard deviation, skewness and kurtosis risk measures are important in explaining property returns. Importantly, the data set includes the impact of the recent credit crisis, where values fell by around 35% between the peak, in June 2007, and December 2008. The data are filtered, to include only returns achieved during 'normal economic conditions'. This analysis is part of a long-term Grosvenor research programme, to identify the correct property risk premium for the purpose of setting appropriate hurdle rates.

Table 9.1 provides the results of regression of returns on the standard deviation, skewness and kurtosis risk measures over a five-year period.

Table 9.1

		Regression Statistics		
Multiple R			0.55	
R Square			0.30	
Adjusted R Square			0.29	
Standard Error			0.04	
Observations			808	

	Coefficients	Standard Error	t Stat	P-value
Intercept	0.09	0.00	35.09	0.00
Standard Deviation	0.56	0.03	16.72	0.00
Skewness	0.00	0.00	1.32	0.19
Kurtosis	0.00	0.00	−4.08	0.00

In this multivariate setting, the estimated coefficient is positive for the skewness risk measure and negative for the kurtosis variable. This is in contrast to expectations that investors would demand additional compensation for investments which displayed negative skewness and high kurtosis. This implies that property investors have given little weight to these variables in assessing risk. However, the recent sharp decline in property values will force investors to reassess their approach to risk, including paying greater attention to the probability of tail risks occurring.

Figure 9.1 presents the data used in this analysis and the risk return line we have estimated. It is, admittedly, a difficult chart to follow and more information is available from Grosvenor Research. As well as the upward-sloping risk return line (which confirms the link between volatility and required returns), Figure 9.1 also shows clusters of returns for a selection of five-year periods. The two periods ending in 1994 and 2008 stand out, as having delivered returns well below those required by rational investors in the long term. The data suggests that, even if investors ignore skewness and kurtosis most of the time during periods of rapid market increase, hurdle rates should be substantially increased to account for the risk of market collapse.

Returns and capitalisation rates in US real estate (August 2006)

Like all investment sectors, the US property market has experienced several cycles over the past 25 years and, while no one believes a major correction

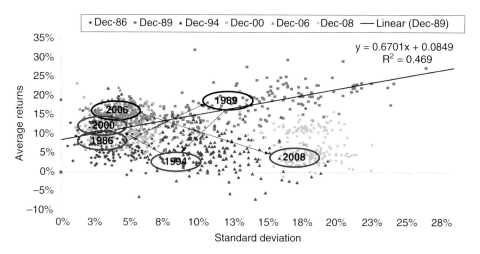

Figure 9.1:   Standard deviation and average returns in UK real estate
Source: IPD UK Key Centres, Ecowin, Grosvenor Research

is just around the corner, numerous signs suggest that returns may have peaked. First, US economic growth is slowing. Job creation has come in below expectations in each of the past three months; the housing market is clearly cooling; high energy prices have taken their toll on consumers; and the equity markets are in the midst of a correction. Second, the Federal Reserve is likely to raise the overnight policy rate at least one more time, as part of its mission to keep core inflation in check. As the yield curve begins to shift, a growing number of investors will require higher going-in returns. Higher rates also reduce the potential of gearing to enhance returns. Finally, it is hard to imagine a scenario in which the main driver of recent returns, cap rate compression, continues. In fact, it is entirely possible that cap rates will actually rise marginally in the coming quarters, more than offsetting the positive effects of improving net operating income.

Assuming that cap rates have plateaued, what lesson can we learn from the historic record? Using data from the National Council of Real Estate Investment Fiduciaries (NCREIF), Figure 9.2 shows the relationship between going in income yields and five year forward average total returns. Income yields, while not the same as transactional cap rates, are closely correlated with cap rates. Because five year forward returns are used, the data series ends in 2001Q3. However, figure 9.2 shows that there is a direct relationship between current income returns and future total returns. Buying when prices have peaked does not pay, on average, because either cap rates shift

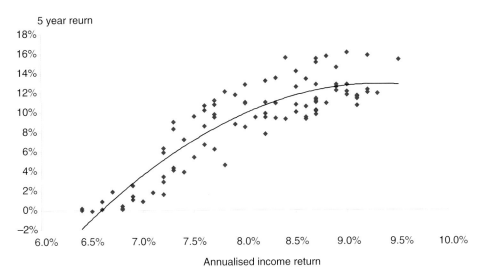

Figure 9.2: 5 Year forward annualised NCREIF returns vs current NCREIF income returns 1978Q1 – 2001Q3
Source: NCREIF

and/or underlying space market fundamentals erode. Since these are averages, some land uses and locations faired better than others, but the message is clear; the lower initial yields, the higher the likelihood that future returns will be disappointing.

That NCREIF income yields are lower today than in 2001 (see figure 9.3) implies that investment returns are more exposed to cap rate risk than any time since 1990. For example, a 50 bps increase in cap rates from 5% to 5.5% reduces total returns by 10%, or approximately three years of compounded 3% net operating income growth.

The observed strength of this relationship leads to two important conclusions. First, even if cap rates do not shift, superior asset and property management skills will be required to produce above average returns. No longer will owners be able to count on the capital markets to produce paper returns that hide management, market and/or property selection mistakes. Cap rate compression, not space market fundamentals, has been responsible for the bulk of returns in the National Council of Real Estate Investment Fiduciaries' (NCREIF) Index in recent years and real estate investors have been more than happy to take the path of least resistance. Second, investors may wish to consider selectively selling properties with limited income growth. These sales have the advantage of freeing capital for opportunistic purchases, as well as minimising the impact of rising cap rates on a relatively fixed income stream.

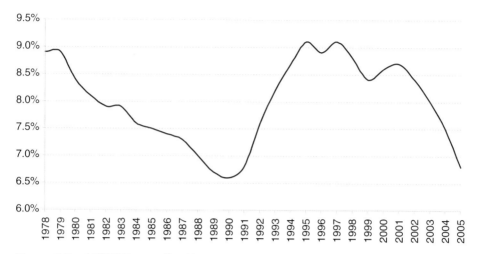

Figure 9.3:   NCREIF annualised income yields
Source: NCREIF

In the early part of this decade, the flood of lower-cost foreign capital and the Fed's aggressive rate cuts were the chief architects of the rapid rise in property prices and the dramatic decline in initial yields. Now that the Fed has reversed course and central banks worldwide seem to be following suit, cap rate compression is probably in its waning days. If that is the case, then investors will need to make even more heroic assumptions about rents, occupancy, and costs to match their current returns. Even if cap rates do not shift because of higher interest rates, slower economic growth will force investors to raise their hurdle rates to compensate for higher risk, reducing the number of purchasers at today's prices.

Just as the US economy has reached a tipping point, so have US real estate markets. The fundamental linkage between economic growth and market fundamentals never disappeared, but was masked by powerful capital market forces. Now that monetary policy has tightened, property owners must make their profits the old-fashioned way, by actually managing properties and fostering tenant relations to maximise cash flows. It is too early to tell how this will affect pricing, but undoubtedly there are a number of fair-weather investors who will seek shelter elsewhere as market returns shift away from capital-driven appreciation to its more traditional cash-flow footing. This will create opportunities for investors who have patiently waited on the sidelines and who are willing to manage properties, not just invest in them. While history does not have to repeat itself, the stage has been set for returns to ease in the coming quarters. Therefore, investors who purchase properties today need to exercise extra caution, since capital markets are no longer moving in their favour and cashflow growth by itself will not be sufficient to generate double-digit short-term returns.

The economics of global property returns (May 2007)

In the UK, there is a reasonably strong relationship between GDP growth and all-property total returns (Figure 9.4). This should be unsurprising: commercial property is not required for its own sake, but to facilitate the production of goods and services. GDP measures the total output of an economy and, as this grows, so also does demand for property.

We decided to investigate the relationship between GDP and property returns, across countries, at a global level, using an econometric technique called 'panel estimation'. What was our motivation for this? First, real estate markets have produced very strong returns in the last five years and there is a growing tendency to think that, as night follows day or famine follows feast, we are in for 'a lean period'. However, if the global economy continues to grow strongly, as most forecasters currently believe it will, and we can show that GDP drives returns in a global context, then maybe the next few years need not look so bleak. Second, in the Global Outlook of

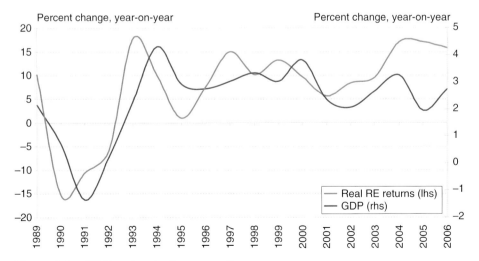

Figure 9.4:   GDP and real returns growth
Source: Grosvenor, Global Insight, IPD

Table 9.2

Variable	Coefficient %
Constant	2.5 (+)
GDP Growth	1.4 (+)
Construction Growth (Lagged 2 Years)	0.2 (−)
UK fixed effect	2.4 (+)
Japan fixed effect	5.7 (−)
USA fixed effect	0.8 (−)
Ireland fixed effect	3.9 (+)
Canada fixed effect	0.8 (+)
Australia fixed effect	0.8 (−)

April 2007, we showed that a substantial construction boom has built up. We wanted to measure how this new supply might dampen real estate returns over the next few years, even if robust economic growth continues. Our model has a general specification: one demand variable (GDP) and one supply (growth of construction activity). Six countries, for which long-run return data are available, form the 'pool' on which the model parameters are estimated.

The estimated equation shown in Table 9.2, is relatively successful in that it explains 73% (adjusted R-squared) of the variance in the returns. Inflation has been removed from the returns, so all of the coefficients are in real terms.

The variables highlighted in green show the generic real estate returns equation. The 'constant' of 2.5% shows that real estate will produce a real return in a country, even when there is no GDP growth. This is due to the fact that, even in recessionary periods, many parts of an economy continue to function, in particular, the public sector. Moreover, recessions tend to be short, whilst users and investors are always looking forward to the next upswing. The impact of GDP growth on property returns is very positive, at 1.4. Every 1% of construction output growth two years ago depresses property returns by 20 basis points. The 'equilibrium' global property return, assuming 2.5% GDP growth and 5% construction output growth and 2% inflation is:

$$2.5\% + (1.4 \times 2.5\% \text{ GDP}) - (0.2 \times 5\% \text{ construction output})$$
$$+ (2.0\% \text{ inflation}) = 7.0\% \text{ (Total Return)}$$

The model also estimates whether countries have, on average, outperformed or underperformed (relative to the estimated equation) in the last 18 years (country fixed effects) and whether a secular trend exists (time-fixed effects). The former are in the Table, the latter in Figure 9.5. The UK

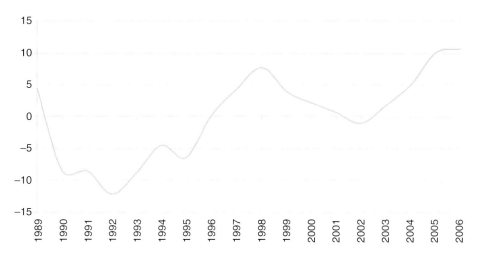

Figure 9.5: Time varying influences
Source: Grosvenor

has outperformed, so that the returns to real estate have been above what would be expected, given GDP and construction activity. Probably, the transition from being a high-inflation economy to a low one in the last 18 years and the consequent fall in long-term interest rates has been greater in the UK than in other countries. Lack of supply due to planning restrictions may be another factor. Other out-performers are Canada, Australia and Ireland. The latter started from a relatively low base in economic terms and became the best-performing European economy over the period (strong growth, set against limited supply). The USA has slightly underperformed, relative to its GDP growth and level of construction, possibly because of relatively high levels of property depreciation. Japan has significantly under-performed, most likely because of massive overcapacity at the start of the period and low levels of business confidence during it.

The time-fixed effects (Figure 9.5) show those periods when property has outperformed or underperformed relative to what it was predicted to have done, because of GDP growth, inflation and construction output. Potentially, the time effects may be a result of interest rates or other monetary variables, though these have not proved significant in our modelling. There is some correlation between the time effects and the stock market; maybe the time effects pick up investment fashions.

What does our work tell us about the future? If the 'fashion' for real estate subsides, but the global economy keeps growing returns should fall to around 6.4%, taking into account the construction boom. If the 'fashion' subsides and the economy falters, returns will be in the 4–5% range. If investors become anti-property and the economy falters, then returns could be in the –7% to –10% range for a number of years. The first scenario is the one we see emerging over the next few years.

Does gearing work? (October 2010)

The impact of the great financial crisis has left a legacy of heart-searching about the use of gearing within the real estate investment community. This is a natural reaction to the embarrassment and real economic hardship of slumped asset values. In addition, recent research has indicated that gearing, even at moderate levels, does not enhance real estate returns over the long term.[1] For these reasons, we have examined the impact of gearing on real estate returns in the long term. The general presumption within real estate is that gearing, apart from in the odd year or so of value falls, is unequivocally good. Possibly this view stems from the theory of corporate finance, which is that gearing improves the value of the firm, because the after-tax cost of capital is lower than the before-tax cost. It is also due to the many individual fortunes that have been built on judicious use of debt.

To analyse the impact of gearing on property returns in the long term, we created a simplified model of a property company balance sheet and Profit & Loss account. The analysis focuses on the UK, so the value changes and income returns generated by this hypothetical property company are driven by the IPD all property index (1981–2009). The interest rate the 'company' faces in the long term is the 10-year bond rate plus a margin of 150 basis points. Two time periods are analysed: 1981–2009 and 1993–2009. In the latter period, interest rates are generally below property yields (cap rates), but this is not so in the earlier period, because of inflation. Table 9.3 and Table 9.4 show the results of three scenarios: (1) gearing is constant, at 53% over the period; (2) gearing is adjusted over the cycle, with the benefit of hindsight; and (3) gearing is adjusted over the cycle with reference only to contemporaneous yield indicators.

Consider Scenario 1 first. Table 9.3 shows that constant gearing over the whole period is unequivocally bad for returns, even after the tax-shelter benefits are accounted for. The poor performance of equity affects the (arithmetic) average total return and the IRR and is particularly noticeable in the risk-adjusted return (average/standard deviation). There appears to be two reasons for this: high rates of interest in the 1980s and the fact real estate recessions, when they occur, are deep and long-lasting. The picture is not so negative for the more recent period (1993–2009): the average equity total

---

[1] Green Street Advisers, 'Capital Structure in the REIT Sector', July 2009.

Table 9.3:   Property and Equity Returns 1981–2009

	Scenario 1: Constant Gearing	Scenario 2: Cyclically Adjusted Gearing/Ex Post	Scenario 3: Cyclically Adjusted Gearing/Ex Ante
Property Return Average	8.7%	8.7%	8.7%
Property Return After Tax Average	5.4%	5.4%	5.4%
Equity Returns Average	8.2%	9.7%	9.0%
Equity Returns After Tax Average	4.7%	6.1%	5.6%
Property IRR	8.8%	8.8%	8.8%
Equity IRR	6.3%	7.8%	7.9%
Standard Deviation of Property Returns	9.1%	9.1%	9.1%
Standard Deviation of Equity Returns	13.5%	10.5%	10.5%
Risk Adjusted Property Returns	0.60	0.60	0.60
Risk Adjusted Equity Returns	0.35	0.59	0.53

return is higher than the property total return and the equity IRR is quite a lot higher. The equity IRR is, of course, not affected by interim volatility of capital values. However, in risk-adjusted terms, geared returns are worse than property returns.

In Scenario 2, gearing is set to zero before the onset of all of the real estate recessions of the period. Over the long period, with these adjustments, geared total returns outperform ungeared total returns, though the IRR is poorer, whilst the risk-adjusted return is the same. Over the 1993 to 2009 period, the ex-post cyclically adjusted gearing provides additional investment return in absolute terms and some in risk-adjusted terms.

Since neither Scenario 1 nor Scenario 2 is very realistic, we created a 'decision rule' which set gearing by reference to global office yields. Why global office yields? First, office markets are the most sensitive to the economic cycle. Second, the global composite 'irons out' a lot of the local market noise and provides a clearer signal of the state of the market. When the composite is below −1 standard deviation of its mean, the market is assumed to be peaking; when it is above +1 standard deviation of its mean,

Table 9.4:   Property and Equity Returns 1993–2009

	Scenario 1: Constant Gearing	Scenario 2: Cyclically Adjusted Gearing/Ex Post	Scenario 3: Cyclically Adjusted Gearing/Ex Ante
Property Return Average	8.1%	8.1%	8.1%
Property Return After Tax Average	5.1%	5.1%	5.1%
Equity Returns Average	8.9%	9.9%	9.6%
Equity Returns After Tax Average	5.2%	6.3%	6.0%
Property IRR	7.8%	7.8%	7.8%
Equity IRR	9.8%	10.5%	10.8%
Standard Deviation of Property Returns	9.5%	9.5%	9.5%
Standard Deviation of Equity Returns	14.2%	10.6%	10.4%
Risk Adjusted Property Returns	0.53	0.53	0.53
Risk Adjusted Equity Returns	0.36	0.59	0.58

the market is in a trough. Gearing is adjusted according to this signal. Over the long term, the *ex ante* gearing adjustment does not work quite as well as the *ex post*, but it does lead to gains in investment performance. The same is true over the most recent period.

It would be easy to say that these results are obvious. Of course, gearing should be adjusted over the cycle. However, as the recent crisis has shown, very few businesses achieve this in practice, particularly in the banking system. Finance is always most easily available at the top of the cycle, just when it would be prudent to reduce gearing. In fact, inappropriately loose monetary conditions are the usual main cause of real estate of real estate recessions. In any case, real estate data is quite easily available nowadays and, with a suitable level of investment in research, gearing can be made to work for real estate investors.

10

Residential real estate

Residential real estate or housing is, arguably, of greater economic significance than commercial real estate. Our analysis, in the article of September
2007, suggests that the total value of the residential market in the UK is
ten times the size of the commercial property market and fully 65% of the
UK's total wealth. In most cities, whether compact and densely populated,
as in Asia, or decentralised and sprawling, as in Europe and the USA, the
majority of urban land (floorspace) is in residential use. One estimate suggests that 90% of urban land is housing land.[1] The aggregate value of the
housing stock is not only due to its physical size, but also the value that
accrues to it from accessibility to jobs and other amenities. Furthermore,
because of the growth of population and income over time, relating to a
relatively fixed supply of land, residential property acquires a scarcity value.
Housing is also a luxury good: as societies get wealthier, people want more
and better residential real estate.

In most advanced countries, though by no means all, the majority of
housing is owner-occupied. However, there seems to be a natural limit to
the level of owner-occupation, at around 65%. Although many governments
promote owner-occupation through the tax system, there will always be a
substantial minority of people in a market-driven economy whose income
or lifestyle does not permit the long-term ownership of residential property.

---

[1] Alan Evans, An Introduction to Urban Economics, Basil Blackwell, Oxford, 1984.

Real Estate and Globalisation, First Edition. Richard Barkham.
© 2012 John Wiley & Sons, Ltd. Published 2012 by John Wiley & Sons, Ltd.

Most recently, in the sub-prime lending crisis in the USA, which triggered the GFC, we have seen what can happen when owner-occupation is pushed too far. People whose incomes are too low or too volatile take responsibility for servicing long-term loans. This is possible when interest rates are low, but when they rise many households are unable to keep up their mortgage payments and therefore default. Our article of July 2010 considers the after-effects of the slump in the residential sector in the USA and points to a revived and substantial increase in interest in renting houses in that market.

Despite the fact that the majority of housing is owner-occupied, the investment opportunities within the residential sector are substantial and potentially highly beneficial to a broadly based multi-asset portfolio. Our analysis, along with that of many others, suggests that the investment characteristics of residential real estate are actually superior to those of commercial property. Our article of September 2007 shows that residential real estate has the highest risk-adjusted returns of all real estate sectors. There are some downsides to investing in residential property; it is difficult to deploy capital in the market quickly, the sector is management-intensive and there is the ever-present danger of negative publicity. In addition, as we show in our article of August 2003, there can be quite long periods when capital value change in the rented sector is quite different from that of the owner-occupied sector. However, good returns and a large quantity of investible stock make the market very suitable for both institutional investment and private capital.

One particular residential sub-market has performed particularly strongly over the last 25 years: the luxury or 'high-end' sub-market. This is a relatively predictable feature of economic growth, with housing as a luxury good, but it also results from the rise in income inequality that has taken place around the world over the period. In part, this inequality is due to the reduction in tax rates that took place during the supply-side reforms of the Thatcher–Reagan era. It is also a function of increasing returns to human capital and entrepreneurship in the advanced economies, which are dominated by a high degree of financial, technological and service-sector innovation and the emerging economies, where production is expanding rapidly. The last 25 years have seen the emergence of a relatively large group of high net worth individuals (HNWIs), the majority of whom have become successful though entrepreneurship of one sort or another, who collectively have bid up the price of the most exclusive residential real estate.

There are also more subtle – urban economic – processes at work. In many of the world's leading cities, certain areas have emerged as the preferred locations of HNWIs. As these areas have attracted HNWIs, local house prices have risen so as only to be affordable only by other HNWIs. As these areas change and become somewhat exclusive, a whole infrastructure develops to support the 'needs' of this group: luxury retailing, fine dining etc.

Sometimes, the inhabitants of these areas gain local political leverage, which allows them to control the development process and negate the normal supply response to rising prices.[2] In other cases there is a political reaction against wealth and affluence which can lead to higher local taxes: for instance, the 'mansion tax' that was mooted in the most recent election in the UK.

We examine the drivers of price growth in the luxury residential markets around the world in three articles: October 2002; September 2005; and September 2006. Notwithstanding the social processes at work, we find that growth of luxury housing values is still very dependent on GDP growth, even if the average rate of growth is higher and the volatility greater. Only in London, one of the world's truly international cities, do we find that luxury housing is not driven by domestic GDP growth but by growth in the global economy, including the performance of the London stock market.

Residential real estate is not only important as an investment asset; it also substantially impacts macroeconomic outcomes. First, the value of the owner-occupied stock net of mortgages outstanding is a substantial part of the aggregate consumer balance sheet. If house prices rise, consumers feel wealthier and spend more. More to the point, in the current environment, when house prices fall, the impact on consumption can be profound and long-lasting. Second, the rate of growth of house prices determines in part the rate of residential construction, which makes a material contribution to overall GDP growth. So, when house prices 'overshoot' or form 'bubbles', there are quite large dangers for the overall economy if the construction sector becomes bloated. Third, as we have recently seen, loans to homebuyers form an important part of the balance sheets of certain lending institutions, whose existence is jeopardised when house prices fall. All of this said, finding the right metrics to identify boom conditions in housing markets is tricky. In some markets, price-to-earnings ratios are appropriate; in others, the ratio of prices to rents works. Our article of August 2005 uses price to rents to diagnose, accurately as it turned out, an unsustainable boom in US house prices. Our article of June 2002, however, points to the difficulties of using such simple metrics in markets that are experiencing structural change. The article of December 2010 continues this discussion, eight years later, in the context of another potentially overvalued housing market: Australia.

Probably the most important thing we have learned over the years about housing markets is that job growth is the biggest single influence on residential capital values. The article of October 2006 shows that, even within a single, small economy, housing markets can vary quite considerably

---

[2] Some would argue that the UK suffers from a more widespread, if less socially exclusive, 'nimbyism' of this type.

between cities, depending on the ability of the local economy to create jobs. This should always be kept in mind when appraising investment and development opportunities in the residential market.

The potential for investment in European residential property (September 2007)

According to the Office of National Statistics (ONS), around 60% of the UK's £6.5 trillion wealth is in residential property. So the value of the UK residential market is around £3.9 trillion ($7.9 trillion). The total value of properties included in the IPD Databank is £192 billion ($390 billion), equivalent to 55% of the total property assets of UK institutions and listed property companies, suggesting the size of the commercial sector is around £349 billion ($708 billion).

Whilst the size of the residential market in the UK is larger than the commercial market, the majority is owner-occupied and not 'investible'. But the sheer size of the residential market means that the sub-sectors which are investible are large, relative to the commercial sector (Figure 10.1). Further, whilst the value of the commercial market does not increase

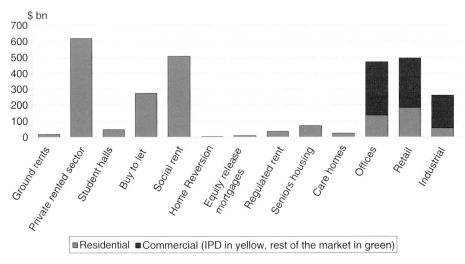

Figure 10.1:   Size of residential vs. commercial market in the UK
Source: Grosvenor on Savills, IPD and DTZ data, 2007

significantly over time, with the exception of retail, the residential market is characterised by sustained long-term capital appreciation.

Official data on the size of the European residential market does not exist, but it is possible to create an estimate. The ratio of the value of the UK residential market to the value of the commercial market is approximately 6.5. Applied to the European commercial market ($8.6 trillion), the ratio suggests a value of the European residential market of $55 trillion. Most of this market is not accessible to professional investors, as owner-occupation is on average 65% of total stock. However, significant opportunities may exist in the social housing market, especially in the larger countries such as France, Germany and Italy. Figure 10.2 shows that owner-occupation is very high in countries such as Spain and Italy, but much lower in France and Germany. Provided that stock is accessible, expected returns attractive and risk manageable, a viable strategy is to acquire private or public stock in those two countries. Government disposals of residential assets and 'corporates' selling off property to finance core investment all represent sources of stock. While Germany is currently the most investible market, acquisitions are also taking place in France and Italy. The size of the stock in a sizeable country is large enough to maximise economies of scale and to justify the launch of specific-purpose-vehicles. As a result, a number of fund managers have recently launched a new plethora of funds focused on European residential investment.

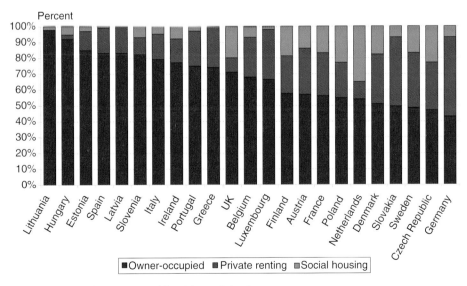

Figure 10.2:   European residential stock by tenure
Source: Grosvenor on local sources data, 2007

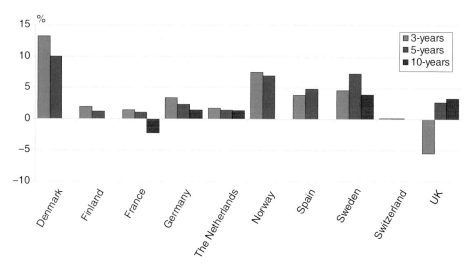

Figure 10.3:   Performance of residential vs. office investment
Source: Grosvenor on IPD data, 2007

Figure 10.3 shows that residential investment has out-performed office investment in almost all European countries selected. Even in the UK, residential has out-performed offices, except in the last three years, during which London offices have produced stellar returns. Similar results occur when returns are risk-adjusted. Capital values in the residential sector are generally less volatile than the equivalent in the office sector. Surprisingly, institutional allocations to residential investment are generally not significant across Europe. On average, residential investment represents around 10% of total investment in the IPD universe. However, there are wide variations across countries. Institutional investment in residential is quite significant in Switzerland (more than 70%) and in the Netherlands (around 45%), but is very tiny in the UK (around 2%).

Why is residential investment not a higher proportion of institutional portfolios in Europe? First, investors may be worried about the ability of residential assets to generate a secure income over time, because of short leases. However, cash flows in the residential sector are generally quite stable and, moreover, there are other segments, such as student housing and senior housing, where the length of the leases is on average longer than in the traditional commercial sector. Investors also think of residential investment as a management-intensive sector. However, companies with a long track record of managing residential investment are probably well placed to do well in other markets as well. Low initial cap rates in the residential market are another reason for concern, but some segments and some countries offer higher cap rates than in the traditional sectors. Finally, investors are worried about a price correction across the continent. However, as it has been already shown, volatility in the residential sector is historically lower than in the commercial sector.

In summary, as competition for commercial property is becoming tougher, investors have to source stock in less traditional, alternative, markets. European residential investment is characterised by attractive risk-adjusted returns, a range of leasing contracts and a sizeable and, increasingly, open market.

Investment opportunities in US housing (July 2010)

The slump in the US housing market did not cause the global financial crisis (GFC), but it did trigger it. Two years on, following a peak-to-trough decline of 32% in nominal terms and 40% in real terms (see Figure 10.4), we review the prospects for US housing.

Since the GFC, the US government has pursued aggressive reflationary policies towards the housing market. The most influential among these has been tax credits for homebuyers. Home sales have surged, just prior to expiration of the last two tax credits, essentially pulling demand forward. The resulting boost to home sales has drowned out the downward price pressures from record amounts of foreclosures and distressed sales. Further helping to stabilise the housing market over the past two years have been

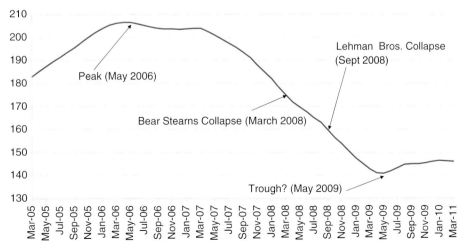

Figure 10.4:   S&P/Case–Shiller 20-city composite index (SA)
Source: IHS Global Insight

foreclosure mitigation programmes and artificially low mortgage rates, prompted by Federal Reserve purchases of residential mortgage-backed securities. Thus, the Case–Shiller 20-City Composite Index posted an increase of 3.7% since the bottom, as opposed to continuing its precipitous decline.

The issue for the US housing market going forward is that the bulk of these stimulus measures have now been withdrawn. The homebuyer tax credit programmes have expired, and the Fed has announced the termination of its programme to purchase mortgage-backed securities. So the housing market is left to fend for itself for the foreseeable future, without the aggressive support of the US government and Federal Reserve.

Forecasts vary on what lies ahead for the market. The more optimistic price projections see a flat year in 2010 and rises of around 2.5% thereafter. Such forecasts are driven by the idea of a sharp recovery in the US economy, with housing, construction and consumption supporting growth. Others see further price declines of between –7% and –12% this year and next, before prices stage a robust recovery. The latter see GDP growth remaining below trend well into 2011. Our view is a mixture of both. We see the economy continuing to recover at just below trend, but with some further weakness in the housing sector due to excess inventory, weak job growth and loss of policy stimulus.

Already, the data is not unfolding particularly well. The latest numbers from the S&P/Case–Shiller 20-City Composite Index indicate two consecutive monthly declines in home prices on a seasonally adjusted basis through March 2010. Not taking into account the adjustments for seasonality, the same index shows that home prices have fallen for six straight months. Although some other price indices have demonstrated increases, it is our view that these prices have been boosted temporarily by homebuyer tax credit activity and will fall again in the near term. In another sign of deteriorating conditions, sales and starts fell sharply from the previous month (see Figure 10.5) – again, from the expiration of tax credits.

In short, activity in the housing market so far this year does not indicate too much promising news to come. However, whilst the market may get worse before it gets better, we do not think that it will cause a double-dip recession. Most of the impact of the slump in housing has already been felt in rising savings rates and construction sector lay-offs. As the market moves through this turbulent period, the economy will continue to grow, slowly adding jobs and rebuilding shaken sentiment. However, very little new stock will be created. Builders will continue to restrain themselves in their production of housing units until inventories deplete and development finance becomes more accessible.

This combination of price weakness and low levels of new construction, set against job formation and household growth, looks set to benefit the

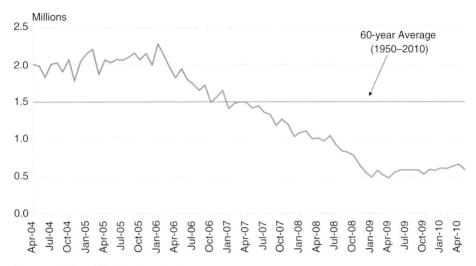

Figure 10.5:   US Housing starts
Source: IHS Global Insight

rental market. A mildly resurgent economy will encourage a younger age cohort to move out of their parents' homes and obtain housing of their own (see Figure 10.6). This segment of the population is set to show strong growth over the next five years. Historically, these younger age cohorts overwhelmingly choose to rent in the 'multi-family' sector. This 'natural' tendency to rent seems to have been enhanced by the events of the credit crunch. Some research suggests that the rate of owner-occupation in the USA will fall from 69% to 65% in the next several years. This means an additional four million households in the rented sector. On the supply side, the boom in owner-occupation of the last 10 years led to multi-family unit production being exceptionally weak. So, against a backdrop of continued weakness in the owner-occupied market, some good investment opportunities seem to be emerging in the multi-family sector.

Trends in owner-occupied residential prices are not always a guide to value trends in the investment sector (August 2003)

As substitutes, owner-occupied and rented residential values could have a negative relationship, because when owner occupation becomes more

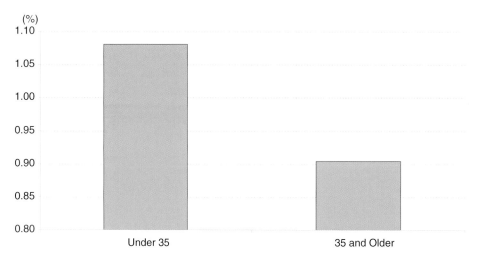

Figure 10.6: Average annual household growth 2009–2014 by age of householder
Source: ESRI

attractive, families move out of rented accommodation and the occupier demand for rented housing falls. But, in practice, a negative relationship is unusual, because assets can transfer between the sectors. When owner-occupied housing becomes more attractive, the value of the rented housing stock rises because of the rising value of its alternative use. Yields fall and investors become more likely to sell their rented stock into the owner-occupied sector. But the movement of housing stock between the two sectors is not free. Owner-occupiers are constrained from selling their houses when prices fall and rental yields rise, because the decision to hold or sell the house is not a purely financial one. For investors in the rented sector, the decisions are easier, although the existence of regulated leases and long lease lengths can prevent investors selling stock out of the rented sector. These imperfections in the movement of capital between the two sectors should be enough to allow relative prices to deviate in the short and medium term, although in the long run we should expect to see very similar trends.

UK market data supports this observation. Official data on the price of owner-occupied housing in London and capital value data on rented residential property values in central London, from Cluttons, show a relatively close long-term relationship (Figure 10.7). There is evidence of outperformance from the rented stock, but the margin is relatively small and is probably due to extended weakness in the owner-occupied market, following the house price crash of 1992. But within the long-term trend there have

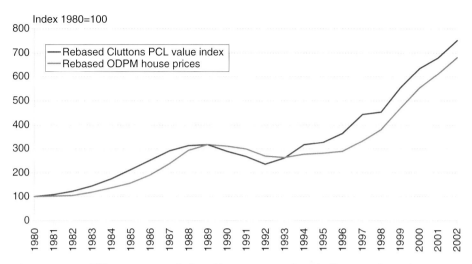

Figure 10.7: UK owner-occupied and investment values in line over long, but not medium, term

been extended periods of misalignment. In the six years up to 1992, the housing market out-performed, then underperformed in the five years to 1997 and has been outperforming since 1998. The London data usefully highlights a major difference between the high end residential rented sector and the wider housing market. Demand in the high end rented sector is based heavily on the flow of expatriate workers within the major international finance and business services firms. Hence demand is closely linked to demand in the office sector in London and this also applies to high-end sector in service-based cities, such as Hong Kong. Hence, it is not too surprising to find that the rented residential sector seems to improve, relative to the housing market in London, when office capital values are accelerating. In fact, residential capital growth is slightly more closely correlated with office capital growth than with London house prices.

In the USA, though, there is even less of a long-term relationship between house prices and rented capital values, based on data from NCREIF and the National Association of Realtors (Figure 10.8). Since the mid-1980s, residential owner-occupation prices have been consistently outperforming the capital values of rented property, so that, since 1986, owner-occupied prices have risen by 97%, while NCREIF capital values have only risen by 14%. Whilst some of the difference might be due to possible differences in the baskets of properties used by the two indices, it seems unlikely that this can explain even most of the deviation. Hence, using trends in owner-occupied markets to assess the investible market has only limited value.

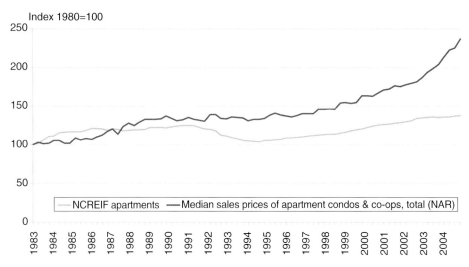

Index 1980=100

Figure 10.8: US owner-occupied and investment values have no clear relationship

How important is confidence in the Asian luxury residential market? (October 2002)

Many leading agents in the Asian market place are firm believers in the power of higher confidence to revive flagging rents and prices. Certainly, stronger investor confidence will boost capital values, but the rental market is more likely to respond to improving fundamentals than higher confidence levels. To test this, we compared the impact of changing consumer confidence in the Tokyo luxury residential market with the impact of changing GDP (Figure 10.9). Our research suggests that consumer confidence has an unreliable and negative relationship with rents, while real GDP seems to drive the market. A 1% rise in GDP today causes an immediate 0.7% rise in rents. In the long run, the relationship is more striking. A 1% rise in GDP today has a total effect on rents of 1.9%. This implies that strategies in Tokyo based on securing standing investment returns are unlikely to deliver very good results, given the relatively pessimistic outlook for real GDP. The fall in the level of real GDP from Q1 2001 to Q1 2002 will feed into rents in the next few quarters, though some relief will come from the rise in real GDP in Q2, 2002. Healthy investment returns will depend on more active investment and development strategies.

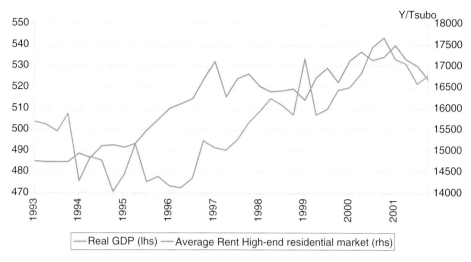

Figure 10.9: GDP is a key driver of luxury residential rents
Source: Bank of Japan/Ken Data Press

Luxury residential – the tale of three cities (September 2005)

Among the three luxury residential markets in Asia, Hong Kong's has the best medium-term potential; Singapore is facing some stiff structural drag that many may not be aware of; and Tokyo's long-term market turnaround has just started.

The Hong Kong story is all about demand–supply mis-match, on the back of robust income growth. Despite a sevenfold income growth since the 1980s, the supply of luxury flats has not kept up with the increased afford-ability and desirability of the population to buy luxury homes. In fact, the average new private flat size has fallen from 53 square metres in 1993 to 43 square metres.

Falling average household size in Hong Kong might have led the planners to think that smaller-size flats would be needed more. But the relative price behaviour of the luxury and mass-market flats suggests that demand for larger and better flats has been stronger. Hence, the price premium of luxury flats over mass-market flats has been rising for a decade. Immigration of rich Chinese will only augment the demand for luxury property in Hong Kong.

Singapore is different. Not only does the city-state not have Hong Kong's favourable demand–supply dynamics; it is also facing some long-term structural drags. Some argue that there is a supply shortage of high-end luxury residences, which are 80% occupied by expatriates. This means that the growth of the expatriate population and foreign investment inflows are crucial for this market. But signs are not encouraging for the outlook.

A strong structural headwind is going against the Singaporean government's massive infrastructure and image-building projects to attract foreign capital. The city-state is suffering from a manufacturing hollow-out, especially towards China, that Hong Kong went through in the 1980s. This process is hurting local and foreign confidence in Singapore (Figure 10.10), because of the lack of a supportive economic hinterland and a stable neighbourhood for the Lion City.

The uncertain structural changes are not conducive to support Singapore property in the long term. While there will still be cyclical ups and downs, Singapore faces the risk of a structural decline, with each market cycle hitting a cyclical top lower than the previous top. This suggests that trading is a better strategy to play the Singapore market than buy or develop and hold.

Tokyo's market is a structural turnaround story. Macroeconomic and structural reform policies are moving ahead in the same direction simultaneously. Even the weak spots of employment and wage growth are showing gains recently. Structural reform progress is seen in both the corporate and

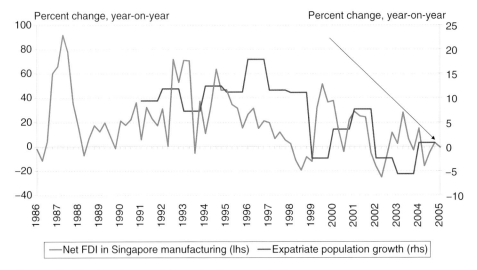

Figure 10.10:   Foreign confidence in Singapore falling
Source: CEIC

banking sectors. Consumer price deflation is fading. Various land surveys released this year have shown that residential land prices in central Tokyo have risen, for the first time in 17 years.

Tokyo is leading the Japanese recovery. It has a growing population, because of migration from other parts of Japan and a growing expatriate population. The service-sector dynamics, which are currently driving internal growth, favour Tokyo over other Japanese regions. The impact of globalisation is also driving a centralisation of business towards Tokyo.

As a result, the central Tokyo market has stabilised and returned to price growth. Further growth will be driven by improving demographics, economic importance, better employment opportunities and affordable prices. Tokyo residential is also benefiting from positive tax changes and a structural change in household formation which favours Tokyo's urban living style.

What drives Prime Central London residential prices? (September 2006)

Since 1992 – approximately the end of the last recession – the average value of Prime Central London (PCL) residential property has risen by 196% in real terms, representing an annual real growth rate of 8.1%. Over the last year, PCL has led the wider housing market out of stagnation, delivering growth of 14.8%. But what exactly is Prime Central London residential property; and is it different to 'ordinary' housing? Like many property terms, the word 'prime' is easier to use than define. Broadly, it refers to the highest-value property in the most sought-after locations. By identifying a representative sample of PCL properties, FPD Savills have been able to track the performance of this sector over 25 years. This is shown in Figure 10.11. For comparison, an index of the average value of All-London and All-UK residential property values is included (compiled by the DCLG); since 1992 All London property has grown by 155% in real terms; and All UK by 130%. For most of the last five years, PCL prices have been static, whilst All London and All UK have, to an extent, 'caught up'. This difference in performance over the last five years provides a hint of the difference between PCL and the wider housing market, which will be explored below. Not that the difference should be exaggerated; as seen in Chart 1, PCL moves in step with the wider housing market in the longer term, albeit with a lead and a slightly higher trend rate of growth.

Why has PCL performed so strongly since 1992; and why has it started to grow so strongly in the last 12 months? On the supply side, over the last

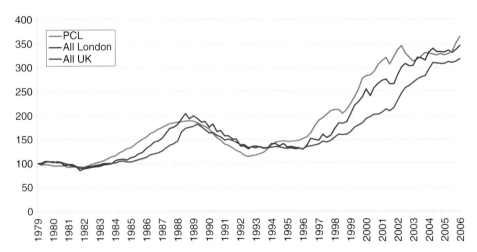

Figure 10.11:   Residential value growth in the UK in real terms 1979-2006
Source: FPD Savills, DCLG

16 years, only 150,000 houses per annum, on average, have been completed in the UK; approximately 0.7% of stock each year. In London, new supply is even lower: 0.5% of stock per annum. It is difficult to establish the supply of PCL property with accuracy, but it must be even lower, since planning restrictions are particularly intense in the prime areas. The effect is to create attractive low-density residential areas close to the one of the highest-paying job markets in the world. Increased demand feeds directly and immediately into prices. In economic terms, the supply curve is nearly vertical in the short, medium and long term.

What are the key demand-side drivers? In general terms, the 'usual suspects': short-term dynamics are provided by GDP growth (providing households with jobs, income and confidence) and interest rates (feeding into user cost of capital), with long-term appreciation driven by population change. In the case of PCL this framework applies, but there are subtle differences compared with the wider housing market.

One difference is shown in Figure 10.12; normally, national GDP growth is the key demand driver but, in the case of PCL, OECD growth is a better explanation. PCL is strongly linked to the international economy, because it is world trade growth that drives key city industries of banking, insurance, currency, commodities and derivatives. The high-value-adding employees of these sectors buy and rent PCL property. In addition, strong global growth creates the 'super rich' entrepreneurs, who buy at the very expensive end of the market and seem to like London for its amenity and governance. A second instance is in Figure 10.13, which shows the relation-

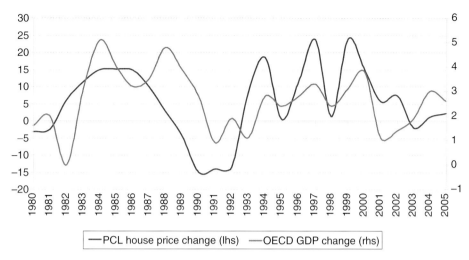

Figure 10.12: OECD GDP growth and PCL price change since 1990
Source: Global Insight, FPD Savills

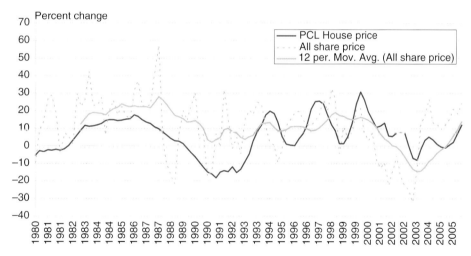

Figure 10.13: UK stock market growth and PCL price change, 1990–2006
Source: Global Insight, FPD Savills

ship between the UK stock market and PCL prices. The 'noisy' quarterly
series has been replaced by a three-year moving average and a relationship
can be seen between stock-market movements and PCL prices, especially
in the last five years. The reason for this is that London's highly paid City
workers' remuneration is directly linked to the performance of the stock

market: the well-known 'City bonus effect'. This is a key reason PCL prices have been static since 2001, and why they have picked up strongly this year. Add to this the fact that London's population has grown by at least 700,000 since 1992 and FBS jobs by 445,000.

What is the outlook? In the near term, it is good: the OECD is growing strongly, the stock market seems to be recovering from its jitters of earlier this year and job generation in London is strong. Rising global interest rates are a negative factor which will dampen OECD growth, feed directly into purchasers' cost of capital and hit stock-market values. Figure 10.11 reminds us that almost all of the growth of the 1980s was lost in the recession of the early 1990s, when interest rates were raised to stamp out inflation.

US home prices looking more exposed (August 2005)

The strongest surge in home prices in American history has left prices looking above underlying intrinsic values in many US markets. In addition, the housing market boosted USA's GDP growth by 0.25 percentage points in 2002, 1.0% in 2003 and 1.4% in 2005, according to Global Insight's US macroeconomic model, and was responsible for nearly all the jobs created since the last downturn.

The frothiness of the market can be measured by looking at the ratio of home prices to rent. The price–rent ratio should reflect the benefits of owning relative to the benefits of owning a rental property, or what an owner of a house saves by not renting. As Figure 10.14 shows, this pseudo-

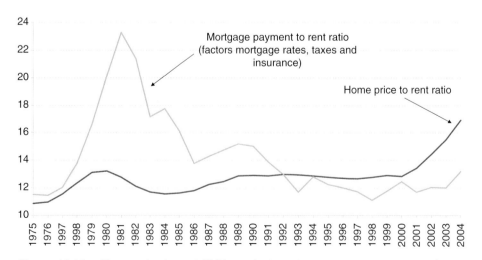

Figure 10.14: Home price to rent (P/E), against mortgage payments to rent ratio

P/E ratio climbed to record highs at the end of last year and has shot up even further since the beginning of the year, because of higher home prices, rather than a decline in rental rates. The chart also shows affordability[3] through the ratio of mortgage payments to rent and accounts for the offsetting impact of lower mortgage rates. Because mortgage rates are expected to increase at a measured pace over the coming quarters, home prices need to fall to keep affordability at acceptable levels.

Why do commentators continue to talk of a UK housing crash that never seems to come? (June 2002)

In every surge in the UK housing market since 1997, pundits have been predicting a subsequent crash and once again UK newspapers are full of similar stories. This time, the evidence looks stronger. House-price inflation is at its highest level for many years and the long-run ratios that map house prices to overall income are becoming inflated. The key measures used are the ratio of house prices to income or earnings. Figure 10.15 shows that both ratios are still well below their last peaks, but are beginning to reach above the long-run average.

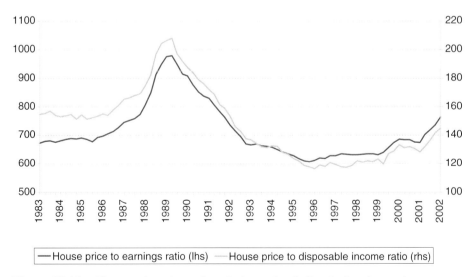

Figure 10.15:   House prices have risen but can rise further before becoming unsustainable

---

[3] A 30-year fixed rate mortgage with a 20% down payment was used in this example. Also, insurance and taxes were assumed to represent 1.5% of total value.

Much higher values, though, would be needed before a downward correction becomes likely. Certainly, house-price inflation of over 15% is unsustainable, but the more likely implication of this is that house-price inflation will fall back, rather than that house prices themselves will fall. A collapse in the level of house prices would probably require a sharp increase in interest rates and, therefore, mortgage rates. Much has been made of the fact that mortgage payments as a proportion of disposable income are still low in the UK, because lower interest rates have compensated for greater loan values. But if interest rates were to rise to over 8% from the current 4%, households would look over-extended and some cutback in the demand for housing and overall consumption would be very likely. Is this a realistic scenario? With underlying inflation around 2.5%, nominal interest rates of 8% plus imply a high level of real interest rates, by historical standards. Only a large external price shock (much bigger than the 2000 oil-price spike) could be expected to cause such a situation, given the Bank of England's record in moving rates early to control inflation increases and keep overall interest rates down, so a collapse in the housing market generated by the general economic situation is unlikely.

Could a collapse come from specific market factors? The current average number of properties for sale per estate agent is at its lowest level for many years and this is undoubtedly driving prices upwards by restricting supply. Falling yields in the increasingly important buy-to-let market could force a number of small-scale investors to sell their properties, causing higher supply and a fall in prices. This remains possible, but while other investment classes offer poor expected returns and little chance for significant gearing, it remains an outside bet.

Box: Have property markets in Asia and the USA overshot downwards?

Cycles in economies and asset markets are generally characterised by an element of overshooting. In property, house prices regularly overshoot on the positive side during the speculative bubbles that develop during periods of sustained price increases, and on the downside when those bubbles burst and households become irrationally averse to purchasing property, because they expect the negative returns of the past to be the pattern of returns in the future. Commercial property markets can be expected to behave in the same way, because many professional investors themselves assess opportunities within the context of recent experience, rather than rational expectations of the future and others use a mix of rational expectations and past experience. The result is that there are always investors who think markets will keep on rising, well after the fundamentals suggest a turning point, and this pushes prices up too far during the upswing. During the downswing, values fall further than they need to, because investor demand remains weak after the markets are ready for recovery. This is, of course, exaggerated by the lead time for new developments, which means that supply is loose when demand turns down and still tight when demand turns up.

This feature of markets creates an opportunity for rational investors to make gains at market turning points, if they can accurately estimate the extent of any overshooting. This is, of course, far from straightforward. One method is to isolate the long-run relationships driving property market values and then assess how far values have diverged in the short term. The GHC team recently carried out this exercise for our principal markets in the USA and East Asia, as these had suffered the most recent volatility. Our aim was to find out whether the downturn in 2001 had driven property markets below their long-run levels. We used an error correction framework that maps property values to the wider economy and is appropriate when there is strong evidence that the market will revert to its long-run trend relationship. Hence, any divergence below the long-run relationship during the downswing can be taken as evidence of overshooting.

The project did show that the sort of underlying relationship we were looking for does occur in many markets. Lack of data in Japan prevented us coming up with anything meaningful there, but elsewhere in Asia we found evidence of under-pricing in the Hong Kong luxury residential sector and over-pricing still existing in the Singapore office market. This second result was a surprise and suggests that the market has yet fully to respond to last year's recession. In the Hong Kong office and Singapore luxury residential sectors there was not enough evidence that an error correction framework applies. In the USA, the Bay Area office market appeared under-priced, suggesting that the downward correction so far has been excessive. In Los Angeles and Washington, DC, markets look to be priced in line with their long-run relationship at the end of the first quarter.

Australian residential outlook – as safe as houses? (December 2010)

Sizeable falls in national house prices were a defining feature of the financial crisis, particularly in those countries which experienced the sharpest rise in household debt pre-crisis (Figure 10.16). A curious exception is Australia. Although it experienced one of the strongest pre-crisis real estate booms and has one of the highest levels of household debt, house prices have continued to trend higher over the past two years.

The persistence of the Australian housing boom has puzzled many observers and raised concerns that there is still a lingering bubble. Against this backdrop, signs are now emerging that the Australian housing market is starting to cool in response to a sharp rise in official interest rates. With

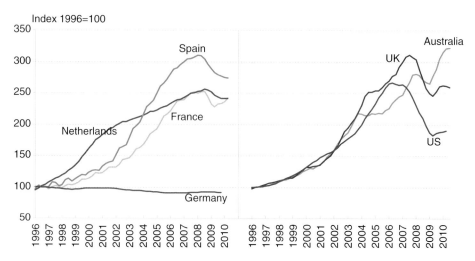

Figure 10.16: International house prices
Source: BIS, ABS & national sources

the standard variable mortgage rate already at 7.75% and with a further 100bp of interest rate increases expected in 2011, is the Australian housing market finally set to crash? We think not.

How overvalued is the Australian residential market? One benchmark that has received a lot of press lately is the house-price-to-rent ratio (the inverse of the rental yield).[4] In theory, this measure should be a relatively stable benchmark of value, as households can always switch between renting and buying if house prices rise too much. In practice, the house price-to-rent ratio is quite sensitive to the method of construction and has little predictive value (see Figure 10.17). In fact, this ratio ignores the structural decline in borrowing costs over the past 20 years. As a result, there has been a marked upward trend in the ratio from the mid-1990s which is unlikely to be reversed.

A better measure of fair value is the ratio of actual mortgage repayments to rents. This ratio incorporates the structural decline in mortgage borrowing costs over the past 20 years and better identifies periods of overvaluation (e.g. the late 1980s, and now). Based on this measure, we estimate that Australian house prices would only need to fall by 15% relative to current rent levels, to bring the ratio back into line with its long-run average – although this estimate rises to 25% if interest rates increase by a further 100bp.

---

[4] This is the measure used by *The Economist*.

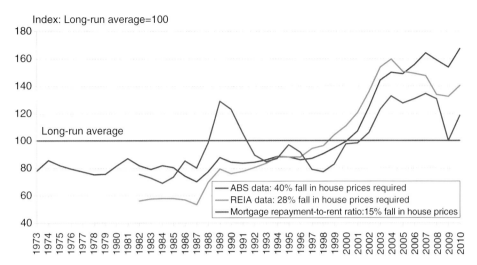

Figure 10.17: Australian house-price-to-rent ratio
Source: ABS, REIA, RBA & Grosvenor

If Australian house prices are around 15–25% above their equilibrium level, how will the correction play out? Given the positive supply and demand fundamentals in the Australian housing market, we think that much of the adjustment will actually come through higher rents, rather than falling house prices. The Australian economy has bounced back quickly over the past two years, boosted by booming commodity exports to China. Unemployment remains well below its long-run average and population growth has surged to a 50-year high of 2.0% p.a., creating strong underlying demand for housing. Dwelling construction has not kept pace. Unlike the US housing market, the Australian housing market remains chronically under-supplied (Figure 10.18). Consequently, there is now significant pent-up demand for new dwellings and tight vacancy rates are now pushing rents sharply higher, with rent growth averaging 8.0% per annum over the past five years.

There are also no immediate pressures from the financial sector. While Australia has a high aggregate level of household debt, Australian banks have been very prudent in their mortgage lending, resulting in very low levels of mortgage delinquencies. While higher interest rates will significantly increase the debt burden of households, this is unlikely on its own to trigger a major fall in house prices, provided the unemployment rate continues to trend lower as expected. More likely, the volume of transactions will slow, as households become unwilling to sell and realise lower than expected prices.

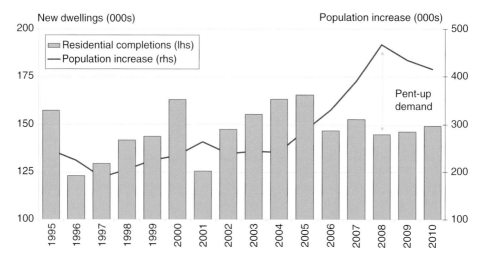

Figure 10.18:   Housing supply and demand fundamentals
Source: ABS

While the Australian residential market looks fully priced, there is no obvious trigger for a large-scale fall in values. House prices will remain flat to slightly negative through 2011 as interest rates rise, but price declines are likely to be minimal. In an environment of chronic housing shortages, much of the correction is likely to come through continued growth in rents and incomes, which will help restore affordability in the sector. This process will be benign, but could take several years. In the meantime, weak capital growth will be offset through strong rental growth and higher investment yields. This pent-up demand for new housing continues to create opportunities for residential development. However, developers will have to proceed with skill and caution in a market that is already fully priced and where buyers are becoming more selective in assessing value.

Australian residential prices – city trends drive performance (October 2006)

Australian house prices peaked at the end of 2003, following their largest boom on record. Despite dire predictions of an imminent crash, the Australian housing bubble has subsequently unwound in an exceedingly orderly manner – particularly in comparison with previous housing cycles. On an inflation-adjusted basis, house prices are now just 1.3% below their peak.

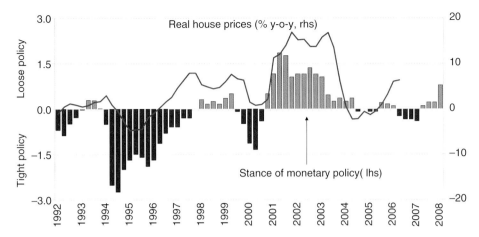

Figure 10.19: Australian house prices and interest rates
Source: ABS

Despite this encouraging performance, a genuine recovery in Australian house prices still looks some way off, given the current interest rate outlook. With the Australian economy now in a mature stage of the cycle, the Central Bank has raised its policy rate to 6.0% and a further 25bp rate rise in November remains a distinct possibility. Figure 10.19 shows the close historical relationship between real house prices and the relative stance of monetary policy.[5] With interest rates now above their neutral level, Australian house prices are expected to remain fairly flat over the next two to three years; while a major crash seems unlikely, Australian house prices are not expected to start to recover strongly until interest rates move into the next easing cycle, sometime in late 2008.

While the national outlook remains fairly benign, the sharp differences in house-price trends across Australia's major capital cities at present suggest that it makes little sense to talk of a *national* cycle. Although individual cities face a common national interest-rate outlook, the performance of house prices in individual cities has varied sharply in the current cycle. Sydney, Australia's largest city, has taken the hardest hit, with median house prices falling (in real terms) by 15% from their peak. At the other extreme is Perth, where real house prices have surged by 55% over the same period.

The increased divergence in performance across Australia's housing market can be partly attributed to the increased divergence in the economic fortunes of individual Australian states (Figure 10.20). Australia is currently

---

[5] 'Tight' monetary policy is defined as when the real cash rate is above its long-run average, while loose policy is when the real rate is below its average.

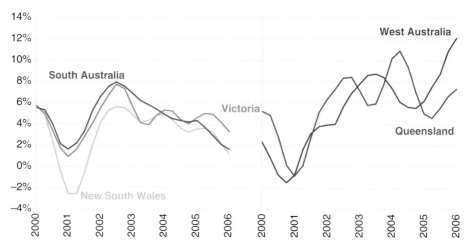

Figure 10.20:   State final demand (trend growth)
Source: ABS

a 'two-speed' economy, with rapid growth in Western Australia and
Queensland (Australia's two biggest mining states) outstripping demand
in the rest of the country, because of their booming resource sectors. Indeed,
the current boom in Western Australia and Queensland is stoking demand
across virtually all the major property sectors (particularly office), not
just in the residential market. As a result, these states have so far been
less vulnerable to the impact of higher interest rates in the current
cycle.

How does the top-end outperform?

Given the sharp difference in the geographic performance of Australian
cities, it is also interesting to consider if there are any major differences in
performance *within* individual cities? Specifically, how have suburbs in the
upper end of the market performed in relation to those at the lower end?
Can investors in a depressed market like Sydney, for instance, protect themselves by targeting a particular segment of the market? The answer seems
to be No.

Using data commissioned by the Reserve Bank of Australia on capital city
property prices by deciles gives us some insights into how individual segments of the Australian market perform.[6] Overall, this disaggregated data
suggests there is surprisingly little difference in the returns performance

---

[6]   Prasad and Richards, 'RBA Research Discussion Paper', 2006-04.

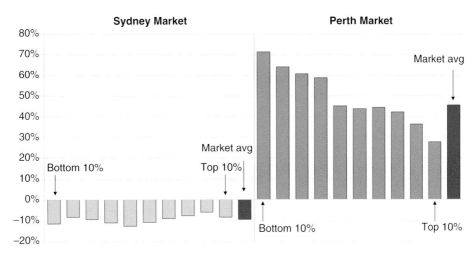

Figure 10.21: City house prices by decile – change since 2003
Source: Australian Property Monitors

between the upper and lower ends of the housing market. Data for Australia's four major markets (Sydney, Melbourne, Brisbane and Perth) show that, while the upper end of each individual city's housing market has enjoyed slightly higher capital growth than the market average, the difference in performance has been surprisingly negligible, averaging just 0.5% per annum over the past decade.

Furthermore, the data shows that, once the overall market turns, it makes little difference which segment of the market you are in. Correlations between individual market segments show there is a higher average correlation between different market segments *within* the same city (correlation coefficient of 0.79) than the correlation between the same market segment *across* different capital cities (correlation coefficient of 0.52). Take Sydney, for example: since the market peaked, the top-end of town has fallen almost as much as the market overall (see Figure 10.21). This would suggest that the top-end may actually be more constrained by issues of affordability and the level of interest rates than is commonly thought. Meanwhile, Perth is at the other extreme, with the top 10% of the market significantly *under-performing* the market average over the past two years.

11

Yields

In Figure 1.2 in Chapter 1, we show the average prime office yield for a sample of the world's largest and most liquid office markets. In retrospect, it is very easy to see that the precipitous fall in yields, immediately prior to the GFC in 2008, was an anomaly driven by a 'super-loose' monetary policy. At the time, however, relatively few investors and property market commentators made that observation. It was more common to laud the arrival of the 'golden age of real estate', wherein the global investment community had finally realised the full benefits of the asset class and were, at last, pricing it appropriately. As will be seen in the articles in this chapter, Grosvenor Research was always somewhat sceptical of the 'golden age' view, preferring to see bond rates as the key driver of falling real-estate yields. In any case the benefits from correctly anticipating yield movements – buying high and selling low – are huge. Timing is the single most important skill in generating alpha or out-performance in real estate investing. For this reason, we have invested a lot of time and effort in investigating the cross-sectional and time-series behaviour of yields. At the time of writing, July 2011, global real estate again seems to be approaching a peak, at least in some markets, as revealed by Figure 1.2 in Chapter 1. Our view is that this is the product of zero interest rates and quantitative easing and that it will not last.

Before we put our research into context and briefly discuss the findings, it is worth making a few points about definitions and data. Yield – or, as in the US, capitalisation rate – is, in theory, the simplest and most complete way of conveying the relative price of real estate in any sector or market. It measures the net operating income from an asset, as a percentage of the market price of that asset. In practice, there are very many variations between countries and property types in the way in which net operating income is defined and measured. In addition, there are very many cross-country differences in the legal terms under which property is owned and occupied. The terms of a lease and their enforceability in the courts sub-stantively determine the security of real estate cash flows and the options available to owners. Since investors price such factors, they affect yields. In conducting international real estate research, it would be easy to get bogged down in a spurious search for an 'international standard' yield. This has not been our approach. We have always taken the best available local data and, where possible, have adapted our models or the interpretation of our results to account for local differences. We have found that there is a growing level of similarity across the world in the factors that influence the movement of yields over time.

Although we have been investigating the drivers of yields since the incep-tion of Grosvenor's research team in 2000, we undertook, in 2008, a major project to model, econometrically, the major drivers of yields in all of the regions in which we operate. The results of this project were only ever published as an internal Grosvenor working paper. This paper is included as an appendix to this Chapter.

A broad conceptual framework has always guided our empirical analysis of real estate yields. In more formal academic research, this might be termed a 'working hypothesis'. At the level of the individual asset, or the sector, or the market as a whole, yields are determined by three factors: (1) the prospects for rental growth; (2) the risk of interruptions to the flow of income from the asset; and (3) the cost of capital. It is, far and away, the last factor that has been and still is the most difficult to 'pin down' theo-retically and empirically. In economics, the concept of cost of capital is clear: it is the opportunity cost of deploying capital in real estate. In other words, it is the return available on the 'next best' investment of equivalent risk and cash flow characteristics. Because of the fixed and relatively certain cash flows that accrue to real estate, the best available alternative invest-ment is government or corporate bonds. So the presumption in research is that, as bond rates change, so, with a lag, will real estate yields. There is some evidence for this, as we show, but as our research evolved we have begun to place more and more emphasis on the 'direct' cost of capital, namely, the cost and availability of debt.

The results presented in the Appendix and the articles of January 2008 and May 2010 show a strong and clear link between long-term bond rates and property yields. However, it is far from clear, as these same articles show, that bond rates are the only monetary variables that affect yields. Growth in credit (or lending), measured directly or by one of the aggregate indicators of money supply, is also important. The article of March 2005 indicates that, in some cases, short-term interest rates are important, because of their link, presumably, with lending conditions. In the article of February 2006, we point out that rising short-term interest rates do not sit comfortably with low real-estate yields and register a degree of nervousness over a looming property-market correction. Although yields are linked to government bond yields, they tend to be higher. The difference is known as the 'spread' and is thought to reflect the greater uncertainty of real-estate cash flows over those guaranteed by sovereign governments. In the article of December 2005, we find evidence that the real estate spread is somewhat similar to the corporate bond spread. In some markets, the link between bonds and real estate is so clear it makes sense to model only the spread. This is the case for the USA, as we show in the Appendix. The articles of May 2010 and May 2006 consider the impact of international money flows on real estate. One of the clear implications of globalisation is that real estate prices are set not only with regard to domestic monetary conditions, but bond rates elsewhere in other powerful economies.

In some of our research, we pick up a link between previous returns and current yields (see the articles of January 2005 and March 2005). This indicates the process by which asset market bubbles are formed. A small compression of yields, perhaps justified by fundamentals, arouses investor interest and stimulates further investment and yield compression. So investors trade on the actions of other investors, rather than underlying fundamentals, so compounding price movements.

Given the uncertainty over which monetary variables drive yields, is it possible to be more definitive on the issue of rental value growth? The answer to this question is, Yes. The articles of March 2005 and January 2008 and the survey presented in the Appendix all point to the central influence of rental growth on yields. Moreover, the best econometric results are derived from the use of indices that measure average rents in the markets being investigated. However, we have found that, in some markets, more general indicators of price movements, such as indices of inflation, work quite well in models. Also, there seems to be some difference, internationally, between the measures of the balance of demand and supply that work well. In some markets, the rate of vacancy is the best proxy; in others, the rate of employment growth works well. These issues are explained in depth in the Appendix.

Although we started this Chapter introduction by stating that, because of the market-timing imperative in real estate investing, we mainly studied the time series characteristics of real estate yields. We have also looked at institutional factors as well. The article of January 2003 shows that GDP per capita can influence the average level of yield in a country, because it proxies for market maturity. The articles of February 2004 and March 2005 show that differences in lease conventions, in particular lease lengths, affect international variations in yield, via cash flow risk. The article of November 2010 explains how changes in banking regulations post-GFC will affect the overall volume of banks' lending and therefore, most likely, yields as well.

Our conclusion, from ten years of research on the drivers of real estate yields, is that we have made substantive progress in understanding the economic determinants of these. However, perhaps the most important findings are: (1) although the broad categories of yield influence are stable, the precise factors in play at any time vary considerably over time; (2) yields are mean-reverting. If yields are low relative to their long-run average, then they are probably too low, whatever the dominant property market narrative of the time.

How far can yields move out? (January 2008)

Mid-2007 looks likely to be the nadir of a 15-year compression of UK yields (575 bps). The second half of 2007 has at least seen a 50 bps outward yield shift, with no sector immune. With the great property party now over, how much further could yields rise? Some recent econometric analysis by Grosvenor may shed light on this question. Our general framework for understanding yields is simple: property's required return (say, bond yields plus 3% risk premium), less expected rental value growth, equals yield. Econometric estimation of this relationship is very difficult, since broader macroeconomic influences are also at play in a very complex and often shifting way. These affect the risk premium and expectations of rental value growth.

We have estimated three plausible, but very different, equations. Equation 1 explains yields using bond rates, rental value growth, inflation, equity returns and savings and explains 95% of long-term yield shift. Equation 2 is based on formal quantification of certain trends and cycles found in long-term yield data. It explains 80% of yield movements. In Equation 3, which explains 62% of the variation in short-term movements, yields are modelled using rental value growth, bond yields and growth of money supply.

Figure 11.1 shows the IPD all-property equivalent yields since 1980 and our forecast series, based on equation 1. The closeness of the two lines shows how effective the model is at predicting yields. The most important variable in equation 1 is the long-term bond rate, which has fallen since about 1992, bringing yields down with it. The other explanatory variables,

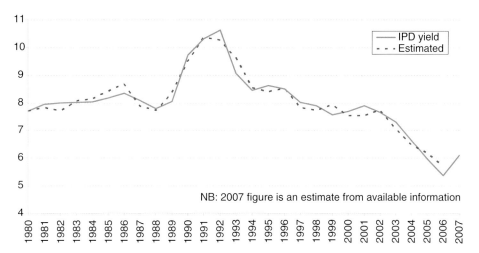

Figure 11.1: IPD all-property yield
Source: IPD, Grosvenor

though less important, also contribute to yield shift: a rise in inflation reduces yields, a rise in rental value growth also reduces yields, an increase in returns from equities increases yields. One surprise in these findings is how weak their impact is on yields, relative to that of bond yields. The stability of the relationships in equation 1, which was estimated over 26 years, should be noted. Interestingly, 2001–2005 is the longest period of consecutive yield falls: the key to the short- and medium-term outlook for yields is probably contained here.

Figure 11.2 shows the 'residuals' from all of our equations. These are the gap between our yield predictions and the actual yield. If the residual is negative, the actual yield is below that predicted by our equation; if positive the model is under-predicting. The residuals show the element of yields unexplained by the equation. Generally, the unexplained part should be random – otherwise it could be explained – and over the 1990s, each of the three equations behaves in this manner. After 2000, however, the unexplained parts of equations 2 and 3 enter negative territory and remain there, with equation 1 doing the same in 2005 and 2006. This is telling us that around 2001, previously long-standing relationships between yields and key macroeconomic variables broke down, at least in part. It is not easy to say what factors caused this overshoot of yields, although the 'herd behaviour' of property investors is a prime candidate.

What of the future? Forecasts created from each equation are shown in Figure 11.3 and are based on an estimated 2007 yield outturn of 6.1% (up from 5.3% in 2006). The assumptions underlying the forecasts are: much

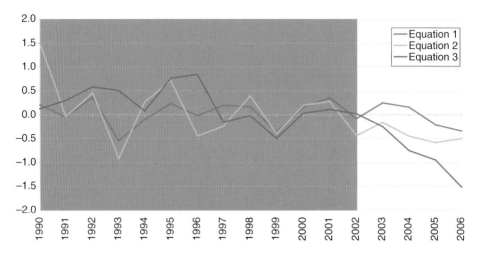

Figure 11.2:   The unexplained
Source: Grosvenor

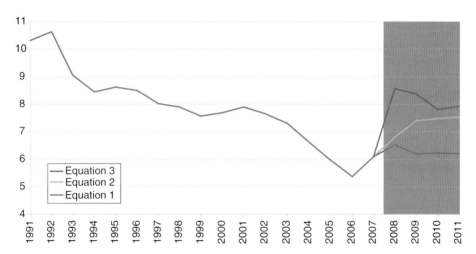

Figure 11.3:   Forecasts
Source: IPD, Grosvenor

reduced growth in money supply in 2008, with some pick-up later; bond rates remaining around 5%; inflation hovering around 2%; savings averaging 3% per annum; returns on equities at 6% per annum; and no rental growth in 2008 and then modest thereafter. Pushed by tightening liquidity, equation 3 shows a large unwinding, with yields shooting up to 8.5% in

2008. With equation 1 the unwinding is more modest, to 6.5% in 2008. Equation 2, the time-series approach, shows yields shifting out to 6.8% in 2008, with outward moves continuing until 2011.

Equation 1 is historically better at explaining yield movements, so perhaps the greatest emphasis should be placed on this forecast. This would give a total yield shift of 120 basis points. Painful, certainly, but not deeply damaging except, maybe, to certain groups of overzealous investors. However, the other models strongly suggest yields are going to move out further, in particular equation 3. Equation 3 contains money supply growth or, put another way, credit supply growth. If the credit crunch gathers momentum, the property market is in for a really hard landing. We should all hope that the Bank of England is successful in its attempts to restore inter-bank liquidity. Finally, to add to the gloom, we have the issue of 'herd' behaviour. It is entirely possible that our models move into a period of underprediction, as sentiment drives investors into other assets. Put another way, we could be moving into a period where yields surprise on the upside.

Bond yields, real estate markets and globalisation (May 2010)

Bond yields are a key determinant of real estate values in the long term. The secular decline in bond yields since the mid-1980s, due to the fall in inflation, has pulled down real estate yields and boosted values. We have presented econometric evidence for this on several occasions in the past. The mechanism is arbitrage across the term structure of interest rates.

Recently, we have observed a second bond market effect, feeding through from globalisation. The story is complicated, but worth sketching out, because it is ongoing and has implications for real estate strategy. In equilibrium, bond yields should be about the same level as nominal GDP growth. Nominal GDP growth is approximately the rate of return investors can expect on real assets. The nominal bond yield is approximately the cost of capital. If the rate of return on assets is higher than the cost of capital, investment will surge and the price of real assets will rise. This is a bit of a simplification, but it is broadly correct, *ex ante* and *ex post*.

Figure 11.4 shows nominal GDP growth for the OECD, alongside nominal bond yields. We can see three distinct periods. In the 1970s, nominal GDP growth was higher than bond yields, because of high levels of general inflation, but also because of the impact of the oil-producing nations taking cash from the Western world and recycling it into Western bond markets. In the 1980s and 1990s, nominal GDP fell below bond yields, as inflation surprised

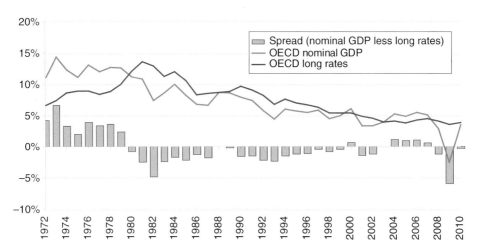

Figure 11.4:   OECD GDP growth and bond yields in nominal terms

on the downside and oil prices were low. In the 2000s, as China and other emerging economies have penetrated OECD markets and recycled the revenue from the associated trade surpluses into Western bond markets, a positive spread has re-emerged.

This positive spread has had an impact on OECD real estate markets. Figure 11.5 shows the OECD GDP–Bond spread against London office yields (cap. rates). We have used London office yields in this analysis, because this is the most liquid and sensitive real estate market in the world. In pricing, at least, London offices can be a considered a proxy for commercial real estate markets in general. Although the leads and lags vary over time, there is a quite clear visual relationship between the spread and London yields. In particular, the big fall in yields that took place in the period 2003–2007 seems to be strongly associated with the positive spread of nominal GDP over bond rates. The jump in yields between 2007 and 2009 is due to the slump in nominal GDP and, therefore, the emergence of a sharp negative spread. As nominal growth has revived and bond rates have stayed low, yields have moved in again.

One problem with London yields is that they are influenced by localised rental pressures as well as international capital markets. To isolate the impact of capital markets, we have created an 'adjusted City yield' by regressing the London office vacancy rate on City yields and working with the residual series. This strips out the impact of local rental pressure and creates a demand and supply stabilised yield series. Figure 11.6 shows the spread and the adjusted yields series. The negative relationship is quite clear and has a correlation of about –4.

What are the implications of this analysis? If, as we expect, the global recovery continues to broaden and deepen, led by the USA and Asia, then

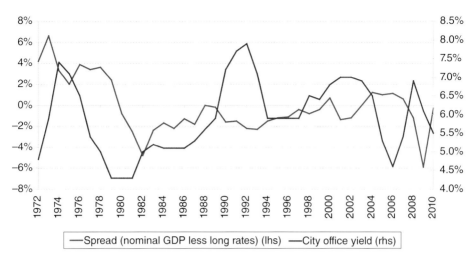

Figure 11.5:   OECD nominal bond GDP spread and city office yields

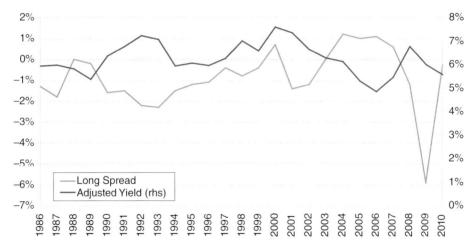

Figure 11.6:   OECD nominal bond GDP spread and adjusted city office yields

nominal GDP will rise above the nominal OECD bond rate and downward pressure on real estate yields will continue. China, OPEC and, indeed, parts of the Euro zone will continue to run current account surpluses. Not all of this revenue can be invested domestically, so it will be deployed in bond markets, keeping long-term rates low. We would ascribe a probability of 60% to 70% to this scenario. Despite the very negative news flow emanating from Greece and the spike in southern European bond yields, the main plausible alternative is a second slump in OECD growth, rather than a generalised bond-market sell-off (though the end result is the same). A negative spread would re-emerge and property yields would rise sharply. In conclusion, it is often said, the real estate is a local business. Nowadays, this is only partly true. In a complex and dysfunctional global economy, investors need to understand the key global drivers of real estate change.

Cross-country determinants of investment yields (March 2005)

The outlook for investment yields is one of the key uncertainties facing the real estate industry at the moment, but for cross-border investors, understanding how yields will move over the longer term has always been one of the keys to success. Some of the strongest returns over the last 10 to 20 years have come from markets that have moved from being speculative to mainstream for institutional investors. With the opposite movement, where markets become speculative after being mainstream being rare, this dynamic has left fewer opportunities to capture future convergence returns. Opportunities do still exist, though, and there is still a wide spread of yields across the global market place.

Working with JLL, we assembled data on yields and their potential drivers from city office markets across the world. We tested them, to see whether the differences could be explained by macroeconomic factors, legal and political conditions, real estate transparency and liquidity or underlying conditions in the occupier markets. In this cross-country comparison, structural factors that do not change significantly over time should dominate, so the results are not necessarily very useful for analysing potential movements over time in a single market. For example, the result that rising GDP per capita reduces yields would not help anyone trying to forecast capitalisation rates in the USA, because GDP per capita is a fairly constant factor there. We analysed the data in a cross-sectional regression framework, but also built in the impact of changes in each market over the last five years.

Our work suggested that a surprisingly effective model to explain differences in yields across sectors and cities is possible; we found a number of potential models that explained an unusually high proportion of the variation for a cross-sectional regression like this. However, there was evidence that a single model to explain all yields is not as effective as a set of models that are designed to explain differences between groups of markets with similar characteristics. Thus, a single model helps explain which emerging markets should converge most quickly with the developed markets, but a model based on, say, the emerging Asian markets, would better explain why yields in Jakarta are different from yields in Kuala Lumpur.

Having said this, the drivers in both the single models and the models based on sub-sectors of different markets were similar. Political and legal factors dropped out, but this could be due to measurement error. Producing a numerical rating to measure the reliability of the legal system or the risk that capital cannot be repatriated is a difficult business. It generates numbers that tend to be unreliable as point estimates rather than ranges and that are correlated with other factors, such as wealth. Both characteristics tend to reduce the data's usefulness in a regression exercise. The result that they did not remain significant probably says more about the techniques of measuring them than their importance.

Interest rates were significant, as expected, but it was the short-term rate that performed better than the long-term rate. Short-term rates are more volatile, so we expected them to have reduced power as explainers of structural differences between markets. But they do reflect inflationary conditions and the level of financial liquidity. More pragmatically, they are also more easily captured than long-term rates, which are less reliable for some emerging markets. Our results suggest that roughly 20% of the falls in interest rates generated as emerging markets converge with developed markets are captured in reduced real estate yields.

Another macroeconomic variable that proved to be important was GDP per capita. Higher wealth seems to drive falling real estate yields. This may be because higher wealth drives the development of the savings and investment industry, which in turn spurs the development of a well-functioning real estate investment market. Alternatively, GDP per capita could also capture most of the legal and political factors that tend to improve as a country gets richer. Using GDP per capita, however, does have important implications for what type of growth is good for the investment market. Strongly rising GDP, driven by population growth, will not be as beneficial as growth driven by rising productivity per person.

One interesting result came from comparing the effect of liquidity and transparency. Both should have a positive effect on yields, so that as markets become easier to operate in, investors pay higher prices to purchase rental streams. Our data on liquidity comes from JLL's surveys of actual transactions in individual office and retail markets by city, whereas the transparency data comes from a qualitative index JLL have constructed, based on the opinions of their local office staff on the informational conditions in the various national markets. The liquidity data remained significant, but the transparency data did not. This may be due to problems with using qualitative indices (as with the indices of political and legal factors), but it may also be a sign that national level data has a limited ability to explain yields at the city level.

At the property level, there were two other variables that appear to help explain yield variation across markets. The first is average lease length,

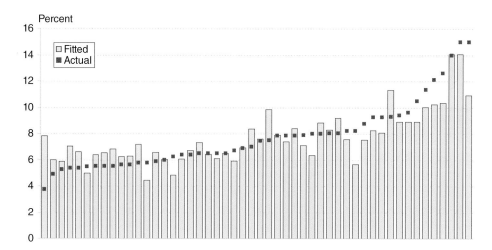

Figure 11.7:   International office yields: actual and predicted
Source: Grosvenor, JLL

which is negatively related, so that higher lease length drives lower yields. The second is the recent path of rents. We used a variable that conditions rental growth for the volatility of that growth. The results suggest that rising rental growth does drive falling yields, but not if that growth comes together with a greater increase in the standard deviation of rental growth.

Summarising the results, yield convergence internationally is most likely to come in high-yield markets where we expect short-term interest rates to fall furthest, GDP per capita and sector liquidity to rise fastest, lease lengths to rise and volatility-adjusted rental growth to rise fastest (see Figure 11.7).

How does the risk of rising interest rates affect property yields and expectations for property performance? (February 2006)

At a recent property investment conference, well-regarded institutional investors and fund managers were optimistic about the ability of global property yields to remain stable, or even compress in 2006. They were not without concern, however, as a rise in interest rates was cited as the risk most likely to affect property values. Over the past 20 years, long-term interest rates declined (see Figure 11.8); the downward movement of the past three years has been a particularly critical element, driving up the value

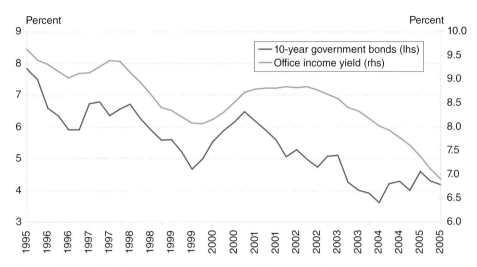

Figure 11.8: US office income yield against 10-year gov't bonds

of property assets and putting downward pressure on yields. Expected returns for property typically provide investors with a risk premium over long-term interest rates, although the relationship lacks stability. (Property investors generally estimate the premium to be between 200 or 400 basis points, depending on the market.) Thus, when interest rates rise, as they will at some point, property's risk premium will contract and the relative attractiveness of property will decline, suggesting that property yields will move out.

The impact that rising rates have on yields has two dimensions: timing (when) and amplitude (how much). With regard to timing, an analysis of the interest rate impact on office yields in the USA since 1995 shows that there was about a 12- to 18-month lag. As for amplitude, since 1995, every 1% decline in nominal interest rates had property yields compressing by 50 basis points. These results are far from being the 'last word' on interest rates' effect on property, but they do put it into context.

Incorporating interest rate expectations into investment forecasts

Grosvenor Research monitors sixty global real estate markets and for each of these it makes a notional five-year IRR forecast assuming the asset is purchased in year 1 and sold in year 5. Rental growth forecasts are based on supply and demand for space; yield forecasts are more complex, because they combine the outlook for local property conditions and wider capital market influences. These include the performance expectations of

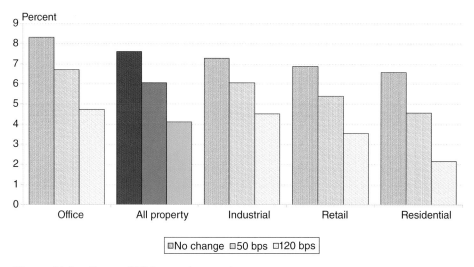

Figure 11.9:   5 year IRR forecast scenarios

competing asset classes and the outlook for interest rates. Thus, to create of a consistent set of yield expectations across a range of geographies is a challenge.

We created three generic forecast scenarios for yields (see Figure 11.9). The three scenarios for each market were: (1) maintaining yields at their current levels (which assumes current interest rates stay roughly where they are); (2) a 'base case' scenario in which yields move out by 50 basis points; and (3) moving yields out by 120 basis points, the 'worst case' scenario.

In the first scenario, the average five-year un-leveraged IRR across all markets was 7.6%. However, the top 15 markets have an average return of nearly 10%. Eleven of the top 15 markets were in the office sector; on average, vacancy rates in office markets in North America and Europe have moved closer to their long-term equilibrium and the rental growth outlook over the next five years has improved. After the steep appreciation in the retail sector over recent years, and given the near-term slowdown in consumer spending, the sector's relative outlook has declined. The residential sector, which tends to trade at lower yields than other property sectors, has also had a run-up in values which appears to have run its course in some markets in North America and Asia.

In the base case scenario (a 50-basis point outward movement in yields), the average return across the portfolio is pushed down about 150 basis points to 6%. This is approaching a level where leverage is less likely to improve returns. However, in this scenario, the top 15 markets still provide investors with an average return of 8.5%.

In the final scenario (a 120-basis point outward shift), the average five-year return is 4.1% and the top 15 markets have an average return of 6.8%. While the outturn in this scenario is not particularly attractive in the light of recent property returns, it shows that the downside risk is relatively limited (compared with equities, for example). This is one of the reasons why so much capital has been drawn to the sector.

How far would yields have to shift out in order for the global portfolio to return an IRR of 0%? By 360 basis points, which implies an increase in long-term interest rates of a magnitude somewhere between 400 and 800 basis points, perhaps. Building an economic scenario that results in such a rise requires a catastrophic event. This appears almost as unlikely as 4% interest rates may have seemed in 1984, when they were 12%.

Can movements in corporate bond yields tell us anything about movements in property yields? (December 2005)

Property, in terms of its risk-return characteristics, is part bond and part equity. With regard to its 'bond-like' characteristics, property may be more akin to corporate bonds than government bonds. Government bonds, backed by the resources of sovereign governments, are generally free of default risk, while corporate bond yields depend on the financial health of the business sector. In fact, it is possible to regard the spread between corporate bonds and government bonds as an indicator of the health of the business sector and the economy at large. Since property cash flows are also linked to the health of the business sector, we investigated the link between property yields and corporate bond yields in the USA and the UK. Figure 11.10 shows property yields and corporate bond yields in the USA. When property yields lag government bonds by four quarters, the two series are highly correlated. In other words, what happens in the bond market is echoed in the property market four quarters later.[1]

It is possible, at least notionally, to disaggregate corporate bond yields into two elements: the risk-free rate (equivalent to the yield on government bonds) and the risk premium (called the spread – see Figure 11.11). In the USA, the spread varied between 80 and 340 basis points in the period of our study. In periods when economic prospects were more favourable, such as the period from the mid-1990s to 2000, the spread was narrow and relatively stable. However, when economic prospects were less auspicious and business risks escalated, during the 2001–2003 period, the spread widened.

---

[1] This refers to the period between 1994 and 2005. The timeframe in the UK was between 1998 and 2005.

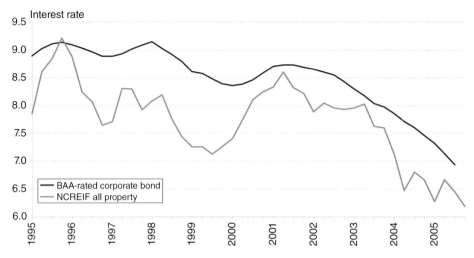

Figure 11.10: US yields with 4-quarter lag and corporate bonds

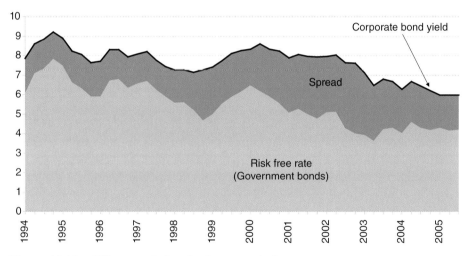

Figure 11.11: US corporate bonds disaggregated

We conducted a statistical analysis to determine which of two factors, the risk-free rate or the spread, had the greater influence on property yields. The US data shows that gilts are most important, but spreads did have a significant effect. In recent years, as risks to the business sector receded, the spread contributed more towards explaining the movement in property yields.

Figure 11.12 highlights the UK data. In the UK, property yields followed corporate bonds by six quarters in the time period observed. However, the

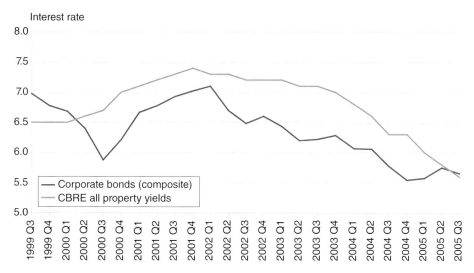

Figure 11.12: UK Yields with 6-quarter lag and corporate bonds

spread's impact on property yields was actually more significant than the impact of government bond yields.

What do these results mean? First, that the corporate bond market has information that is relevant to the property market. Potentially, corporate bond yields are a leading indicator for the direction of property yields, not just because of the correlation with government bond yields, but because they are an index of the health of the business sector. Second, more generally, the impact of falling interest rates has a dual impact on property yields. The direct impact is that arbitrage leads to falling property yields. The indirect impact is that falling rates increase corporate creditworthiness and reduce spreads. This also contributes towards lower property yields.

Capital flows to emerging markets (May 2006)

Given the ease with which capital can move around the globe, we look at potential currency realignments, as interest rates in developed markets begin to rise.

In recent years, the flow of private capital to emerging markets has increased markedly. These have now overtaken official (government and multilateral institutions) flows as the largest source of foreign funds into emerging markets. Overall, net private capital flows to emerging markets are now almost back to the levels witnessed before the Asian financial crises of the mid-1990s. Purchases of financial instruments, particularly bonds (both government and corporate) account for a large proportion of these flows. The increased willingness of private investors to lend to emerging economies reflects a number of factors. Among these factors are a possible reduction in investors' risk aversion and, particularly, the relatively low rates of return that have prevailed in many advanced economies in recent years.

Over the past five years, the major economies (Japan, USA and the Euro zone) have pursued a low interest-rate policy, on the back of weak economic growth. The Japanese interest rate has been near zero per cent (in real terms, this has been zero at various stages of the period of quantitative easing), while the US interest rate has averaged 3%. At the same time, the economic boom in some emerging economies, including Iceland and New Zealand, has brought higher interest rates, as monetary authorities attempt to fend off high inflation. The interest rate in Iceland now stands at 11.75% and in New Zealand, at 7.25%. The existence of a significant and positive interest-rate differential between the emerging and the advanced economies has encouraged investors to borrow in low-yielding currencies (the Japanese yen, in particular) to purchase high-yielding assets in emerging economies. This arbitrage has been prevalent in Iceland, particularly, and New Zealand, where foreign flows have mushroomed in recent years (see Figure 11.13).

The high demand for Icelandic and New Zealand assets had, until the beginning of the year, two main effects; the currencies in both economies

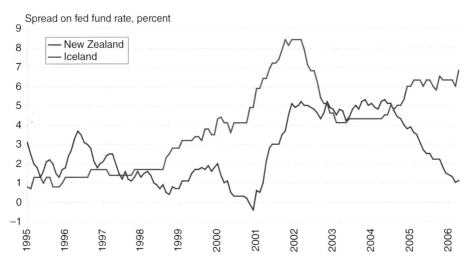

Figure 11.13: Falling interest rate spread
Source: Reserve Bank of New Zealand, Central Bank of Iceland

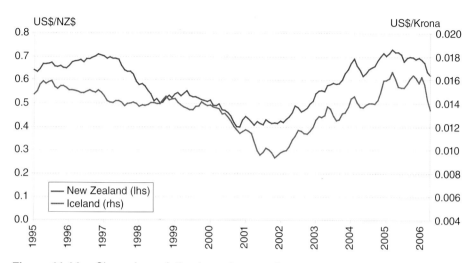

Figure 11.14: Sharp depreciation in exchange rate
Source: Reserve Bank of New Zealand, Central Bank of Iceland

appreciated strongly against the US dollar (see Figure 11.14) and, buoyed by a strong currency, record current account deficits have developed. Given that the appreciation of the currencies is largely due to the favourable interest-rate spread, it is reasonable to expect that a realignment will occur when the interest-rate spread begins to evaporate. Thus, when interest rates in advanced economies begin to rise (as they are now), the interest-rate spread that has existed between assets in these countries and in the advanced economies will begin to fall. Investors might then begin to ask whether it is worth seeking high-yielding assets in emerging markets, if they can get attractive returns closer to home. Such thoughts may lead investors to unwind their arbitrage positions. This will increase the demand for the US dollar and the Japanese yen, relative to the currencies of Iceland and New Zealand, leading to depreciation in the value of these currencies. The questions we ask are, when and how will such a realignment of currency values take place?

The answer to the first question is that the realignment has already begun. Since the beginning of the year, the Icelandic krona has fallen by 16% against the US dollar and the New Zealand dollar has fallen by 11%. The principal cause of the depreciation is tightening monetary policy in the advanced economies; but a recent downgrade of Iceland's government bonds has also played an important role. Interest rates in the USA have now risen from 1% in 2003 to reach 5% (a five-year high). More importantly, earlier this year the Bank of Japan announced the end of its policy of quantitative easing, which has seen interest rates at near zero per cent for over a decade and the massive injection of liquidity into the Japanese economy. The monetary policy-tightening cycle is likely to see investors closing out their arbitrage positions, with the effect that exchange rates in the emerging economies will fall further.

We do not expect that currency realignment will occur as abruptly as many are predicting. As we indicated in last month's issue of the Global Outlook, the end of the Bank of Japan's zero interest rate policy is unlikely to see interest rates increased sharply, or in the near term. Therefore, we expect the attractive differential in the rate of return in Japanese assets and that in the emerging economies to prevail in the near term and only diminish gradually. This will see investors unwind their positions slowly, leading to a gradual realignment of exchange rates. This, at least, is the theory.

One reason for looking closely at currency events in emerging markets is that they often act as a harbinger of broader global events. Substantial capital has flowed into emerging markets' real estate in recent years. What's happening to exchange rates is likely to be impacting property in 12 months or so. In other words, rising interest rates, we believe, will lead to yield decompression and the correction will start in emerging markets. Currency movements are the start of the process.

Real estate investment yields – bouncing up or down? (January 2005)

The real estate investment world is still trying to deal with the effects of a widespread, but not universal, fall in investment yields. Concerns that the market is experiencing some kind of bubble are high and many analysts are rightly concerned that an increase in interest rates will pull the rug out from underneath the market and leave it exposed to rising yields and falling capital values. In 2004, up to end Q3, yields have fallen by up to 80 basis points, producing capital value increases of up to 22% (Figure 11.15).

Short-term interest rates could play a key role in bursting any potential bubbles. As short-term rates rise further, as they inevitably will, financing terms will deteriorate and demand based on exploiting the positive differential between investment yields and finance costs will evaporate. For that play to completely disappear, though, finance costs would have to rise to 6–7%. Short-term rates of around 5% are quite realistic, based on long-term analysis, but the likelihood of the key overnight money market rates reaching the level of real estate investment yields is much lower.

It may be, instead, that higher long-term yields force real estate investment yields up. Investment theory suggests that real estate investment yields are priced at premium (to reflect risk) above the (risk-free) rate on the

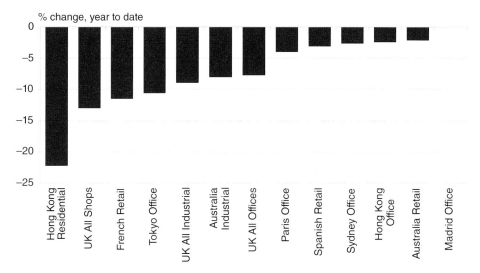

Figure 11.15: Yield shift from end 2003 to Q3 2004
Source: JLL, CBRE, PCA, IMMOSTAT, CWHB

public sector long bond. Therefore, as bond rates rise, so too must real estate yields, unless the risk associated with taking on real estate investment is falling. Bond yields should rise if inflationary expectations pick up, which normally happens in a cyclical recovery.

The main problem with this theory is that the relationship between bond yields and real estate investment yields has not tended to behave the way it ought to. Regression analysis shows that the one-to-one causality from the bond market to real estate has not existed. Further, there is only patchy evidence that any relationship has existed. The history of the two variables helps explain why. Bond yields were actually higher than property yields over much of the last 30 years, implying that real estate investment not only carried no risk, but was safer than a 'risk-free' investment.

We can put the relationship in context using CBRE's unusually reliable and extended UK data. Figure 11.16 shows that UK property yields are not particularly low at the moment and are higher than they were throughout much of the 1980s and 1990s. In the early 1980s, yields were stable in the range 5%–5.5%, compared to the current average for all property types of 7.0%.

The same pattern, where real estate yields switch from being below bond yields to being above, is shown by the IPD UK data and by investment data from other markets. The relationship between the two shifted in the mid-late 1990s and it is worth considering the risk that it could shift back again. This would cause a further – and possibly dramatic – reduction in real estate yields.

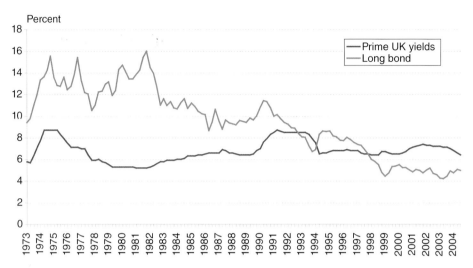

Figure 11.16:   Prime yields and the risk-free rate in the UK
Source: CBRE, Global Insight

Looking at investment data from the USA and Australia (Figures 11.17 and 11.18), a clear candidate to explain the shift was that poor total return performance drove yields higher. After the initial deterioration, the consequent rise in yields reinforced the negative impact on total returns, as institutional investors left the market. The lesson from the 1980s and 1990s is that yields rise when property returns collapse. Shifts in the risk-free rate had little discernible impact and it may be appropriate to think of real estate yields as being some independent target rate, plus a premium based on expected performance. It is important to make a caveat, though; that the investment indices from which these conclusions are drawn were in their very early days during the 1980s and, hence, their coverage and quality was still developing.

If this analysis were to hold, the real estate market has more control over its future than when yields are a function of the risk-free rate, plus a risk premium. Changing government bond yields would not necessarily drive the real estate market up or down. Only good or bad performance would.

Signs of change in the investment market? (January 2003)

Investment yields around the world's property markets have remained firm throughout the last year, despite a marked worsening in the underlying

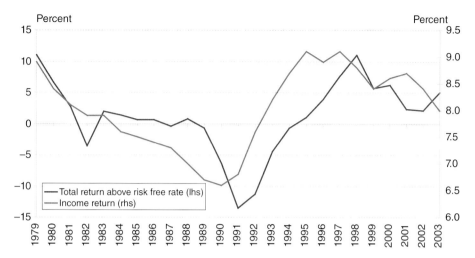

Figure 11.17: NCREIF all-property USA returns
Source: NCREIF, Global Insight

Figure 11.18: PCA all-property Australia returns
Source: PCA, Global Insight

occupier markets. Yields should represent a premium against the risk-free rate, offset by the likely growth in rents. So, with rents tumbling in many markets, the marginal movements in yields imply a significant reduction in the property risk premium. This has made sense so far, given the lack of investor desire to invest in stock markets, but the equity falls already seen

GDP (US$) per head

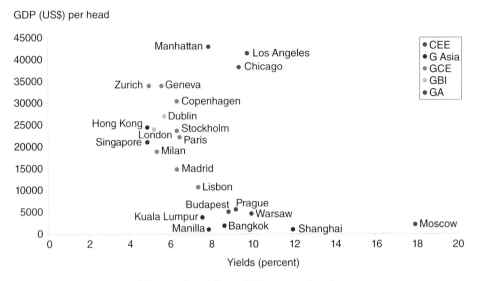

Figure 11.19:   Office yields tend to fall as GDP per capita rises

make further collapses much less likely. In addition, the rent drops that have been largely discounted in many transactions as a temporary phenomenon are looking more permanent in a number of cases. Thus, the outlook for property investment versus stock market investment may be deteriorating and the sellers' market may be coming to a close, amid anecdotal evidence from around the world of deals beginning to collapse, because the realised price is below the seller's expectation. Figure 11.19 shows the relationship between yields and GDP per capita and suggests that the main driver of yields is average income. We may be about to see a shift of the relationship to the right, however, implying higher yields at all income levels.

Lease flexibility and income security in international property markets (February 2004)

The trend in the UK property market away from leases characterised as long-duration with upwards-only rent reviews focuses attention on the impact of adopting different lease conventions. The current system delivers security of tenure to the occupier, but little control over costs, while owners get security of income, but little chance to alter the tenant mix. In an attempt to more closely balance the risks borne by the occupier and the owner, the industry is being encouraged to offer more flexible terms to occupiers. A comparison of leasing conventions around the world shows that there are a range of possible alternatives to offer. Leases could be shorter; they could feature upwards and downwards marking-to-market or indexation to a broad price index; or they could offer break options. Recent trends suggest the move to shorter average lease lengths will continue, even though many retailers prefer the security of tenure from longer lease lengths.

To help us put UK lease conventions in context, DTZ Research developed a measure of lease flexibility that quantifies the impact of different features by assessing their impact on a fair-value yield. This fair value yield rises in response to measures that increase flexibility, because higher flexibility should reduce security of income for a given market environment, causing higher target rates of return and a fall in capital values for any given income stream. As expected, the UK market emerges as particularly secure, under-lining the attraction for non-UK investors of accessing stable UK income profiles. There are other markets as safe, though, with Dublin and Amsterdam marginally out-scoring London on the DTZ measure (Figure 11.20).

UK leases did generally outperform continental European leases, but in many cases the differences were small, partly because of indexation in the euro zone. Indexation reduces the opportunity for investors to gain large increases at periodic review from rental market swings, but the upside is that rents still tend to increase, even when property markets fall. More importantly, annual indexation allows rents to increase more rapidly than under periodic reviews. With a five-year review structure, an increase in market rents can take up to five years to feed into passing rent and this can significantly reduce the value of leases in a rising market. Once lease length drops to five years, though, the cost of lower income security to the investor

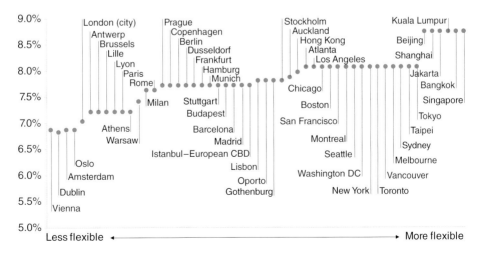

Figure 11.20: Lease flexibility and fair value

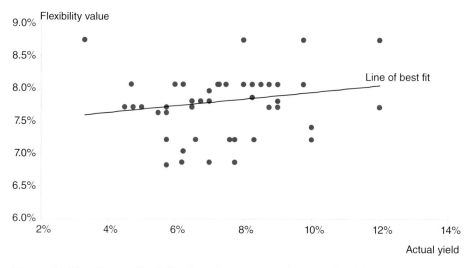

Figure 11.21:   Greater flexibility does lead to some increase in yields

increases. German and Italian leases scored less well than French and Dutch leases, with North American leases further behind. The differences were significant, with US lease conventions equivalent to losing around 100 basis points from the yield on a UK lease.

The flexibility of lease conventions is one of the factors that determine market yields. Higher flexibility and lower income security should increase the target return on an investment and, therefore, the initial yield or capitalisation rate. Comparing the market yields reported by DTZ with their measure of flexibility, we did obtain a positive correlation, but the value was only 20% (Figure 11.21). This is high enough to be a significant effect, particularly in a cross-section study like this, where high correlations are often difficult to obtain; but clearly, there are other factors to take into account. Our previous research has suggested that income per capita is a major determinant of yields and both transparency and liquidity should have a role to play. Building a model to explain the difference in yields across markets is therefore an important area for future research.

Impact of tighter regulations on bank lending (November 2009)

As a result of the damage to the world economy from the financial crisis, banking regulations are set to be tightened. Details of the revised regulations are sketchy, but the direction of change is unmistakable: bank capital and liquidity requirements will be increased.

Banks fund their lending activities by taking deposits and issuing equity and debt. Banks prefer to hold minimum equity capital, because it is more expensive than debt. Interest on debt is tax-deductible and equity investors generally demand higher returns than creditors. Nonetheless, bank capital plays an important role in absorbing unexpected losses and funding ongoing activities. Capital also protects depositors and creditors in the event that a bank is wound up, since the first losses are borne by equity investors. Liquidity, by contrast, is the ability of a bank to meet withdrawals and other liabilities as they become due. Banks also prefer to keep their liquidity levels to a minimum, since liquid assets generate lower returns than illiquid assets.

Whilst banks try to maintain sufficient liquidity and capital to survive under 'reasonable' conditions, the recent crisis showed that the capital and liquidity levels of most OECD banks were insufficient to meet liabilities and remain solvent during a serious shock.[2] Although governments stepped in to bail out the banks, considerable damage has been wreaked on the economy; banks have cut lending, resulting in lower levels of investment and consumer spending, relative to pre-crisis levels.

Two main changes will aim to limit the potential damage of future crises. On the liability side, banks will be forced to hold more capital against riskier assets and more of the 'right type' of capital (i.e. equity capital, which absorbs losses during periods of stress). On the asset side, the banking sector will be forced to hold more liquid assets, such as government bonds, which can be easily sold during periods of financial stress to meet liabilities.

Further steps will be taken to minimise the impact of the 'implicit' guarantee that key banks, deemed 'too big to fail', will be bailed out by the state. As we have seen, banks take advantage of this 'downside insurance' by taking on more risk than they would in a fully competitive market. The 'guarantee' also reduces the incentive of creditors to monitor a bank's activities, allowing banks to raise funds more cheaply than other sectors of the economy.

To overcome these problems, these 'too big to fail bank' banks will be forced to hold higher capital buffers and increase the amount of capital they hold against risky assets. For instance, in addition to requiring banks to hold a proportion of securitised loans on their balance sheets, they will be forced to hold some capital against these assets. Banks will also be required to build up their capital buffers during the good times or, alternatively, hold a layer of debt that converts to equity in the event that a minimum capital ratio is breached. These rules will help the sector withstand future crises.

Tighter capital and liquidity requirements will improve the stability of the banking system by reducing the probability of bank default. These

---

[2] Australian, Canadian and Spanish banks were exceptions, because of tighter banking regulations in these jurisdictions.

measures will also reduce the cost of any taxpayer involvement, since a higher proportion of losses will be incurred by shareholders. However, these tighter regulations will push up the banking sector's cost of capital. These higher costs will be passed on to lenders via higher interest rates and reduced lending. This will take place even when conditions return to normal. The regulatory scope will also be extended, to include the unregulated sector of hedge funds, off-balance sheet vehicles and investment banks. However, the different regulatory response across the world is likely to see 'footloose' borrowers moving to less regulated jurisdictions.

Tighter regulations will force companies to look for other sources of finance. Large firms will raise more finance through equity and bond markets. This is already taking place across the UK, where the corporate sector is using equity and bond finance to repay loans (Figure 11.22). Low interest rates and quantitative easing are aiding this adjustment, since investors earn much higher returns from corporate securities than cash. However, this won't last forever.

The real losers from the contraction in lending are likely to be small to medium companies, because of their inability to access bond and equity markets. Therefore, on balance, tighter regulations are likely to lead to lower levels of entrepreneurship and investment, because these companies will be forced to fund their expansion out of profits. This will lead to lower levels of trend economic growth in the future.

In the real estate sector, mezzanine, other types of niche finance, and higher equity injections will play an increasing role in plugging the funding

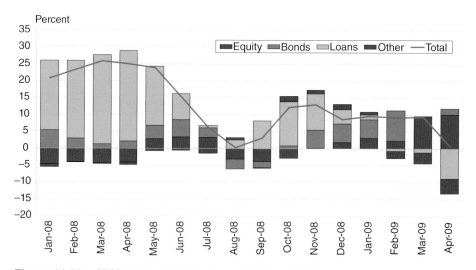

Figure 11.22:   UK banks' capital raising in 2008 and 2009
Source: Bank of England

gap. This mezzanine finance is likely to be sourced from investors, seeking higher returns in a low-inflation and interest rate environment. However, reduced loan to value ratios and higher mezzanine and equity financing will lead to lower-geared returns. This is not good news for investors looking for high returns. On the other hand, a real estate sector that is not geared to the hilt may force investors to focus on property's real attribute: namely, income returns rather than capital growth.

Appendix

Modelling global real estate yields (November 2008)

For each of Grosvenor's markets we have estimated an equation to explain yield movements. The choice of explanatory variables was driven by theory, but also by judgement and exploratory analysis. The methodology and model specification was often dictated by the nature of the available data. For instance, the lack of volatility in yield data, from valuation smoothing, means that many of the explanatory variables need to be similarly smoothed: to do this a variety of moving averages and other transformations have been employed. Where there was data for several markets, i.e. cities in a country or sectors in a country, panel estimation techniques were used, because these provide more robust estimates of the underlying relationships. For the USA, national level property sector data was used and in France, Spain and Australia the panel was based on one sector in a number of cities. The periodicity of the models was determined by the data: both annual and quarterly models, spanning different time periods, were estimated. In most cases, the yield was directly modelled as a function of a number of explanatory variables, but in the case of the USA yield spreads, or the difference between yields and the risk-free rate, was used as the dependent variable.

The quality of yield data varies between countries and it is highly nuanced. In some cases the data is derived from transactions; in other cases, it refers to the spot values of 'hypothetical' prime properties. We discuss the data sources in more depth in the individual country sections. This is not the only factor that makes international yield modelling difficult. Broader

Table 11A.1: Explanatory variables across the world

	Occupier market factors			Capital market factors			
	Vacancy / stock	Employment / GDP	Rents / inflation	Credit / money flows	Other asset performance	Exchange rate	Bond / interest rate
United States	✓✓			✓✓✓		✓	✓
Australia			✓✓✓	✓	✓✓*		✓
France Retail		✓		✓✓			
France Offices			✓	✓✓			✓✓✓
Spain	✓		✓	✓✓✓			✓✓
Ireland			✓	✓✓			✓✓✓
UK		✓	✓✓✓		✓✓		✓✓✓
Japan			✓✓✓				
Hong Kong			✓✓✓				✓✓

macroeconomic influences are also at play, in very complex and often shifting ways, affecting the risk premium and rental growth.

Table 11A.1 shows all of the markets where, in our judgement, satisfactory equations were estimated and the key variables were found to be statistically significant in their explanatory power. Where a variable was found to have a small impact, it is marked with one tick; a medium impact would be two ticks; and a substantial impact is shown by three ticks. Given the caveats above, it was very interesting to see that, in broad terms, similar explanatory variables were found to be significant in the individual markets.

The rest of this appendix looks in greater detail at the individual equations for each country, with a discussion on the data used, the equation specification and the results. A technical appendix at the end contains the full equation specifications and statistics. The appendix finishes by summing up the key results.

United States

The yield data we used in the US was provided by Real Capital Analytics (RCA): the series reflects the capitalisation rates from all deals closed in a particular quarter for a given property type. Since RCA collects information on deals as small as $2.5m, RCA capitalisation rates represent a broader spectrum of properties than those found in the NCREIF database. In addition to data on yields, the equation uses times series information on 10-year Treasury yields, commercial mortgage flows adjusted for inflation, trade-weighted exchange rates and vacancy rates by property type provided by REIS. Lags and moving averages were used, to try and mimic investor and market behaviour, as described above.

Because there is a relatively clear long-run relationship between Treasury yield and real estate capitalisation rates, which has been well described in previous research, the dependant variable in the USA was specified as the risk premium (e.g. the gap between yields and 10-year Treasury yields). Panel estimation techniques were used. The risk premium was found to be influenced by three main factors, shown in Table 11A.2. Changes in the exchange rate and changes in mortgage amounts influence yields similarly. The impact of vacancy is sector-specific: vacancy has a bigger, 0.05, impact on retail yields than for apartments at 0.02 or offices at 0.007. The 'fixed effects' variable allows the model to control for idiosyncratic factors not captured elsewhere in the model: here, it may be thought of as the varying risk premium of each sector, relative to the others.

The exchange-rate variable measures the change in the exchange rate between one period and the next, lagged by one period. The mortgage variable is in levels and is a four-quarter moving average, with the same data for offices and retail and a separate residential mortgage series for apartments. The vacancy is the average of the last two quarters' vacancy, relative to a moving average of the last 12 quarters. Figures 11A.1, 11A.2 and 11A.3 show the explanatory variables against the dependent variable.

The results were in line with our prior expectations. A positive change in commercial mortgage commitments should reduce the risk premium and

Table 11A.2:   Explanatory variables

Variable name	Coefficient	Historic range of variable[1]
Effective exchange rate	−0.027	0.01
Mortgage amounts	−0.00007	87
Vacancy relative to trend for: Apartments	0.02	0.7
Offices	0.007	0.8
Retail	0.05	0.2
Fixed effect – Apartment	−0.02	
Fixed effect – Offices	0.03	
Fixed effect – Retail	−0.01	

(1) The historic range of the variable combined with the coefficient gives an indication of how large the change in the explanatory variable has been in the size of changes in the dependent variable.

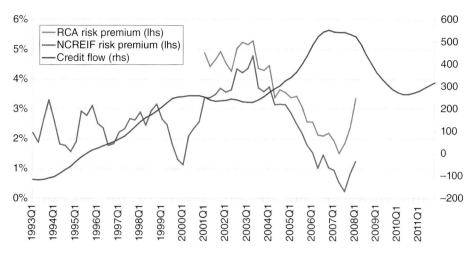

Figure 11A.1: US risk premium vs. credit

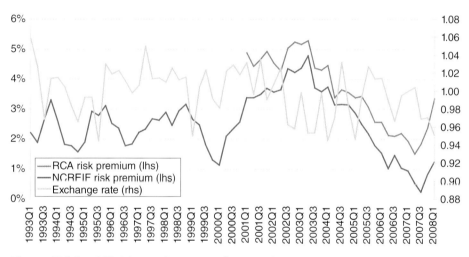

Figure 11A.2: US risk premium vs. exchange rate

so have a negative sign, which is what we found. The higher the vacancy rate relative to its long-term trend, the higher the required risk premium; again, confirmed by the data. Finally, a positive sign is expected on the exchange-rate variable, as a stronger dollar makes US properties less attractive to foreign investors and also encourages foreign investors to sell US holdings, to take advantage of favourable pricing. This was confirmed.

Commercial mortgage flows were found to be significant across the sectors. More liquidity leads to lower spreads. In other words, increased capital flows are a proxy for lower cost of capital and investor interest in the asset class. Although the models were estimated on RCA data, the

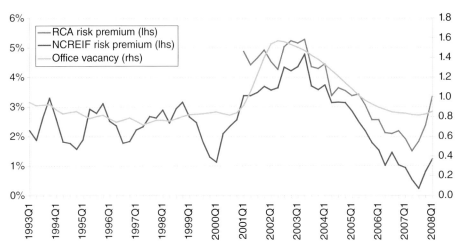

Figure 11A.3:   US office risk premium vs. vacancy

charts show the risk premium estimated from both the RCA and NCREIF data. In both series, the risk premium falls from 2003 Q3 through to the end of 2007. Mortgage amounts were relatively flat from 1999 through to 2003, before they began their rapid expansion through to 2007. Starting in 2007, lending began to tighten in the first rounds of the GFC.

The change in the trade-weighted exchange rate was also found to influence spreads. The weaker the dollar relative to the previous quarter's exchange rate, the narrower the spread, all else being equal. Our interpretation is that as the dollar weakens or strengthens, the US property market becomes more (or less) attractive to foreign buyers.

The difference between a one-year moving average of vacancy rates and its long-term trend also helps to explain yield spreads. When this difference is positive, it implies that space market conditions are weaker than their long-term equilibrium levels, so markets are more risky and spreads higher. When the two-quarter moving average is below its long-term trend, it implies that the market is tightening, rents are rising and spreads decreasing. The long-term trend is defined as a three-year moving average for the office and retail sector and a two-year moving average for apartments, because of due to multifamilies' shorter leases and, potentially, more volatile cash flow.

The equation for the US yield spread explains 90% of the movement, although the use of fixed effects pushes the explanatory power up. Nonetheless, the results are useful, in that they quantify many of the key driver variables factors and the time that it takes before investor behaviour modifies market prices.

Australia

For the Australian market, an office yield equation was constructed using a quarterly series of average prime office yields. Since prime office assets in Australia's major CBDs are, in investment terms, close substitutes a pooled equation was estimated for the three markets of Brisbane, Sydney and Perth, where long-run data was readily available. The equation is estimated over the period 1985 Q1 to 2008 Q1.

The equation explains the level of Australian yields, using the Australian real 10-year bond yield, the level of rental growth in each market, business credit growth and, somewhat surprisingly, UK office yields. A 'fixed-effect' variable was included for each market, to capture the different average level of yields in each city (e.g., reflecting differing market risk premiums, due to different market size and liquidity). Not surprisingly, Sydney was found to have the lowest risk premium, whilst Perth had the highest. The equation results are shown in table 11A.3. The relationship between yields and the individual explanatory variables is shown in Figures 11A.4, 11A.5, 11A.6, 11A.7 and 11A.8.

The real risk-free rate was found to explain most of the movement in Australian office yields (see Figure 11A.4). This was constructed using the nominal bond rate and subtracting the tax-adjusted inflation rate. This has a positive coefficient of 0.089, which means that a 1% increase in the real bond rate would be associated with a 0.9% increase in the office yield.

As might be expected, the rental growth outlook in each market was also a major driver of Australian yield movements. A three-year moving average of rent growth was used to proxy the state of the rental cycle in each market. Figure 11A.5 shows yields and the rental change variable for the Sydney market. The equation estimates that a 1% increase in rental growth is typically associated with a 30-basis-point inward yield shift.

International influences also seem to play an important role in determining Australian office yields. Australian office yields were found to be highly correlated with shifts in global office yields, as captured by CBRE's UK prime office yield series (Figure 11A.6). This is not that surprising, given that office demand has become increasingly correlated globally and given the increasing global investor base for office assets. UK office yields are good general proxy for global shifts in investor sentiment toward the office sector. The chart shows UK prime office yields against Sydney office yields. Since the early 1990s, the Australia yield has tracked the UK series, when it is lagged by a year (see Figure 11A.6). UK yields were found to have a statistically significant leading relationship with Australian office yields. Overall, a sustained 100-basis-point movement in UK yields were found to raise

Table 11A.3:   Explanatory variables

Variable name	Coefficient	Historic range of variable
UK CBRE prime office yield	0.19	3.7
Real Bond yield	0.089	6.0
Three year moving average of rental growth	−0.034	30
Business Credit	−0.007	39
Fixed effect − Brisbane	−0.13	
Fixed effect − Perth	0.87	
Fixed effect − Sydney	−0.74	

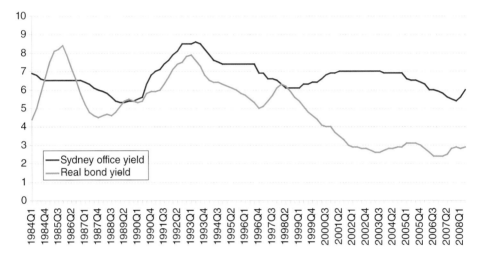

Figure 11A.4:   Sydney office yield and real bond yield

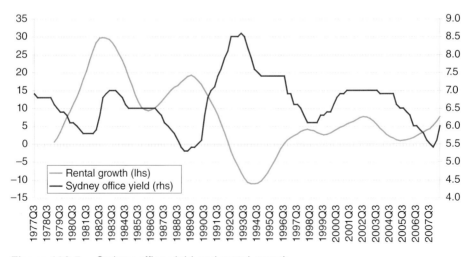

Figure 11A.5:   Sydney office yield and rental growth

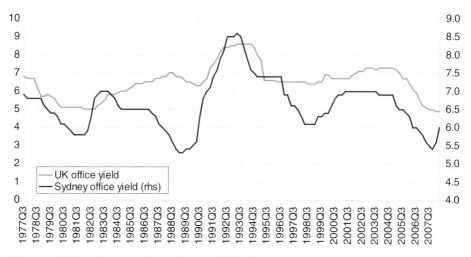

Figure 11A.6: Sydney office yield and UK office yield

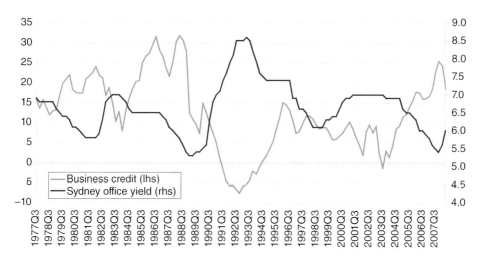

Figure 11A.7: Sydney office yield and business credit change

Australian office yields by around 20 basis points, with a lag of four quarters.

Change in private business credit in Australia is also associated with office yield shift (Figure 11A.7). A 1% increase in this variable is associated with a very small inward yields shift of 1 basis point all else equal. Figure 11A.7 shows the inverse relationship between the two variables. Business credit has only increased by 11% over the long term, which only accounts for 10 basis points of yield movement. However, in the period leading up to the GFC, credit growth was well in excess of the long-run average, accounting for 25–50 basis points movement in yields.

Table 11A.4:   Explanatory variables

Variable name	Coefficient	Historic range of variable
Real 10 year government bond	0.41	4.3
Construction cost index	−0.1	9
Changes in credit	−0.05	14
Fixed effect − Paris	−2.47	
Fixed effect − Lille	1.13	
Fixed effect − Lyon	0.67	
Fixed effect − Marseille	0.77	

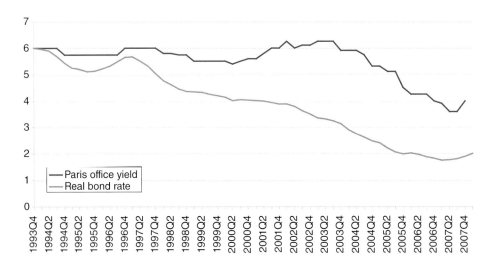

Figure 11A.8:   Paris office yield and real bond rate

France offices

In the investigation of French office yields, the data used was quarterly prime office data from CBRE running back to the early 1990s. The four big cities of Paris, Lille, Lyon and Marseille were included in the pooled estimation. Our equation explains 85% of the yield movement, but the model is not entirely satisfactory as there are some issues with serial correlation.

The real bond yield was found to be an important explanatory of French yields (Figure 11A.8). As before, it is the nominal bond yield less the rate of inflation. The coefficient on this is quite large, at 0.41, which suggests that for every 1% increase in the real bond yield, then real estate yields will increase by around 40 basis points. However, over our sample period, inflation, bond yields and real estate yields have all been moving inward.

French rents are linked to the construction cost index (CCI) and so, in the French case, we used this as a proxy for rental expectations (Figure 11A.9). We lagged the construction inflation by four quarters and took a four-quarter moving average. The coefficient on this variable is relatively small, suggesting that a 1% increase in the CCI is associated with a 10-basis-point yield movement. The CCI series does not have much variability in it, so its impact on yields, on average, is around 25–50 basis points.

The change in the amount of credit used by non-financial institutions in the economy was also statistically significant in the equation. As Figure 11A.10 shows, the relationship between this measure of credit and real estate yields looks more stable after 2000, at the point when the cost of

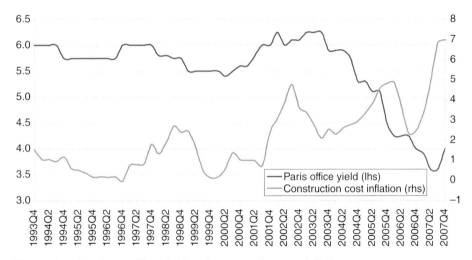

Figure 11A.9: Paris office yield and construction cost inflation

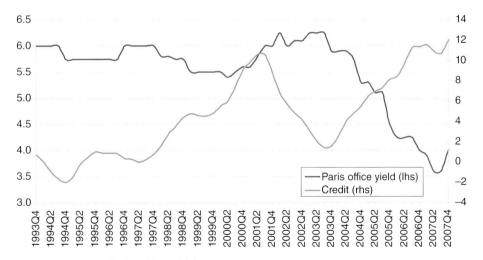

Figure 11A.10: Paris office yield and credit

credit dropped dramatically. In our equation, we find that a 1% change in our credit variable is associated with a five-basis-point change in yields. Credit growth has averaged around 6% on the entire sample period and so accounts for around 25 basis points. As in the case of Australia, credit growth was very strong in the run-up to the GFC and probably accounted for 50–75 basis points of inward yield shift over the period.

The cross-sectional variation has been picked up by the fixed effects in the estimated equation, with the ranking, from lowest to highest, being: Paris, Lyon, Marseille and Lille. These fixed effects pick up the idiosyncratic behaviour that isn't captured by the explanatory variables, part or all of which could be thought of as the risk premium. This suggests that Paris has the lowest risk premium and Lille the highest.

Spain offices

The Spanish market has seen a number of cycles since 1986. Using quarterly CBRE prime yield data from 1986 Q1 for Barcelona and Madrid, a panel estimation method was used.

Our prior expectation for the Spanish market was that it is driven a lot by market cycles, with construction booms and busts and credit availability which is also related indirectly to construction and business activity.

Our final equation had credit, stock, rents and bond yields explaining yields. The variables are not smoothed and this may suggest that the Spanish market moves more quickly to market changes in rents, stock, credit and bonds. The coefficients on the fixed effects variables suggest that Madrid had, on average, a slightly higher yield. Yield compression in Spain, as elsewhere, is (i) a negative function of the growth of credit as well as rental values; and (ii) a positive function of total level of stock. Such relationships are quite intuitive and are explained by the charts. The value of the econometric models is to appraise quantitatively the values related to each variable, the highest negative elasticity being the change in credit.

Figure 11A.11 shows Madrid yields against the change in credit for the entire economy. As the rate of credit expansion falls, yields rise and con-

Table 11A.5:   Explanatory variables

Variable name	Coefficient	Historic range of variable
Change in credit	−0.054	23
Change in stock	0.051	6
Change in rents	−0.008	87
10 year bond yield	0.064	9.5
Fixed effect – Barcelona	−0.056	
Fixed effect – Madrid	0.039	

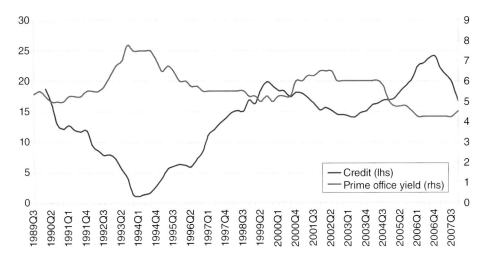

Figure 11A.11: Madrid office yields and credit

Figure 11A.12: Madrid rental growth and yields

versely, when credit growth picks up, yields move in. The relationship looks less strong after the introduction of the Euro, when other factors, such as cross-country convergence, played a bigger part. The coefficient of –0.05 on this variable suggests that a 1% increase in credit will have a 5 basis points inward shift in yield. As credit has grown in double digits, then the overall impact is somewhat larger; somewhere between 75 basis points and 125 basis points.

The picture is somewhat similar with rental growth, where, when rents are falling, yields rise and vice-versa (Figure 11A.12). Again, there seems to be a slight disruption to the relationship after Euro entry, especially in the early 2000s, when rental falls were only associated with sideways yield movements. The coefficient on the rental growth variable is quite small, at –0.008, although rental growth has been extremely large, ranging from –40% to +50%. This means that a 1% change in rents would be associated with a 0.008 basis points in yields, so 50% would be associated with a 40 basis points inward shift in yields.

The stock data for Barcelona is very volatile and not available as far back as for Madrid (Figure 11A.13). The chart for Madrid shows that, as the rate of additions to stock increases, so the office yield moves out and as the rate eases, then yields move in. The coefficient on this variable is 0.05, which suggests that a 1% change in the change in stock is related to a 5 basis points change in yields. The growth in stock has ranged from 10% to 1%, so the impact on yields is marginal; at most, 50 basis points.

The relationship between bonds and property yields in Spain is not overly strong, with a positive correlation between 40% and 65% for each market (Figure 11A.14). However, it may be that during the period the risk premium and risk-free position changed, as Spain went into the Euro. Bond yields fell from the beginning of 2000 until the end of 2005, when they began to increase again. Prime Madrid office yields fell from 2002 until their recent up-tick, at the back end of 2007. The spread of property over bonds narrowed and is likely to return in the future, which suggests that property yields will need to move out. The coefficient on the variable is 0.063, which is small, given that 1% change in bond yield would be associated with a 6 basis points change in real estate yield. Given that bond yields do not have a wide spread, then the impact on prime office yields over the sample studied has been marginal.

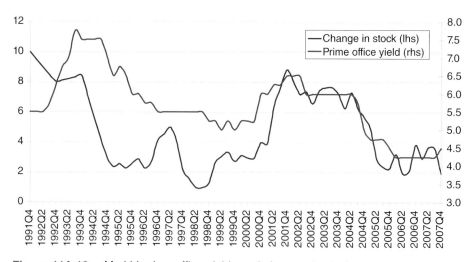

Figure 11A.13:   Madrid prime office yields and changes in stock

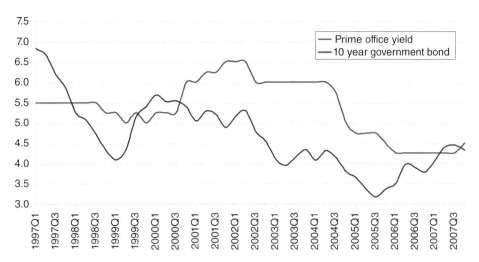

Figure 11A.14: Madrid office yields and 10-year bonds

Ireland

In Ireland, the annual IPD equivalent yield was modelled. The series begins in 1984 and is for all property. Since 1993, Irish yields have been on a downward path, with only a minor shift out during the early 2000s, which was soon reversed.

The key explanatory variables were found to be the long-term bond rate, rental value growth and the change in the broad money supply.

Figure 11A.15 shows how both bond yields and all property yields have been shifting inward over the last 20 years. Ireland, like Spain, has undergone a significant structural change over the modelling sample period. The coefficient on the long-term bond rate is 0.56, which suggests that a 1% change in the long-term rate is associated with a 56 basis points change in property yields. The bond rate is lagged by one year, so that this year's bond rate influences next year's property yield.

The relationship with the money supply is less visually clear, but as the money supply increases, on the whole, property yields fall (Figure 11A.16). The coefficient on this variable is –0.17, which suggests that a 1% change in broad money supply will change yields by 17 basis points. The range of growth of money supply suggests that changes in this variable of the modelling period could account for up to 125 basis points on the all-property yield.

Rental growth has had an inverse relationship with yields over most of the sample period (Figure 11A.17). The coefficient on this variable is –0.04, which is small and could explain 40 basis points in yield shift over the period. If the equation is estimated from 1992 to 2007, the coefficient increases to –0.11, which would explain more yield movement. Although

Table 11A.6:   Explanatory variables

Variable name	Coefficient	Historic range of variable
Long bond rate	0.64	8
Rental change	−0.11	20
Money Supply	−0.17	9.5

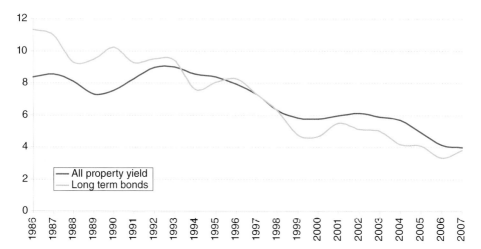

Figure 11A.15:   Ireland – yields and long-term bond rate

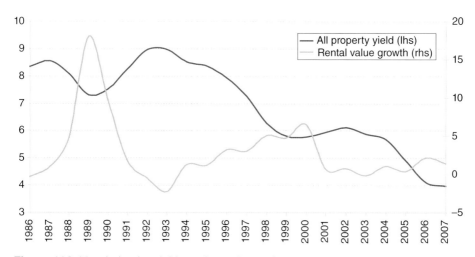

Figure 11A.16:   Ireland – yields and rental growth

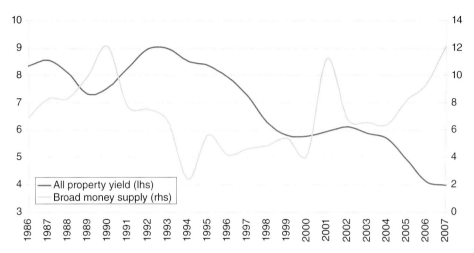

Figure 11A.17: Ireland – yields and broad money supply

Table 11A.7: Explanatory variables

Variable name	Coefficient	Historic range of variable
UK Long term bond	0.66	8.2
UK inflations	−0.33	11.8
UK IPD rental growth	−0.07	35
UK GDP growth	−0.17	6.6
UK all equities total returns	0.02	46

this may seem a more sensible magnitude, the sample period is somewhat shorter.

United Kingdom

The year 2007 was the nadir of a 15-year compression of yields (575 basis points) in the UK. The estimated equation, which explains 96% of IPD all-property equivalent yield movements over the period 1980–2007, is shown in Table 8. The variables in the equation are: long-term bond rates, inflation, rental growth, the performance of equities and economic growth. A dummy was used in 2006, as this was an unusually extreme year in terms of yield compression.

We used a 10-year moving average of government bond yields and we found that a 1% decrease in a 10-year moving average in long rates is associated with a 70 basis points decrease in yields. This is by far the biggest influencing factor and reflects the importance of bond rates in property's cost of capital. It also reminds us that property is more like a bond than an equity, at least in the UK. The 10-year moving average means that the UK market has adjusted slowly to the fall in bond rates: the property market seems relatively impervious to short-run bond market volatility.

We used a 10-year moving average of inflation, where we find 1% increase in the 10-year moving average of inflation would be associated with a 33 basis points decrease in yields. This we see as picking up the long-term expectation that property is a good preserver of real value (i.e., rents rise at least in line with inflation). Additionally, inflation is often associated with periods where the output gap is positive, which is also correlated with rental growth expectations.

We found current rental growth to be statistically significant in the model, with a 1% increase in rental growth being associated with a 7 basis points point fall in the all-property yield (Figure 11A.18). The relatively small impact of rental growth on yields is probably due to the fact that other variables in the model, such as inflation, GDP and the bond rate are better at picking up underlying economic growth.

In our equation we used a five-year moving average of equity returns (lagged one year), where a 1% increase in equity returns is associated with a 2 basis points increase in yields. Our casual observation is that, at times when equities are booming and are 'in favour' with fund managers, UK real estate tends to be neglected and, sometimes, even sold off. This said, the performance of equities appears to play only a marginal part in the determination of property yields.

We employed a current and future economic activity variable, using an average of this year's and next year's GDP growth, where we found a 1% increase is associated with an inward shift of around 17 basis points. GDP

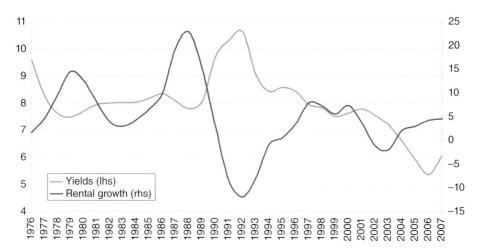

Figure 11A.18:   UK IPD all-property yield and rental growth

growth expectations are an underlying driver of performance expectations for real estate. True expectations are difficult to measure, so we have used actual GDP growth one year ahead as a proxy. Over the period in question, when the volatility of GDP growth was relatively low, this year's growth rate is a good predictor of next year's.

Japan

The paucity of data in Japan means that the modelling has of necessity had to be more parsimonious than in other markets. The dependent variable is the quarterly CBD office (effective) yield from JLL. The series starts in 2001, Q3. Over the sample period yields rose from 4.5% to just under 6.0% in 2003, before declining into 2007, where they stabilised before moving out marginally. The stylised results are in Table 11A.8.

Although the sample period is short, there does appear to be a relationship between rental growth and yields as shown in the chart (Figure 11A.19). The rental growth variable is a 4-quarter moving average, lagged two quarters. The coefficient on this variable is –0.049 and is statistically significant. Rents have grown by 44% in the period of the analysis in the past and this would explain over 200 basis points movement in the yield.

Table 11A.8: Explanatory variables

Variable name	Coefficient	Historic range of variable
Rents	0.05	65

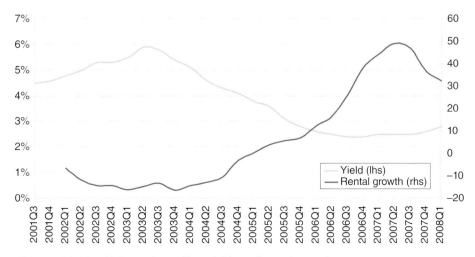

Figure 11A.19: Tokyo prime office yields and rental growth

This simple equation, which links yields to a constant and rental growth, explains nearly 80% of the variability in the data over the sample period. There are some problems with the model; the residuals are serially correlated. This suggests that we have a missing variable. However, all relevant variables that we tried were not statistically significant or correctly signed. Again, it may be that the residual series is picking up sentiment or changes in real estate risk premium. To date, we have been unable to measure these factors.

The relationship with the bond yield is not evident and the two appear to be negatively related, so that as bond yields increase, property yields fall.

Hong Kong

In Hong Kong, the office market was modelled using JLL quarterly data on equivalent prime yields, over the period 1994 to 2008. The yield movements appear to be highly cyclical.

The explanatory variables fit with our standardised framework, with a risk-free rate and some measures of potential income growth through rents and inflation. In the Hong Kong equation, a couple of dummy variables were used; one in 2003 (2003 Q4–2004 Q2) for SARS and one in 1996 (1996 Q3–1997 Q2) for the Asian crisis. This highlights the fact that, whilst statistical models can help analyse trends, there are certain situations which are not predictable and these can have a significant impact on markets. Yields only settle into their 'equilibrium level' when economic conditions are somewhat normal.

For a significant portion of the sample period, the long bond and property yield move in line, but this relationship breaks down for a number of years in the early 2000s (Figure 11A.20). The coefficient on the bond rate in the equation is 0.22 which suggests that a 1% change in the t-bill would be associated with a 22 basis points change in yield – but this is probably an underestimate of the relationship during normal times.

Table 11A.9:   Explanatory variables

Variable name	Coefficient	Historic range of variable
Treasury bill	0.22	9.3
Inflation	−0.08	16
Rental change	−0.03	120
Rental change lagged a year	−0.01	120
SARs dummy	−0.66	
Asian crisis dummy	−0.95	

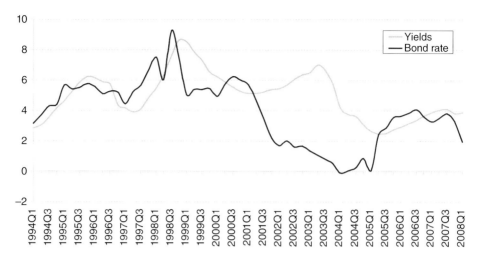

Figure 11A.20: Hong Kong office yields and long bond rate

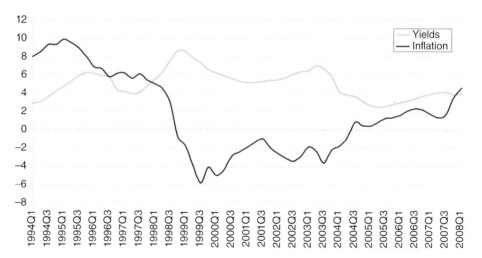

Figure 11A.21: Hong Kong office yields and inflation

In most countries, the inflation rate and rental change appear to pick up expectations about future income performance (Figure 11A.21). It should be noted that this is not true in those equations where the real bond rate has been used. In the case of Hong Kong, the relationship between yields and the inflation rate is significant, but the coefficient is relatively small, at –0.08 which indicates a 1% change in inflation is associated with 8 basis points on the yield. Furthermore, it would seem that during the period of falling prices yields were pushed upwards and, during this period, the inverse relationship shown in Figure 11A.20 is much clearer than in other time periods.

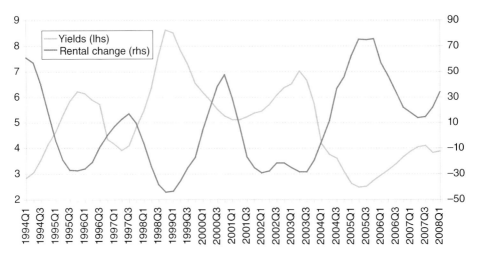

Figure 11A.22: Hong Kong office yields and rents

Rental change enters the equation as a contemporaneous and lagged (by a year) variable. Both are significant, but the coefficient on the current period rental change is larger, at 0.033 where, as the lagged coefficient is −0.01, so the combination explains about 50 basis points for a 1% change in rents. Figure 11A.22 shows clearly the inverse relationship between the rental change and yields.

Concluding comments

The factors that explain yields are similar, across the markets we have investigated. These are:

- Some measure of the risk free rate;
- Some measure of the demand–supply balance in occupier markets;
- Some measure of investor interest in real estate.

Some debate remains as to whether a real or nominal bond is the correct variable to use in the risk-free framework. In our empirical work we have used both and in cases where inflation has stood alone as an explanatory variable, we have used nominal bonds. In the case of France, the real bond rate was used and the construction cost index used in rental indexation was also found to have explanatory power.

That the balance of demand and supply in occupier markets is generally significant is reassuring; it suggests that investors are not only driven by capital market events, but also prospective income growth from the use of real estate in the production of goods and services. This said, there is ample evidence in the equations that the strong availability of credit over the period the models cover strongly drives investor demand. Generally, either a credit variable or a money supply variable was found to be a significant driver of yields. The change to a period of tight credit conditions (now unwinding) will push yields outward and investors may be looking more at the underlying real estate fundamentals. Generally, the oncoming credit crunch is likely to push yields out.

At the current juncture, almost all factors are pointing to a continued outward shift in yields. In the medium term there may even be a complete loss of appetite for real estate on the part of investors, which would probably disturb some of the relationships which have held for the last 20 years or so. One area in which this work is weak is the examination of the time varying influence of investor sentiment towards real estate on yields.

Notwithstanding this, the analysis has provided some understanding of the key drivers of property yield movements over time and in a huge variety of market contexts.

Hong Kong office yield model

Dependent Variable: Hong Kong office yeilds

Method: Least Squares

Sample (adjusted): 1994Q1 2008Q1

Included observations: 57 after adjustments

	Coefficient	Std. Error	t-Statistic	Prob.
Constant	4.65	0.14	32.27	0.00
TBill lagged 1q	0.22	0.03	6.85	0.00
HK CPI	−0.08	0.02	−4.58	0.00
YoY % Growth HK office rents	−0.03	0.00	−18.16	0.00
YoY % Growth HK office rents lagged 4q	−0.01	0.00	−4.72	0.00
2003 dummy	−0.66	0.29	−2.31	0.03
1996 dummy	−0.95	0.25	−3.73	0.00
R-squared	0.93	Mean dependent var		4.98
Adjusted R-squared	0.93	S.D. dependent var		1.55
S.E. of regression	0.42	Akaike info criterion		1.23
Sum squared resid	8.90	Schwarz criterion		1.48
Log likelihood	−27.96	Hannan-Quinn criter.		1.32
F-statistic	117.17	Durbin-Watson stat		0.95
Prob(F-statistic)	0.00			

Australia – office markets model

Dependent Variable: location specific yield

Method: Pooled Least Squares

Sample: 1985Q1 2008Q1

Included observations: 93

Cross-sections included: 3

Total pool (balanced) observations: 279

Period SUR (PCSE) standard errors & covariance (d.f. corrected)

Convergence achieved after 17 iterations

Variable	Coefficient	Std. Error	t-Statistic	Prob.
Constant	5.75	0.60	9.53	0.00
UK CBRE office yields lagged 4q	0.19	0.07	2.73	0.01
8q MA 10 year real bond yields	0.09	0.03	3.47	0.00
12q MA location specific growth in face rents	−0.03	0.01	−3.96	0.00
Y0Y % growth in business credit	−0.01	0.00	−10.53	0.00
AR(1)	0.95	0.02	42.31	0.00
Fixed Effects (Cross):				
Brisbane constant adjustment	−0.13			
Perth constant adjustment	0.87			
Sydney constant adjustment	−0.74			

Effects Specification

Cross-section fixed (dummy variables)

R-squared	0.98	Mean dependent var	7.24
Adjusted R-squared	0.98	S.D. dependent var	0.98
S.E. of regression	0.14	Akaike info criterion	−1.05
Sum squared resid	5.38	Schwarz criterion	−0.95
Log likelihood	155.00	Hannan-Quinn criter.	−1.01
F-statistic	1899.79	Durbin-Watson stat	1.25
Prob(F-statistic)	0.00		

Ireland – all property model

Dependent Variable: Ireland all property IPD equivalent yield

Method: Least Squares

Sample: 1992 2007

Included observations: 16

	Coefficient	Std. Error	t-Statistic	Prob.
Constant	3.99	0.55	7.20	0.00
Long rate lagged 1 y	0.64	0.05	13.21	0.00
IPD all property rental growth	−0.11	0.04	−2.59	0.02
YOY% growth in money supply	−0.17	0.04	−4.42	0.00
R-squared	0.98	Mean dependent var		6.52
Adjusted R-squared	0.97	S.D. dependent var		1.62
S.E. of regression	0.28	Akaike info criterion		0.53
Sum squared resid	0.97	Schwarz criterion		0.73
Log likelihood	−0.27	Hannan-Quinn criter.		0.54
F-statistic	159.45	Durbin-Watson stat		1.64
Prob(F-statistic)	0.00			

Japan – Tokyo office market model

Dependent Variable: Tokyo office yield

Method: Least Squares

Sample (adjusted): 2002Q1 2008Q1

Included observations: 25 after adjustments

White Heteroskedasticity-Consistent Standard Errors & Covariance

	Coefficient	Std. Error	t-Statistic	Prob.
Constant	4.24	0.12	34.31	0.00
4q MA of YoY growth in office rents lagged 2q	−0.05	0.00	−10.41	0.00
R-squared	0.79	Mean dependent var		3.89
Adjusted R-squared	0.78	S.D. dependent var		1.28
S.E. of regression	0.60	Akaike info criterion		1.90
Sum squared resid	8.33	Schwarz criterion		2.00
Log likelihood	−21.74	Hannan-Quinn criter.		1.93
F-statistic	85.64	Durbin-Watson stat		0.24
Prob(F-statistic)	0.00			

United States

Dependent Variable: sector specific RCA income yield minus ten year bonds (i.e. spread)

Method: Pooled Least Squares

Sample (adjusted): 2001Q2 2008Q1

Included observations: 28 after adjustments

Cross-sections included: 3

Total pool (balanced) observations: 84

Period SUR (PCSE) standard errors & covariance (d.f. corrected)

Convergence achieved after 7 iterations

Variable	Coefficient	Std. Error	t-Statistic	Prob.
Constant	0.05	0.01	9.25	0.00
Ratio of lagged Exchanges rate	−0.03	0.00	−5.42	0.00
4q MA sector specific activity	−6.72	9.23	−7.28	0.00
REIS Apt. 2q MA vacancy relative to 16q MA lagged 1q	0.02	0.00	14.54	0.00
REIS Off 2q MA vacancy relative to16q MA lagged 1q	0.01	0.00	1.77	0.08
REIS Ret 2q MA vacancy relative to 16q MA lagged 1q	0.05	0.01	4.77	0.00
AR(1)	0.57	0.07	8.77	0.00
Fixed Effects (Cross):				
Apartment constant adjustment	−0.02			
Apartment constant adjustment	0.03			
Retail constant adjustment	−0.01			

Effects Specification

Cross-section fixed (dummy variables)

R-squared	0.92	Mean dependent var	0.03
Adjusted R-squared	0.91	S.D. dependent var	0.01
S.E. of regression	0.00	Akaike info criterion	−8.33
Sum squared resid	0.00	Schwarz criterion	−8.06
Log likelihood	358.66	Hannan-Quinn criter.	−8.22
F-statistic	102.95	Durbin-Watson stat	1.85
Prob(F-statistic)	0.00		

Dependent Variable: sector specific RCA income yield – ten year bonds (ie spread)

Spain office model

Dependent Variable: location specific yield

Method: Pooled Least Squares

Sample (adjusted): 1992Q1 2007Q4

Included observations: 64 after adjustments

Cross-sections included: 2

Total pool (unbalanced) observations: 108

Period SUR (PCSE) standard errors & covariance (d.f. corrected)

Convergence achieved after 15 iterations

Variable	Coefficient	Std. Error	t-Statistic	Prob.
Constant	5.82	0.27	21.86	0.00
Change in credit	−0.05	0.01	−7.36	0.00
Location specific change in stock	0.05	0.01	5.06	0.00
Location specific change in rents	−0.01	0.00	−1.77	0.08
10 year government bond rate	0.06	0.02	3.46	0.00
AR(1)	0.91	0.05	18.83	0.00
Fixed Effects (Cross):				
Barcelona constant adjustment	−0.06			
Madrid constant adjustment	0.04			

Effects Specification

Cross-section fixed (dummy variables)

R-squared	0.94	Mean dependent var	5.64
Adjusted R-squared	0.93	S.D. dependent var	0.82
S.E. of regression	0.21	Akaike info criterion	−0.19
Sum squared resid	4.60	Schwarz criterion	−0.02
Log likelihood	17.23	Hannan-Quinn criter.	−0.12
F-statistic	246.58	Durbin-Watson stat	1.93
Prob(F-statistic)	0.00		

French office model

Dependent Variable: Location specific office yield

Method: Pooled Least Squares

Sample (adjusted): 1993Q4 2007Q4

Included observations: 57 after adjustments

Cross-sections included: 4

Total pool (unbalanced) observations: 220

Variable	Coefficient	Std. Error	t-Statistic	Prob.
Constant	6.85	0.44	15.61	0.00
8q MA 10 year real bond yield lagged 4q	0.41	0.08	5.20	0.00
4q MA construction cost index lagged 4q	−0.10	0.05	−2.26	0.02
2q MA YoY %growth in credit lagged 1q	−0.05	0.02	−2.63	0.01
Fixed Effects (Cross)				
Paris constant adjustment	−2.47			
Lille constant adjustment	1.13			
Lyon constant adjustment	0.67			
Marseille constant adjustment	0.78			

Effects Specification			
Cross-section fixed (dummy variables)			
R-squared	0.85	Mean dependent var	7.95
Adjusted R-squared	0.85	S.D. dependent var	1.82
S.E. of regression	0.72	Akaike info criterion	2.20
Sum squared resid	108.98	Schwarz criterion	2.31
Log likelihood	−234.89	Hannan-Quinn criter.	2.24
F-statistic	201.87	Durbin-Watson stat	0.13
Prob(F-statistic)	0.00		

12

Global office markets

There are few more potent symbols of modern capitalism than the gleaming office blocks that form the central core of most sizeable cities. In the same way, there are few more salutary reminders of the failures of modern capitalism than the swathes of offices left vacant in the wake of a stock market crash or the onset of recession. The size and prestige of cities can easily be measured by the volume, in square meters, of the office space located there. Less easy to measure, but no less important to a city's brand, is the signature architecture embodied in its office stock, enhanced, as it often is, by dramatic lighting. When China wished to announce to the world that it was opening its doors to international capital, it set about constructing the Pudong office market in Shanghai.

The service sector creates about 65% of the value added in an OECD economy. Offices provide the platform for most of this activity to take place. Even as car ownership and communications technology has allowed houses, shops and some offices to decentralise in the latter half of the twentieth century, the service sector has remained rooted in the city centre. There are two reasons for this. First, the central area of a city commands the largest 'white collar' labour market. Second, substantial efficiency gains tend to emerge when service sector firms locate near to each other. These derive from inter-company specialisation and ease of information exchange

Real Estate and Globalisation, First Edition. Richard Barkham.
© 2012 John Wiley & Sons, Ltd. Published 2012 by John Wiley & Sons, Ltd.

between senior managers in different firms. Offices use about 40% of total commercial floor space.[1]

Offices are beloved of the real estate community. For developers, offices represent the opportunity to make substantial profits, often with relatively little equity input in a relatively short period of time, if projects can be brought to market at the right time. Of course, timing is the key to success. The office market is highly cyclical and average long-run development profits are actually quite low.[2] Investors also like having offices in their real estate or multi-asset portfolios. This is despite the fact that most studies, including our article of February 2003, show that the office sector has the lowest risk-adjusted returns of all real estate sectors.[3]

Poor risk-adjusted returns stem from a number of factors. In the long run, office rental values tend to fall in real terms. This is because it is very easy to increase the supply of space in most office markets by building upwards, or extending the market outwards a little.[4] As we show in the article of January 2004, even in markets which are relatively constrained in terms of new supply, there is relatively little long-term superior rental appreciation. This is because there is, in the long term, a high degree of substitutability between office locations: if rents get high in one location, firms move to another. Only where there is a very compelling reason for firms to stay in the city, such as its position as a global financial centre, and the degree of space constraint is extreme, do rents appreciate in the long run. These conditions can be found in markets such as London's West End and Hong Kong (see the article of April 2004 for a comment on London's West End and some analysis of office cycles).

The other cause of poor long-term office performance is periodic, or cyclical, over-production of new office space. Our article of June 2005 gives a brief commentary on the impact of office supply on performance. Many reasons have been put forward for this. The cycle of over- and under-production is explained in traditional microeconomics by the existence of lags in the supply side. It takes a long time to build an office so, when demand initially increases, although construction starts up, there is no new supply (because buildings are unfinished) and prices escalate at an increasing rate. This induces a second round of potentially excess new supply. In financial economics, the cycle of under- and over-supply is thought to derive from the rational desire of developers at the start of the cycle to maximise

---

[1] In the UK, commercial floor space is about 15% of the total built environment, with housing being the other 85%.

[2] IPD, Development returns project.

[3] Risk is usually conceived of as the volatility of annual total returns; and risk-adjusted returns are measured by the Sharpe ratio.

[4] If an office market or central business district (CBD) can be represented, for the sake of argument, by a circle then a small increase in the radius of the circle leads to an 'exponential' increase in the land area. I owe this argument to James Clifton Brown of CBRE Investors.

the value of their projects by delaying their start. Later in the cycle, when the option to develop has been exercised, there is a 'free for all' as developers compete to get their product to market. Whatever the cause, office markets typically suffer cycles of 'feast and famine', which create negative returns and volatility.

It would be wrong, however, to attribute all of the volatility in office markets to the supply side of the market; volatility in demand is also important. One of the objectives that Grosvenor and many other investors set themselves is diversification. In seeking to find markets that are relatively uncorrelated, we have noted that global office markets are actually becoming more correlated over time. The cause of this is globalisation. Economies have always been quite integrated through trade, but now production systems and capital markets are so interconnected that economic shocks are almost instantaneously transmitted from one market to another. Office demand in the main financial markets is also directly linked to the level of the stock market, which imparts further volatility. The article of April 2008 shows that office markets in the world's great financial centres, such as London, New York and Tokyo move almost in 'lock step' with one another and well ahead of their respective domestic hinterlands. The article of July 2003 shows that globalisation also affects markets at a more local level. The articles of June 2006 and July 2006 show that correlation is trending up in the main economic blocks of the Americas, Europe and Asia Pacific.

Our analysis of the correlation, in the article of July 2006, between office markets has also revealed that correlation is itself somewhat cyclical. In the trough of the global office cycle, up to the mid-upswing point, there is a relatively low level of correlation between markets. As markets peak and slump, the correlation rises. It seems that there is the least potential for diversification in office markets when it is most needed. This suggests that those two well-known components of real estate performance, timing and stock selection, are becoming more important over time, not less. One way to identify 'under-pricing' is to conduct 'cross-sectional' analysis of markets. Our article of November 2005 on office rents and the 'Gini coefficient' is an attempt to identify markets in which rents are above or below their predicted level.

Having spent some time discussing the limitations of offices as investment assets, it is worth reflecting on the fact that they are an essential part of the real estate strategy of most large and well-informed investors. There are probably a number of reasons for this. First, offices are large and relatively liquid, so they provide investors with the ability to quickly increase their real estate exposure. Second, again due to 'largeness', offices allow investors to increase their allocation to real estate quickly. Third, compared with shopping centres or business parks, offices are easy to manage, to the point that they are often regarded as 'passive investments' like equities. Fourth, since the majority of economic growth in the OECD over the last

30 years or so has been in the service sector, investors intuitively understand the underlying economic drivers of office returns.

Just how rewarding is office sector investment? (February 2003)

The current problems in property markets around the world have highlighted the vulnerability of the office sector to economic downturns. Whilst it has been clear for some time that offices are a particularly risky sector to invest in, because of a more volatile cycle, what has emerged in this recession is a high degree of correlation between the different office cycles around the world of investment-grade real estate. As investors scratch their heads and wonder where exactly they can expect to find reasonable returns in the international office markets, the benefits of diversifying an office portfolio internationally look thin.

But, more importantly, the long-term return to office investments is limited by an unhappy characteristic. Rents do not tend to show an upward trend in real terms. Figure 12.1 shows the experience of the UK investible sector, as measured by the IPD universe. Drawing long-term trend lines on charts like this is sensitive to the start and end points, so does not always make good sense. But, even with this proviso, it seems clear that, over the last 20 years or so, there has been no increase in rents beyond what has been delivered by general inflation. In fact, there are signs that rents have

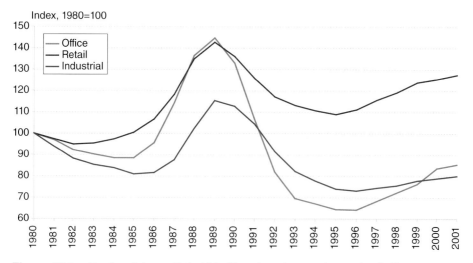

Figure 12.1:   Real rental growth in UK offices is unimpressive and volatile

actually fallen in real terms (although that conclusion can change, depending on the particular measure of rents used and the time period covered). Crucially, this flat long-term growth profile has not been achieved with the benefit of smooth year-to-year variation. Office rents appear to increase far more rapidly in an upswing and fall faster in a downswing. Based on the IPD annual data, office rents increased 60% from 1980 to their peak in the late 1980s, compared with rises of 50% and 43% in retail and industrial respectively. From those market peaks, office rents fell 56% in the subsequent downturn, compared to 24% and 37% in retail and industrial respectively, and then rose 33% to end 2001, while rents in retail and industrial rose just 17% and 9% respectively. Using quarterly data would give higher estimates of the rise and fall in all sectors, but would not alter the relativities between sectors. The office market tends to deliver a disappointing long-run rental return, then, and at the cost of relatively high market risk.

Is this a signal that the UK office market is a poor performer? Not really. In many other countries, the evidence is similar and supports the general conclusion that good returns can only be made in the sector from development, active management, yield falls and timing the cycle. But strategies based on development, active management and falling yields are also available in other property sectors that do not suffer from the same flat underlying growth profile and very volatile cyclical pattern, so the decision to be active in the office sector may well depend on a belief in being able to time the cycle.

The total returns achieved by mainstream investors suggest they have not been able to do this very well. Figure 12.2, with total returns by sector in the NCRIEF database of US investor returns and the Property Council of

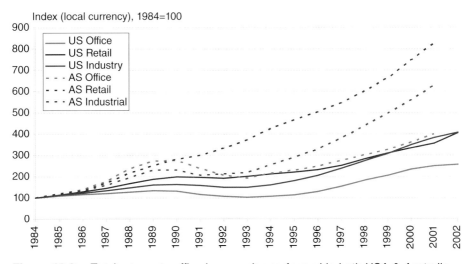

Figure 12.2: Total returns to office have under-performed in both USA & Australia

Australia's corresponding database, is typical of data in other countries. Average returns tend to be lower for office investments, although the differences are not enormous and do not explain the under-performance. In the UK, Australia and the USA, office returns were just under 1% below retail returns and just over 1% below industrial returns. In Asia, there were some cases of stronger office market returns, but this was in Singapore, where retail returns have been particularly bad and in Japan, where the dynamic has been distorted by the adjustment to the last bubble. But the under-performance of offices tends to come from much higher volatility for relatively similar average returns. This has caused the historic risk/return ratios for each sector, that measure the amount of return generated for the risk taken on board, to highlight office investments as the least rewarding activity in the USA, the UK, Australia, Hong Kong (although industrial there did badly also) and Spain. Once again, the peculiar factors in Japan and Singapore retail make the result in those markets less clear.

The reason for the poor returns comparison is that the extra market risk of being active in the office sector is not reflected in higher yields (cap rates). Yields in offices tend to be lower than yields in industrial and only slightly higher than yields in investment-grade retail. Is this a failure in market pricing? Liquidity considerations may justify the pricing to some extent, particularly as an explanation for why relatively illiquid industrial assets trade at higher yields, but this does not help greatly in explaining the comparison between retail and office yields (Figure 12.3). Investors should think twice, then, about office market activity.

Supply-constrained office markets do deliver stronger rental growth – but not always (January 2004)

It is not rare in the property world to target supply-constrained markets in the belief that these markets deliver better rental growth. Markets without supply constraints are less likely to deliver long-running surges in rental values, because property shortages can be reversed more quickly. But even in supply-constrained markets, shortages may last longer but could be eventually relieved, meaning there are extended periods of rental growth but, over the long run, growth is no higher than in other markets and carries higher volatility. Even without a supply response, extended periods of rental growth could result in supply-constrained markets pricing themselves out of business, causing demand to fall and rents to finally ease off.

We tested this, using CBRE data from TortoWheatonResearch on the 50 most important office markets in the USA, by estimating how important rental increases were in stimulating construction. Our theory was that in

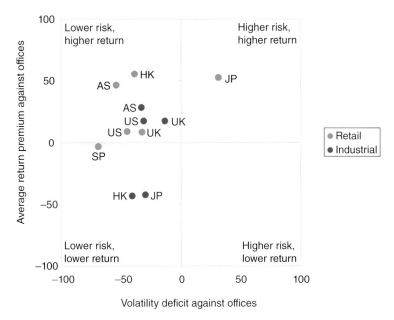

Figure 12.3: Historic performance argues against holding offices for long periods
Sources: IPD, NCREIF, PCA, JLL

markets without supply constraints, rental increases will stimulate construction, causing increased supply over the following one to three years. The supply constraints might be physical or policy-related. We used regression techniques to examine the impact of rents on future supply and the results allowed us to segment the 50 office markets into those with and without evidence of supply constraints (Figure 12.4). We then looked at long-run rental growth in all these markets and found that there was a positive correlation between the degree of supply constraints and rental growth rates. However, this correlation was only around 25%, which is high enough to take note of but low enough to allow a large number of exceptions. As a rule, then, targeting supply-constrained markets should be a rewarding strategy, on average, but is no guarantee of universal success.

Europe's largest office markets are set to lead the recovery (April 2004)

Sentiment has turned quickly in the London office market, on the heels of a rapid turnaround in Hong Kong. In the prime Hong Kong market, rental

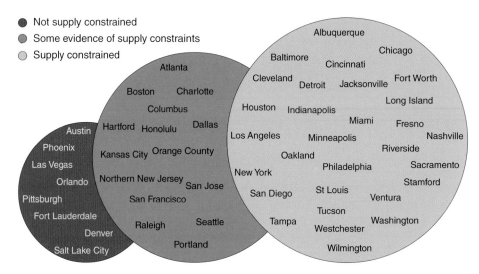

● Not supply constrained
● Some evidence of supply constraints
○ Supply constrained

Figure 12.4:   Size of bubble relates to total stock across all markets in each category

values had started to rise by Q4 (although year-on-year growth rates were still around -20%), as occupiers relocated to better locations, following massive rental declines during 2001 and 2002. The mechanism in the main European markets will be different, though, just because these markets did not witness such great declines from their respective peaks and the opportunities for occupiers to relocate without increasing their rental rates are much more limited. In Europe, the recovery depends much more on a classic demand recovery within a restrained supply environment. On that basis, the West End of London and Paris emerge as the best candidates for an early turnaround.

In London, a rise in interest from prospective occupiers is raising expectations of an imminent rental recovery in the West End market, immediately after vacancy rates have peaked. This compares with the last cycle, when positive rental growth only materialised five quarters after the peak in vacancy. The difference this time is that vacancy peaked in 1992 at 15.3% (according to CBRE), while vacancy in Q3 2003 peaked at 10.8% and was down to 9.9% in Q4 (Figure 12.5). In the last cycle, rental growth had kicked in by the time vacancy was down to 12.8%. The IPD monthly index also signals a recovery, with central London rents down just 0.1% in January and West End rents holding steady. A quick turnaround would mean that the recent slump remains a far cry from the problems of the early 1990s. The cycle then was much more like Hong Kong's recent experience, with rents dropping 70% in real terms from their peak, compared with a fall of just 34% from March 2001 to December 2003. These dynamics leave rents much higher in real terms now than they were during the last trough.

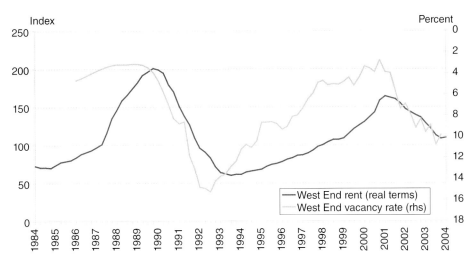

Figure 12.5: Vacancy rate supports stabilisation or recovery in the West End market
Source: CBRE, PMA

Of course there is, as always, another side. Markets seldom return to rental growth so quickly after the vacancy cycle has peaked. More pertinently for the West End, London's other major sub-market, the City, is in a worse position and rents should fall further there in 2004. This raises the issue of how far rents in two such similar and geographically close sub-markets can diverge, given that the premium for West End locations is already at record levels, after being on an upward trend for the last decade (see Figure 12.6). Will occupiers pay more than 60% extra for West End space, given the similarity of the markets? Part of the increased cost to occupiers of a stronger demand environment will also be to reduce incentives that currently stretch to an 18–20 months' rent free period off a 10-year lease in the West End and 28 months' rent free in the City. This should offset growth in headline rents to some extent, although owners will be keen to support headline rents. So, while the market should support some rental growth in 2004, expecting much more than inflationary growth (2–3%) in 2004 is much less certain.

Europe's other leading market, Paris, is also characterised as having tight supply conditions. Comparing vacancy rates across markets is rarely advisable, given the widespread methodological differences in estimating both stock and the level of availability. Despite this, supply in central Paris seems, if anything, to be even more tightly constrained than in London. Vacancy was just 1.0% at the end of 2000 and had risen to just 5.5% by the end of 2003, according to CBRE/Bourdais (Figure 12.7). As in London's West

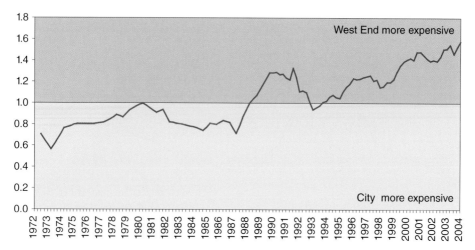

Figure 12.6: Ratio of West End and City nominal rents
Source: CBRE

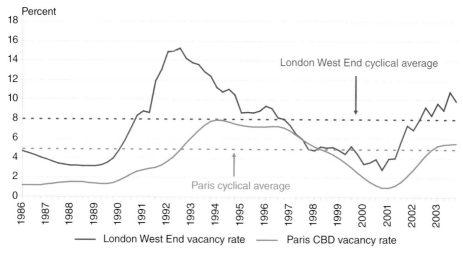

Figure 12.7: Both London W.E. and Paris are close to their long-run average vacancy
Source: PMA, Bourdais

End, take-up increased in the second half of the year. But in Paris, availability has not yet shown signs of peaking and a further small increase is likely in the first half of 2004, because both of new completions and the surrender of unwanted space. The main difference with the West End is the economy, which is expanding at well above trend rates in the UK, but is struggling to reach trend in France. Thus, demand has not yet been strong enough in

Paris to spark a recovery, despite the tight supply conditions. Our own econometric models suggest a recovery will not be long in coming, however, and the market should have returned to growth by the end of the year.

Paris and London are the region's largest markets and, out of the next rank, Madrid is also approaching a turning point. By contrast, Milan, which avoided the downturn, is now building up a supply pipeline that is beginning to cloud the medium-term outlook, while the German markets remain extremely problematic. Madrid has suffered a supply issue since 2000, but the majority of new completions have been in the suburban markets. This, together with a trend for occupiers in peripheral markets to relocate to the centre, once rents there fell in 2002 and 2003, has helped insulate the CBD market and kept the increase in vacancy in line with the trend in Paris. There is still a significant amount of new space to come to the Madrid market, though, which should generate further rental declines in 2004 and delay any turning point until 2005, when relatively strong demand growth should stabilise the market and lead to rental growth by 2007.

Supply risk in international office markets (June 2005)

The relatively slow recovery in the world's major office markets is clearly linked to the disappointing employment growth in their underlying economies. In some markets, though, employment growth is robust (such as Madrid), but the market has still disappointed. The supply picture settles some of these apparent contradictions. Figure 12.8 shows the current available supply, together with the next two years' pipeline construction, as a proportion of the historic average demand. The Sydney CBD market, at four, indicates that current vacancy plus expected new supply is equal to four years of forecasted demand. Some of the currently best-performing markets are in the low-supply risk group, such as Washington, DC, and Hong Kong. These markets already price in low-supply risk, because availability is low. The medium-risk markets are the potential rising markets, in the short term. A strong demand year in London and Sydney would push these markets much higher up the international rankings. But the prospects in the Bay Area must be considered medium-term at best.

Office markets and the global economy (April 2008)

In the current economic turmoil, most real estate comment has focused on the outlook for housing and, via the link between housing and consumer

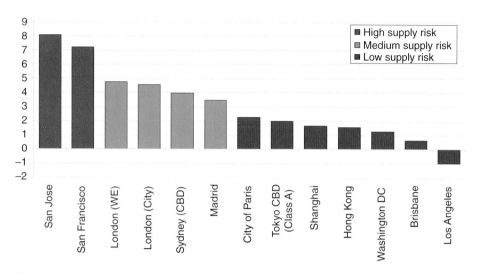

Figure 12.8:   Supply risk in office markets
Source: Grosvenor, Torto Wheaton, Jones LangLaSalle, CBRE

spending, retail values. Undoubtedly there are dangers in these areas, with intense credit rationing likely to put downward pressure on US and European house prices for at least the next 12 months. However, it is possible that the weakening global economy will have a greater impact on offices. Office markets, especially those in the big global cities, are driven by financial and business services employment growth. This, in turn, is linked to debt and equity issuance, which is a direct and geared function of global economic conditions. Residential and retail property is driven by a much more diverse economic base, because of a high level of spatial disaggregation, and may actually prove more resilient than expected.

The close link between office markets and the global economy is shown in Figures 12.9 and 12.10. The performance of the global economy is indicated by the deviation of world economic growth from its trend of 3.3% per annum. This is a standard method of illustrating economic cycles. Figure 12.9 shows annual rental growth in the London office market. The correlation between the two series is remarkable. Over the whole period, the correlation coefficient is 0.5, but since 1996 it is much higher, at 0.8. The increasing correlation between London and the rest of the world is due to globalisation. National economies are increasingly interlinked through trade, multinational corporations and communications technology and these linkages are most extensive in the capital markets.

Figure 12.10 shows the same world economic growth series alongside rental growth in two other office markets: New York City and Tokyo. In

Figure 12.9: Office markets and world economic growth
Source: Global Insight, CBRE, Grosvenor

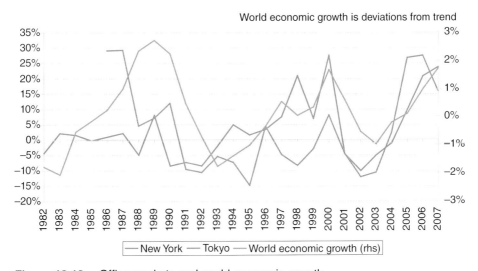

Figure 12.10: Office markets and world economic growth
Source: Global Insight, CBRE, Grosvenor

the case of Tokyo, despite near-recessionary conditions between 1990 and 2005, the correlation between world economic growth and office rents is 0.5. However, it does not seem to be increasing over time. In the case of New York (prime Midtown offices), there is a very weak link between rents and the world economy in the early period, up until about 1993, but then

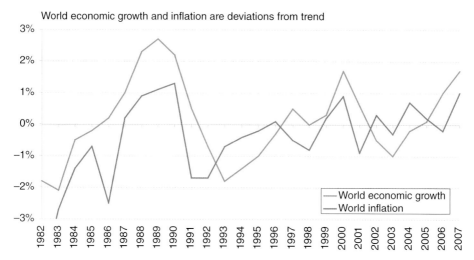

Figure 12.11:   World economic growth and world inflation
Source: Global Insight, Grosvenor

a much stronger correlation sets in. The correlation coefficient for New York is 0.3 for the whole period, but 0.8 since 1996. Again, this demonstrates how profoundly the forces of globalisation are impacting the capital markets and their associated operating platforms. As might be expected, the correlations between the office markets themselves are increasing over time. Over the whole period, the correlations between New York and Tokyo, New York and London and Tokyo and London are 0.4, 0.5 and 0.3 respectively. Since 1995, the correlations have been 0.6, 0.8 and 0.5.

To assess the outlook for these markets, we need to consider what the economic data is saying. Figure 12.11 shows the same economic series, world economic growth relative to trend, alongside world CPI inflation relative to trend. When economic growth is above its trend level, the world economy is growing too fast; the overall level of demand for goods and services is greater than the economy's ability to produce these goods and services. As can be seen, under such conditions there is a tendency for inflation to build up. The correlation between the economic growth relative to trend and inflation relative to trend is high, at 0.7. The implication is clear: the world economy needs a considerable economic slowdown to eliminate inflationary pressures, so, with the exception of the USA, we should expect interest rates to stay at around their current levels for at least the next nine months. Interest-rate cuts in the USA are likely to be very supportive of economic growth, but the Fed is taking a big risk with inflation. As for office markets, we should expect rental growth to disappear over the next two years, with a strong possibility of rental decline.

What are the investment implications of this analysis? The first and most obvious conclusion is to go 'underweight' on London, Tokyo and New York offices for the next year or so, until the outlook for the global economy becomes clearer. Second, those running international office portfolios or with a slightly longer-term time horizon should look at Tokyo offices; a relatively low correlation with the other main office markets suggests that this market continues to offer diversification potential. Entering this market through the hugely discounted Japanese REITs would allow an early execution of this strategy. Given the high degree of correlation between international office markets and the access to increasingly well-established property derivatives markets, pairs trading or relative value strategies offer opportunities to generate alpha. The latter approaches provide scope to outperform even as market fundamentals weaken, as the above analysis suggests they will.

Can local office markets buck international market trends? (July 2003)

The current office market cycle has featured a much higher degree of synchronisation than usual, as markets across the developed world turned down at around the same time. This makes perfect sense in globalised markets dominated by international occupiers such as investment banks, accountants and legal firms. But office demand in some markets is still characterised as being mainly locally driven, and in such markets the space requirements of the main international occupiers should have less impact. In Spain, the two main office markets of Madrid and Barcelona are usually described as being different in this respect. Madrid is more sensitive to national and international trends in occupation, while Barcelona is perceived to be a more 'local' market that is more sensitive to the needs of the regional economy.

We have recently completed a modelling exercise to analyse the determinants of office rents in both cities, using both national and regional level economic data as possible drivers. Given the local nature of the Barcelona market, we expected to find that national trends in the finance and business services (FBS) sector (which moved in line with trends in the more internationally exposed FBS sectors) would be less important than in the Madrid market. But in fact, the best model in each market was heavily dependent on the output of the national FBS sector (Figure 12.12). In addition, our models suggest that Madrid is also affected by both the size of the office stock and employment in the local financial services sector,

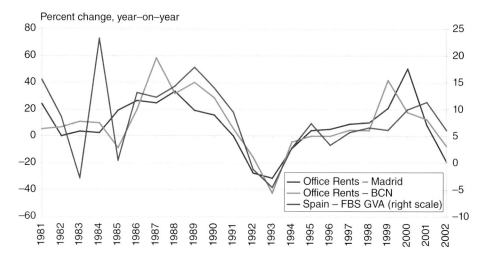

Percent change, year–on–year

Figure 12.12:   Financial and business services drive rents in both Spanish markets
Source: Eurostat and CBRE

while Barcelona is affected by the local unemployment rate and new office supply.

This work suggests that globalisation among office occupiers has been strong enough to affect markets that are often viewed as regional, rather than national, hubs and challenges the view that regional hubs can provide a diversification shelter.

Euro zone convergence – economic myth and property reality (June 2006)

One of the main economic arguments for the introduction of the Euro was that the main economies of Europe were increasingly moving together, that is, converging. This, it was argued, provided the opportunity for the harmonisation of monetary policy and the introduction of a single currency. Exchange rate stability between Euro zone countries, alongside stable inflation and price transparency, would provide substantial opportunities for improved allocation of economic resources. And so it has been, by and large. An important question, at least from the perspective of a property investor, is: to what extent has the increasing correlation between European economies and, therefore, property markets reduced the opportunity for risk reduction by diversification? The idea that the global property market is becoming increasingly harmonised is a common theme at property conferences at the moment. Is it actually true?

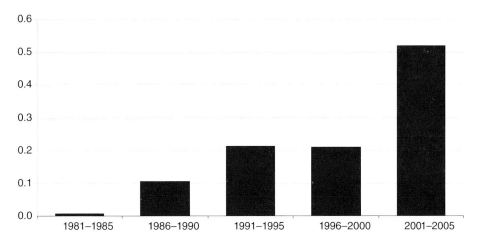

Figure 12.13: Correlation of euro zone office yield shift over time

Figure 12.13 shows the five-year correlation in prime office yield shift (quarterly), across the main Euro zone office markets, for consecutive five year sequences. The data were kindly provided by Cushman & Wakefield Healey & Baker. There is a clear indication that, over the last 25 years, and in particular in the last five, office market yields have become more highly correlated. The same pattern is observable in shop yields, though the peak in correlation is only 0.35, whereas in offices it is 0.5.[5]

The same analysis was conducted on quarterly growth in prime office rents across the Euro zone. A lower level of overall correlation was expected because rental values are, to a greater extent than yields, determined in local markets. At a local level, supply constraints induced by land use planning and urban form have strong influence on rent levels. Nevertheless, the idea that financial and business services, which drive office take-up, are increasing integrated across national boundaries caused us to think that correlation in rental movements would show an increase over time.

Figure 12.14 shows that correlation in office rental change has increased over the last 20 years, but also that it was fairly highly correlated at the start of the period. The correlation in shop rent changes is much lower generally (0.1) and shows no trend, up or down. This analysis confirms that office market fundamentals are more integrated across the Euro zone than in retail. If investors require cross-country diversification, the retail sector is better than offices, because rental outcomes are more highly influenced by local factors.

The 'one market for global real estate capital' hypothesis appears, to an extent, to be true: cap rates in offices and retail are increasingly correlated.

---

[5] Lack of space prevents publication of the chart; it is available from Grosvenor Research.

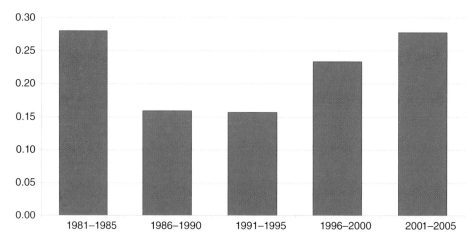

Figure 12.14: Correlation of office rental change over time in the Euro zone

For the time being, the level of correlation in yields is low enough to provide investors with plenty of scope for diversification. However, if the trend continues, some of the benefits of international diversification look set to diminish over the next 10 years.

There is an interesting codicil to this research. In order to check the basic premise on which the research was based, namely, increasing economic integration of Euro zone economies, the correlation of quarterly GDP growth rates over time was examined. The results are in Figure 12.15.

Figure 12.15 shows little evidence of an increase in economic integration over the time period. In fact, 'integration' appears to be cyclical. At times of strong global growth, Euro zone economies have done well together. At times of weak performance, integration declines. In the period up to the launch of the single currency, economies appeared to be strongly converging; subsequently, this died away. This evidence might be stretched to suggest the Euro was launched partly on a false premise, though, to be fair, the co-movement of quarterly GDP growth is only one way of looking at convergence. Quarterly GDP growth is quite a 'noisy' series. In any case, from the perspective of an international investor however, non-synchronous economic activity is a very good thing.

Convergence continued – the US case (July 2006)

Last month, we examined the correlation between real estate and economic activity across European countries, to see whether economic convergence

Figure 12.15: Five-year rolling correlation between quarterly GDP growth in Euro zone countries

has fed through into property markets. This month, we turn our attention to a longer-established and highly successful single currency zone: the United States. We expected to find a much higher level of correlation between regional economies and regional property markets and, in this, some indication of how the Euro zone might develop.

The principal benchmark used to measure performance of direct real estate in the USA is the National Council of Real Estate Investment Fiduciaries (NCREIF) index. The quarterly index is composed of appraisal-based valuations of institutionally owned commercial properties. Data differences meant that we used total returns for the US analysis, in contrast to rents and yields used in the European analysis. Our initial analysis was done for offices in the four NCREIF regions. After the recession of 1989, the five-year rolling correlations were very high, well over 0.7, across all pairs of geographical areas. However, the very large NCRIEF regions do not allow for the individual performance, good or bad, of specific states or cities or properties, to influence the correlation number.

For a more localised analysis, we looked at NCREIF annual total returns in 10 large office markets in the United States: New York, Boston, Philadelphia, Washington, DC, Dallas, Chicago, Los Angeles, San Francisco, Miami and Atlanta. The five-year rolling correlation coefficients of total returns (Figure 12.16) are lower than for the more aggregated regions, but still quite high. Over the time frame studied, the correlation coefficients are between 0.35 and 0.7. In the European case, correlations of rental growth were consistently below 0.3 and the correlation of yield shift was below 0.3 until recently. The level of the correlation coefficient seems to be related

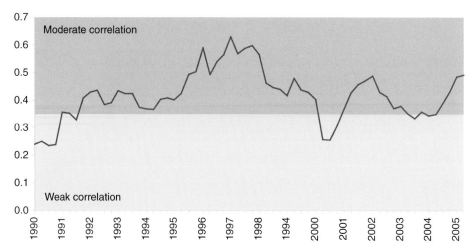

Figure 12.16: Five-year rolling correlation between ten top US office market returns
Source: NCREIF, Grosvenor

to the economic performance of the entire economy, with low correlation coefficients being aligned to periods of weak economic growth.

Using NCREIF data again, a five-year average rolling correlation coefficient across all sectors was calculated for the entire United States. 'All sectors' includes: hotels, apartments, offices, industrial and retail. Figure 12.17 shows the results for all sectors and ten office markets. The results are similar for the sectors and offices, which suggests there is as much correlation between sectors as within them (or there is as much diversification potential within a single sector as between sectors).

In the UK, Brown and Matysiak found that correlations between properties tended to be lower than in other asset classes. Interestingly, they also found that the correlations were equally as low within a sector, as they were picking from different sectors. They concluded that: 'although market factors have an influence on property returns it is evident that non-systematic factors are of considerable importance'. Our basic analysis from the USA seems to concur with this, in so much as there is little difference in the rolling average correlation coefficient between the single sector offices, across markets, and the average rolling correlation between sectors.

Moving to the economic fundamentals, Figure 12.18 shows the average correlation coefficient of GSP (Gross State Product) growth across States over various time periods. During the early 1980s all US states were performing poorly – hence the high correlation coefficient. The late 1990s saw a low correlation of 0.2, which may suggest that, as the technology boom

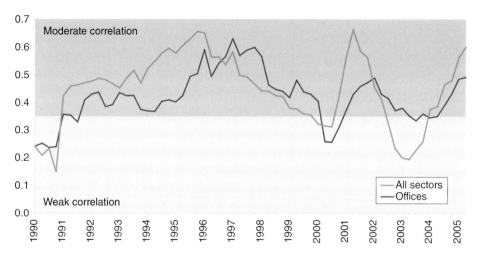

Figure 12.17: Five-year rolling correlation – offices and sectors in the US
Source: NCREIF, Grosvenor

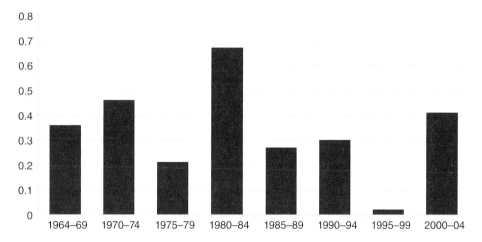

Figure 12.18: Average correlation of US States' GDP
Source: Global Insight, Grosvenor

took off, some states performed better than others, producing divergence between states. However, there is a discontinuity in the GSP time series at 1997, which may, also, explain this low figure.

In Europe, we found that there was a move towards property convergence across markets, whereas the economic convergence argument looked less robust. In the USA, real estate returns appear more correlated than in Europe. As expected, the US economy has a higher degree of correlation across States, the late '90s not withstanding, than Europe has across countries. These findings fit our expectations, but we probably expected to find a higher degree of correlation. Some suggest that true international diversification can only be achieved by investing inter-continentally, but our results suggest there are still considerable diversification benefits to be had within a sector, or across sectors, in the USA.

Does income inequality affect office rents? (November 2005)

In this article, we examine the relationship between economic development and office rental levels. Understanding what affects rental levels can assist in determining which markets are above or below their expected rental level and so help to spot potential opportunities or over-extended markets.

The rental information was taken from CB Richard Ellis's global market rents publication for 2000 to 2005. The analysis covered countries in each continent; a total of 93 locations. The rental data was in US dollars (per metre, per annum), converted using the exchange rates given in the CBRE report.

Based on a statistical analysis, rents can be explained by a country's real GDP per capita *and* its share of world GDP. The equation suggests that for each 1% increase in GDP per capita, there is a 0.6% increase in real rents. If a country increases its share of global GDP by 1%, then its real rents will increase by 0.2%. This model explains 60% of the real rental level in each of the markets.

Figure 12.19 shows rents ranked by country share of world GDP. London's two main office markets, the City and the West End, stand out with the highest rents. Countries with a smaller share of world GDP, on the left side of the chart, tend to have lower office rents than those with bigger shares. This is demonstrated by the trend line.

In the dataset, China has the largest share of world GDP and has seen the strongest GDP per capita growth over the last 10 years. On this basis, rental levels in Chinese cities (the three bars at the far right of Figure 12.19) are lower than expected. The structure of the Chinese economy, with a high proportion of manufacturing and small service sector, might explain this anomaly. It also hints at quite strong rental growth in China in the years to come.

The level of GDP is not the only potential indicator of economic development. The distribution of income within a country, the income of the rich

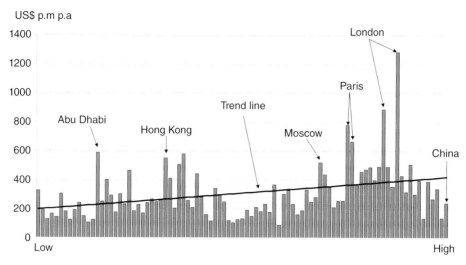

Figure 12.19:　Locations ranked by a country's share of world GDP

relative to the income of the poor, is also important. According to Simon Kuznets, as a country develops, income inequality first increases then decreases. A country's income distribution can be described by its 'Gini coefficient'. A Gini has a value between 0 and 1; the lower the value, the more equal is a country's distribution of income. Latin America is the world's most unequal region, with a Gini coefficient of around 0.5; in the developed world, the figure is close to 0.3. Austria, the Czech Republic and Sweden have the lowest Gini, with Brazil, Chile and Colombia having the highest.

Thus, in another exercise, the Gini coefficient was used in a model to explain real rental levels. The model suggests that a 1% increase in inequality corresponds to a 1.4% decline in the rental level. For example, a country with a Gini coefficient of 0.35, all things being equal, would have a rental level around $60 per square metre per annum, less than a country with a coefficient of 0.3. Figure 12.20 ranks locations by their country's Gini coefficient. Locations on the left side have a more equal distribution of income.

The red bars show countries with Gini coefficients of less than 0.3. These are the most 'equal' countries, the lowest being Austria with 0.24. Dublin and Paris have higher rents than their peer group.

The blue bars show countries with Gini coefficients between 0.3 and 0.4. London office rents are significantly higher than other locations.

The green bars show countries with Gini coefficients above 0.4. These are mainly South American countries, but also include some Asian and Eastern European nations. Hong Kong and Moscow stand out as having significantly higher rents in this block.

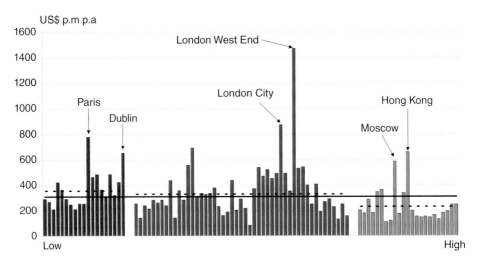

Figure 12.20:   Locations ranked by Gini coefficient

The solid black line shows the mean of all locations; the dotted lines show the mean for each Gini-block. The rental level mean for countries with a Gini above 0.4 is statistically lower than the overall mean, at a 5% significance level. For the other two groups, the group mean is not significantly different from the entire sample average.

Conclusions? First, GDP per capita and world GDP share are good determinants of the level of rent. Second, where GDP is more evenly distributed, rental levels tend to be higher, on average.

13

Looking forward

The outlook for the world economy – as at late 2011 – is bleak. In the USA the housing market remains in the doldrums, which is preventing the construction industry from making its normal early cycle upturn and creating jobs. Unemployment remains high and consumers are focused on rebuilding their balance sheets. In Europe, a reasonable recovery in economic activity is being derailed by a sovereign debt crisis. Portugal, Ireland, Greece, Spain and Italy are having problems funding their fiscal deficits and refinancing previously issued bonds that are maturing. Greece has the biggest problem, because of its poor growth, structural deficit and high debt-to-GDP ratio and urgently requires emergency aid from other EU members. This funding is available, but is contingent on Greece making very painful cuts to its bloated public sector and other labour market reforms. Elsewhere in the Euro zone, governments which have the resources to bail out Greece and the other countries with fiscal and sovereign debt challenges are facing mounting domestic opposition to doing so. Doubts about the ability of the Euro zone to remain intact are undermining economic sentiment and reducing the motivation of firms to invest.

So it is becoming clear in late 2011 that the monetary and fiscal policy stimulus that was put in place after the GFC in 2008 has failed to restore the economy of the OECD to its pre-crisis growth trend. As Japan found in the 1990s, even extreme monetary stimulus, quantitative easing as it is called, cannot be relied on to generate growth during a 'balance-sheet

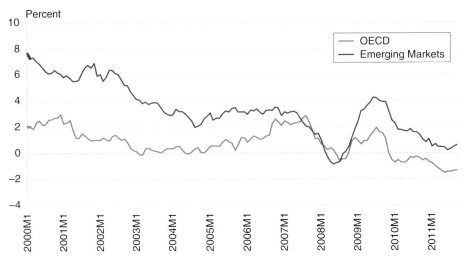

Figure 13.1:   Extreme monetary policy is having little effect
Source: IHS Global Insight

recession'. Until all commercial banks have fully marked to market their non-performing loans, including sovereign bonds, and have been recapitalised, credit growth will not be strong enough to drive private sector demand, no matter how much quantitative easing is undertaken. At best, the OECD is facing a weak and volatile recovery; at worst, it faces a 'lost decade', as in the case of Japan. It has been estimated by Reinhart and Rogoff[1] that it takes as long to 'unwind' a financial crisis as it does to create one. If we see the origins of the crisis as the zero interest policy pursued in the wake of the tech-crash, then the GFC was seven years in the making. Ergo, in 2011 we are facing another four years of weak growth and balance-sheet adjustment. If, as we have argued in Chapter 1, the cause of the crisis is the flow of savings from Asia – in particular China – into Western bond markets, then the origin of the GFC might be as early as 1995. This means the OECD is facing another 10 years of de-leveraging. Figure 13.1 shows real interest rates in the OECD and emerging markets. So far, extreme monetary policy has mainly succeeded in reflating asset markets and inducing some restocking. It has not had much impact on restarting consumption.

   If there is a bright spot in the global economy it is in the continued growth of the emerging economies, with China as the main driving force. If China's initial growth impetus was from export-orientated production based on cost advantages, economic development is now being driven by urbanisation. That China has been able to maintain real GDP growth of around 10% per

---

[1] C.M. Reinhart and K. S. Rogoff, This Time is Different: Eight Centuries of Financial Folly, Princeton University Press, 2009.

Table 13.1: Change in monetary policy between Q1 2010 and Q3 2011 by country

	Policy Rate	Reserve Requirements
China	+100 bp	+600 bp
Brazil	+350 bp	+460 bp
Russia	−50 bp	+150 bp
India	+275 bp	+100 bp
Korea	+125 bp	
Turkey	−75 bp	+840 bp

annum in the face of a major global downturn is not only remarkable, but also central to the survival of the near-bankrupt OECD economies post GFC. However, it is becoming clear that China and the other emerging markets are running into the real economic problem of widespread accelerating inflation. It is possible that emerging market inflation is merely the result of a series of bad harvests and elevated food prices. Food, in emerging markets, can be up to 30% of the basket of goods used to calculate CPI. It is more likely that China and the other emerging markets, despite seeming to have an endless supply of labour, have actually run into medium-term capacity constraints. Table 13.1 shows how emerging market policy-makers have had to act in order to curb the growth of demand and bring inflation down. These measures will destroy demand.

The rise of China, because of its size and quasi-socialist economic policy mix, remains at the heart of the policy challenge facing the global economy. Some argue that China's negative real interest rates and undervalued currency is creating the biggest resource misallocation in history, with fixed capital investment running out of control. The logical consequence of this is that China, like Japan before it, will in due course suffer massive over-investment and its own debt crisis. For the time being this is going too far; most countries undergoing economic development need to build cities and infrastructure and, according to most independent observers, China is making a good job of it. Nevertheless, China's policy-makers are walking a narrow path between overheating and resource misallocation and keeping demand high enough to provide jobs and improved living standards to rural migrants and the emerging middle class. Similarly, OECD governments need China's growth to help maintain global demand, but are failing to deal with the restructuring required as a result of its rising share of world manufactured goods markets (see Figure 13.2). China has the ability and reserves to help finance struggling Euro zone governments by purchasing their bonds. It may be willing to do this, but probably at the price of greater access to Euro zone markets.[2]

---

[2] China seeks 'market economy status'.

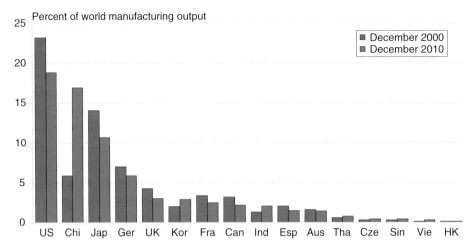

Figure 13.2: Growth has been export led
Source: EcoWin

Will the next 10 years turn out to be as problematic as the economic circumstances at the end of 2011 suggest they will? Even now, it is possible to put forward an optimistic outlook, even if it is unfashionable to do so. First, the economies of the OECD have shown themselves in the past to be highly resilient to all manner of economic shocks, including financial crises, oil-price rises, natural disasters, wars and political change. As long as entrepreneurship is encouraged and technology makes progress, societies can shift resources from declining to expanding sectors quite quickly. Second, periods of economic crisis can engender a much more cooperative and creative approach by policy-makers than is the case in times of easy prosperity. So, in the same way that the complacency of the period of the 'great moderation' led to the GFC, the subsequent period might well see the creation of new institutions that better regulate the global economy.

How might the world look in 10 years' time if politicians and entrepreneurs are able to 'seize the moment'? First and foremost, China will be much more integrated into the world economy than it currently is. In return for increased access to OECD markets and access to technology, China will have allowed the value of the Yuan to rise quite quickly. The rate of growth of China's share of world markets will have slowed, but the spending power and the living standards of its consumers will have risen. Importantly, Western companies will be selling more goods and services to China. The growth of Chinese foreign currency earnings will have slowed, so long-term interest rates in the USA and the OECD will be trending up. Because of its role in engineering these currency adjustments, the G20 will be firmly established as the dominant force in global economic management. The

Euro zone will have survived its trial by fire; fiscal policy will be federalised, or at least substantively centrally coordinated, and the Euro bond will have made its debut on world markets. Greece, Spain, Portugal, Ireland and Italy will be restructured and competitive. The ECB will have replaced the Federal Reserve as the world's most important economic institution. The USA will be facing up to the fact that it is slowly losing the unchallenged benefits of reserve currency status, but its technology, branding and culture will still dominate consumer markets, particularly in Asia. Growth will have been weak in the first three years of the decade, but will have picked up thereafter, leading to a slow decline in unemployment. Living standards and consumption will have risen much faster in emerging markets, relative to the OECD. Because of the rising demand for food and commodities, Africa will be the most exciting place to do business on the planet.[3]

If we accept the idea that the next ten years, and particularly the next three, will contain some difficult adjustments, but also many unforeseen upside events, so that growth – overall – will not be as weak as currently expected then we should expect quite a lot of change in the pattern of resource usage. Put simply, if growth is to continue the world will have to use its resources much more efficiently than it currently does. This will be difficult to achieve in the emerging markets, where rapid, resource-intensive growth is the quickest and easiest way to lift millions out of poverty (and ensure political stability). It will be easier in the OECD, where populations are older, better educated and more affluent and are already putting pressure on governments to create legislation that obliges consumers and businesses to behave with a much greater level of resource efficiency and a much lower level of carbon emissions. It is quite possible that this points to a substantial and fairly rapid adoption of nuclear power. However, the politics of this change are far from straightforward as the reaction to the nuclear disaster at Fukashima has shown. Perhaps more likely, as in war time, the scale of the problem and the degree of government support for change will lead to quite rapid, interesting and beneficial changes in technology. The OECD economies will have begun a major public-sector-led programme to refit and decarbonise their economies. The scale of the investment undertaken will have led to a much lower level of consumption growth than has been the case in most of the post-war period.

Even if we take a relatively optimistic view of the outcome to the current crisis, it is not surprising that the outlook for real estate is mixed. It could hardly be otherwise during such a period of transition and potential turbulence. Figures 13.3 and 13.4 show the current yields or capitalisation rates

---

[3] For reasons of brevity, we do not comment on the implied relative decline of the USA as the world's pre-eminent military power. The USA and China will work very hard to prevent confrontation in Asian waters, but it might be inevitable.

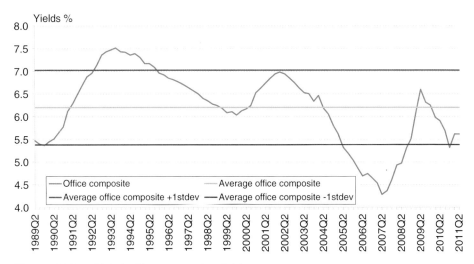

Figure 13.3: Global office composite yield
Source: Brokers, Grosvenor Research, 2011

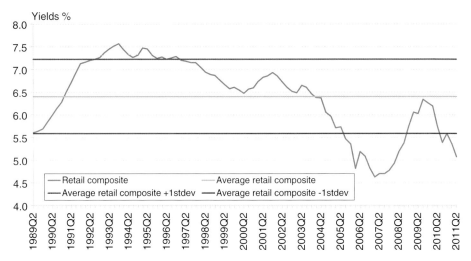

Figure 13.4: Global retail composite yield
Source: Brokers, Grosvenor Research, 2011

for a weighted average of the word's major core real estate investment markets. One of the most surprising features of the post-GFC period was just how quickly world real estate markets bounced back. There can be little doubt that the cause of this revival was the aggressive fiscal and monetary policies pursued in the wake of the GFC, particularly the latter.

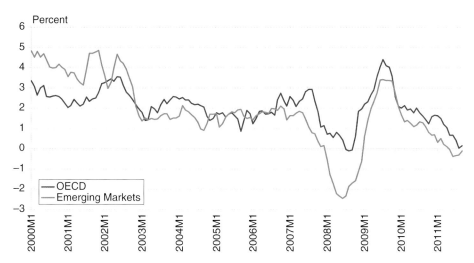

Figure 13.5: Real long-term bonds in OECD and Emerging Markets
Source: IHS Global Insight

Quantitative easing was introduced in the USA and the UK specifically to reduce long-term interest rates (Figure 13.5 shows real long-term bond rates in the OECD). This has acted, in the ways described in Chapter 11 of this book, to substantially reduce real estate yields. So, if economic growth in the OECD revives more strongly than we currently expect, more strongly in fact than in the optimistic scenario outlined above, then it would be likely that bond and real estate yields would actually rise. By the standards of the last 20 years or so, core real estate is trading at the very top of its 'price band'. Actually, although we have referred to the changes we see taking place in the global economy as 'optimistic', we do see growth in the OECD remaining very weak well into the medium term, with ample spare capacity and very little inflation. So, for the next three to four years, current yield levels seem sustainable, because of the reasonable 'spread' over bonds that they offer in most economies. However, investors will have to keep a very alert 'weather eye' on the evolution of bond markets over the next five years, because at some point these markets will fall, taking, in all probability, real estate markets with them.

Notwithstanding current pricing, given the ageing of the world's population, it seems very unlikely that real estate will do anything other than grow in importance as an investment asset class. Figure 13.6 shows that real estate is around 40% of global wealth and, as such, requires a larger place that it currently has in institutional portfolios. Our article of September 2010 at the end of this chapter deals with the way in which the need for

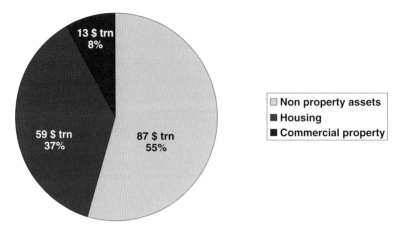

Figure 13.6:   Global wealth – 2000 prices
Source: UN, IPD, Grosvenor, 2009

Table 13.2:

Date	Living in Cities	World Population	City Inhabitants
1900	10%	1.6 bn	160 m
2011	50%	6.1 bn	3.05 bn
2050	75%	9.2 bn	6.9 bn

all societies, OECD and emerging, to provide pensions will drive the demand for real estate as an investment asset. This investment demand will be complemented by strong fundamentals. According to the London School of Economics 'Urban Age Project', the number of people living in cities will double over the next 40 years (see Table 13.2). As long as economic growth does not suffer a catastrophic 'Malthusian check', population growth plus economic growth and urbanisation add up to strong demand for real estate. Not only does city growth provide demand for real estate, it also increases supply. City growth is likely to add around 3.5% per annum to the global stock of investment-grade real estate for the foreseeable future.[4] As long as the real estate advisory community take the trouble to provide investors with thoughtful advice on the urban and social context in which they deploy their capital and the appropriate time frame for holding real estate

---

[4] Grosvenor estimate. Does not include the transfer of stock from the owner-occupied sector to the investment market. If this is included, that rate of investment-grade stock growth increases to 4%.

assets, there is no reason why real estate cannot be as important as equities and bonds as an asset class in the next 20 years.

If the future of real estate as an asset class look reasonably assured the channel by which capital is deployed and managed is much less clear. As we noted in Chapter 1, the last ten years have seen a substantial growth in the REIT sector. Approximately 15%[5] of the investment grade stock of global real estate is owned and operated by REITs. REITs offer investors a more liquid form of exposure to real estate at a cost of greater volatility and lower control over portfolio and leverage decisions. The better managed REITs also offer investors access to highly specific real estate management skills and advantageous access to debt markets. We should assume that, as in the USA, the global REIT industry will slowly mature, with companies increasingly specialising and offering investors the opportunity to access highly professional management. As such, the REIT sector will offer an increasing challenge to non-listed real estate fund managers and increase its ownership share of the real estate market.

In terms of fundamentals, the residential sector would seem to have the most assured future. In 100 years, if mankind survives, people will still be living in houses and, most probably, shopping in shops. However, the outlook is quite different for the residential sector in the developed world, than the emerging markets. In the latter the challenge is to build homes in cities for rural migrants and the burgeoning middle class. The scale of the challenge is huge. For instance, China intends to build 36 million affordable homes between 2011 and 2016, according to its most recent (twelfth) five-year plan. In any case, the pace of nominal GDP growth in emerging markets, as well as rising raw materials and land costs, suggest strong price appreciation in these markets, as well as many investment and development opportunities. The danger for emerging markets is not only that their housing booms will come to an end at some point, but also that they are likely to construct too much low-quality stock, which becomes obsolete or involves high maintenance quite quickly. In the OECD, housing markets look set for an extended period of low or negative capital value appreciation. Low growth, combined with weak growth of credit, will impede house prices in the short and medium term. Further out, rising interest rates and, most likely, rising tax rates will also have a negative impact. As we point out in Chapter 10, we are likely to see a strong move out of the owner-occupied sector into private rented accommodation in the USA. This trend will probably establish itself elsewhere in the OECD, as consumers de-leverage and house prices stagnate.

Retail property also faces a different future in the OECD than in the emerging markets. In the OECD, consumer de-leveraging, low growth and

---

[5] Grosvenor estimate.

cost–push inflation mean that the growth of retail sales is likely to be low for some time. So also will be levels of new development. The very best destinations will continue to perform well, as will discount retail centres and convenience formats. However, centres which do not offer cost leadership, convenience or powerful consumer experience will struggle. By contrast, the growth of consumer incomes in the emerging markets will continue to stimulate a very high level of value growth and development activity, particularly malls. It is likely that emerging markets will not realise until it is too late just how bland cities can become when they are dominated by malls. A significant proportion of the malls in emerging markets will be obsolete in a relatively short time, because of poor construction, poor design and poor location.

The sector which, perhaps, faces the greatest uncertainty over its future is the office sector in the OECD. In the big financial sectors, demand for space over the last 20 years has been driven by the equity market boom and the expansion of the banking sector. None of these drivers of demand look set to perform strongly in the medium term. This is not to say offices face a bleak future. As the OECD economies restructure, in the face of increased competition from China and the other BRICs, it is likely that advanced financial services will remain a growth industry. However, the form which service sector expansion takes over the next 10 years is very unclear. It could be those office clusters that best service the creative industries that perform best, particularly if they offer a convenient live–work environment. Of course, it almost goes without saying that the reverse is true in emerging markets. Here, growth of the service sector will remain strong, driving office demand. The big danger for the high-growth BRICs, due to the extreme elasticity of supply, is extreme volatility. Come what may, the office cycle is as inevitable as death and taxes.

We started this book by describing the period roughly from 2000 to 2010 as 'a remarkable decade for real estate'. Although the recovery from the great financial crisis was rapid, it is apparent that the OECD economies are still hamstrung by consumer, corporate and government debt levels that are way too high. Moreover, the economic structures that produced the crisis are far from reformed or revived. Whilst it is possible to see the current period of uncertainty and volatility as providing the motivation to create more robust and legal and institutional arrangements for economic growth, we are not there yet. Apart from serving their clients to the best of their ability the challenge for the real estate industry is to play a constructive role in shaping the new world order. In explaining how economic growth drives real estate outcomes, we hope that we have also demonstrated how important the real estate industry is in providing a platform for that growth to take place.

The case for increased pension fund allocation to real estate (September 2010)

The legacy of the last economic and financial crisis on the global pension system is still very noticeable. The asset losses experienced in 2008 have not yet been fully recovered (Figure 13.7). Global pension assets are still more than US$2 trillion short of their 2007 level, even though 2009 witnessed significant market revival. In fact, investment data show that pension funds in few markets acted in a countercyclical way during 2008 and 2009, purchasing stock as markets sank and reducing their acquisitions as markets recovered.

The global pension 'system' has a general under-funding problem, as the ratio of pensioners to workers in the developed countries is rising rapidly and this is compounded by the weakness of OECD public finances. Whilst we expect governments to take action to increase pension savings over the next several years, it is also clear that policy is moving to reduce liabilities by increasing the age of retirement. Either way, the last thing the system needs is a further fall in asset values.

Unfortunately, in the majority of OECD countries, bonds are still the main asset class, though equities rank first in Australia, the UK and the USA. This exposure to equity prices has been the most important factor behind the large swings in the size of pension fund assets across these

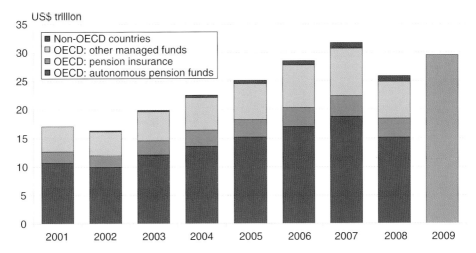

Figure 13.7: Global pension assets
Source: OECD, UBS, IFSL, Towers Watson, Grosvenor Research, 2010

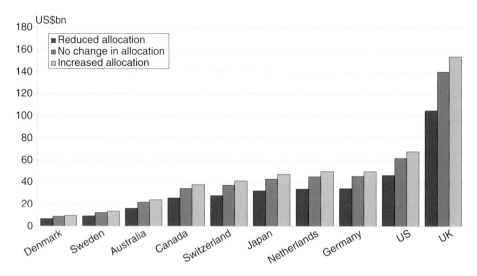

Figure 13.8:   Capital potentially investible into property 2010–2015
Source: PFR, Grosvenor Research, 2010

countries. Going forward, we think bond markets are the main source of risk, because of the potential build-up of inflation in the medium term. Rising bond yields would hit the baby-boom generation hard, as it approaches retirement.

In most OECD countries, real estate accounts for a relatively minor share of pension assets, although some exceptions exist. For example, real estate is a significant component of pension fund assets in Switzerland, Finland, the Netherlands and Australia (around 10% or more of total assets). While a strategy targeting mainly bonds and equites may be appropriate for investors seeking to maximise returns, the first objective of a pension fund is to make sure it meets its liabilities. With populations ageing across the developed world, pension funds are approaching the point at which they will pay out more to pensioners than they receive in contributions. With bond markets over-inflated and equities subject to high levels of volatility, this suggests a change to stable, income-producing assets such as real estate.

With an average weighting to real estate of 5.0%[6] and global pension assets growing by 7% per annum,[7] we expect around US$440 billion to be generated for sole allocation to real estate over the next five years. However, if the average allocation were to rise by 10%, global inflows of net real estate

---

[6] Grosvenor Research calculations, based on PFR data.
[7] This is based on the average growth rate of global pension assets between 2001 and 2009 (source, OECD). It may understate the future growth rate of total assets if governments implement further measures to promote savings.

investment would rise by an additional US$40 billion. The pension fund markets with the most capital to spend on real estate will be the mature pension markets, with the USA the dominating source. Other important contributors would be the UK, Germany, the Netherlands and Japan. Our analysis is based on the major OECD economies, but we should not underestimate the growing importance of the emerging European economies and, more importantly, China and the Far East, where the likely improvement of the welfare system will, in turn, create a major new source of capital for real estate investment.

Is there enough real estate to support a substantive switch in asset allocation? It is currently estimated that there is around US$1.5 trillion of institutional investment in real estate globally. The global turnover of the investment market in normal conditions[8] is approximately US$400 billion. An additional $65–95 billion per annum as a result of an increased allocation to real estate of 20% would be substantial in this setting and would have a positive effect on real estate pricing. So, with populations ageing and bond markets looking vulnerable, it can be argued that pension funds urgently need to re-allocate capital to real estate. Those that make an early switch will gain the most.

---

[8] With the exclusion of boom years, such as 2006 2007, and depressed years, such as 2009.

Index

This index is in a word-by-word arrangement, and covers the introduction and following chapters. Figures are indicated by the page number in italics, and tables are indicated by the page number in bold. An 'n' following a page number indicates a note at the bottom of the page.